Techno-logic & Technology

Techno-logic & Technology advances an ambitious new framework for studying the development of stone tool technology, with the goal of integrating humanity's earliest and longest-lasting technology into a comprehensive questioning of the interaction between humanity and the material world.

Michael Chazan provides a translation of Éric Boëda's authoritative work *Techno-logique & Technologie*, which draws on the latter's career of research on stone tool assemblages from archaeological sites in Europe, the Middle East, China, and South America, together with a theoretical apparatus influenced by the work of Gilbert Simondon. This book presents a major challenge to all archaeologists studying ancient technology to reconsider how they think about artifacts and how to approach the question of progress through time in human technology. Lithic analysis is a highly empirical field of study that rarely has an impact on issues of broad theoretical interest, and Boëda's book is a welcome exception. Michael Chazan, himself a Paleolithic archaeologist specializing in stone tool technology, includes an interview with the author to help equip the reader to engage with this challenging text.

Chiming with the growth of interest in the work of Gilbert Simondon in the English-speaking world, this book is an important resource for Paleolithic archaeologists and lithic specialists. It will also be of interest to researchers in material culture studies, technology studies, and human evolution.

Éric Boëda, a professor at the Paris Nanterre University, is among the pioneers of the French technological approach to stone tool analysis and the most active Paleolithic archaeologists working today. His fieldwork includes projects in Brazil, Mali, Syria, France, and China. His research challenges some of the most established ideas about prehistory, including the timing of the first arrival of humans in the Americas, the evolutionary context of *Homo erectus,* and the hunting capabilities of Neanderthals. Professor Boëda's reputation is built equally on his influential work on the theory of technological evolution and the methodology of stone tool analysis.

Michael Chazan is a professor at the University of Toronto. He co-directs the Wonderwerk Cave Research Project, with fieldwork at Wonderwerk Cave and the sites of the Kathu Complex, both located in the Northern Cape Province of South Africa. He is the author of *The Reality of Artifacts: An Archaeological Perspective* (Routledge, 2019).

Techno-logic & Technology
A Paleo-history of Knapped Lithic Objects

Éric Boëda

Translated by Michael Chazan

LONDON AND NEW YORK

First published 2023
by Routledge
4 Park Square, Milton Park, Abingdon, Oxon OX14 4RN

and by Routledge
605 Third Avenue, New York, NY 10158

Routledge is an imprint of the Taylor & Francis Group, an informa business

© 2023 Éric Boëda and Michael Chazan

The right of Éric Boëda and Michael Chazan to be identified as authors of this work has been asserted in accordance with sections 77 and 78 of the Copyright, Designs and Patents Act 1988.

All rights reserved. No part of this book may be reprinted or reproduced or utilised in any form or by any electronic, mechanical, or other means, now known or hereafter invented, including photocopying and recording, or in any information storage or retrieval system, without permission in writing from the publishers.

Every effort has been made to contact copyright-holders. Please advise the publisher of any errors or omissions, and these will be corrected in subsequent reprints.

Trademark notice: Product or corporate names may be trademarks or registered trademarks, and are used only for identification and explanation without intent to infringe.

British Library Cataloguing-in-Publication Data
A catalogue record for this book is available from the British Library

ISBN: 978-1-032-41647-2 (hbk)
ISBN: 978-1-032-41650-2 (pbk)
ISBN: 978-1-003-35908-1 (ebk)

DOI: 10.4324/9781003359081

Typeset in Times New Roman
by Apex CoVantage, LLC

Contents

List of figures	*x*
Preface	*xxiii*

	Introduction	1
1	**An epistemological perspective**	4

From typology to technique, from technique to technology 4
Typology: a necessity with limited utility 5
Techné without logos 9
On the necessity of a technology of change 11
> *The notion of tendance 11*
From form to structure, from tendance *to individuation 13*
From structure to lineage 15
> *The direction of evolution: from abstract to concrete 15*
The place of the human 17

2	**The techno-logic of evolution: a key to understanding human technicity**	20

Tools 20
> *The contribution of a techno-functional approach 20*
>> *The necessity of theorizing the tool 20*
> *What is a tool? 21*
>> *The process of instrumentalization: a techno-centric approach 24*
>> *The process of instrumentation: an anthropo-centric approach 26*
> *The techno-functional approach 27*
> *The internal structural relationship of incising artifacts 28*
> *The processes of individuation of the lineage of incising artifacts 28*

vi *Contents*

The absolute beginning: a naturally incising object 28
Abstract or additional anthropic structure 30
Concrete or integrated anthropic structure 31
Modalities of structural evolution: confection, debitage,
shaping 32
The tempo of production 33
The passage from debitage to shaping 33
Change of perspective: from morphology to structure, from
the object to the ensemble 34
The tempo of the bifacial phenomenon 38
The tempo of the post-bifacial phenomenon: from partial to
full debitage 42
The "circum-Mediterranean" Levallois option 45
The option of debitage and confection 47
The case of the Umm el Tlelian 47
The case of the Yabrudian 51
The case of the Hummalian 55
Conclusions 59
The structures of production 60
What is a core: an additional or integrated structure? 60
An additional structure (abstract) 60
The non-homothetic or falsely homothetic character of
additional structures 60
True non-homothety 61
A misleading homothety 63
An integrated structure (concrete) 63
The homothetic or non-homothetic character of
integrated structures 65
An integrated structure of homothetic character with a
phase of reinitialization 65
An integrated structure of homothetic character with
continuous debitage 66
An integrated structure of non-homothetic character
with continuous debitage 66
The process of concretization 67
Structural stages of evolution 68
Characteristics of predetermination of the technical criteria
of removals 69
The assemblages with an abstract structure and the
corresponding classes of removals 69
Useful volume of Type A/undifferentiated flakes 70
Useful volume Type B/removals with a distinctive
transformative part 70

Contents vii

Useful volume of Type C/removals with differentiated transformative and prehensile parts 71
Useful volume of Type D/removals with differentiated transformative and prehensile parts 71
Archaeological production structures 73
Abstract volumetric structures 73
Useful volume of Type A 73
Useful volume of Type B 74
Useful volume of Type C 74
Variability of the modes of initialization, selection, and production 76
Method of initialization, method of production 81
The resilience of the morphology of the blocks of raw material 81
The removals 82
Useful volume of Type D 85
Variability of the modes of initialization and production 88
Type D1 88
Initialization of Kombewa type 89
Initialization that can resemble Levallois without being Levallois 91
Initialization: Victoria West Cores 93
Type D2 94
In the archaeological context, the exploitation of Type D2 is very common 96
Debitage of blades of Type D2 96
Debitage of bladelets of Type D2 97
Type D3 98
Debitage of Levallois typo-points 98
Debitage of pseudo-Levallois typo-points 104
Conclusion 105
Concrete volumetric structures 106
Type E 106
Type F 106
Useful volume of Type E 107
Type E1 107
Type E2 108
Conceptual specificity 108
Useful volume of Type F 116
The phase initialization 117
Objectives of configured cores of Type F 119
The specific characteristics of Types F1 and F2 120

viii *Contents*

First factor: normalization of the prehensile part 120
Second factor: production in series, diversity/unity 121
F1 production or the necessary diversity of artifacts:
  a structural advantage 121
Debitage of Type F2 or the option of normalization of a
  single type of artifact 129
Third factor: a linkage between the volume of the core
  and the volume of the artifact 132
An addition to the definition of debitage of Type F1:
  autocorrelation 134
The "autocorrelation" of Types F2 136
Specificities of production of Type F3 137

**3   The anthropological sense: a paleo-history of the lineages
of blade production and blade products in the Middle East
during the Pleistocene**   **153**

The blade phenomena 154
  Evolutionary preamble 154
  Historical preamble 155
  Techno-logical temporality 156
    The modes of production 156
    The products 156
    The modes of production and the products 157
  Chronological temporality 158
    The production of blades 158
      First phase 158
      Second phase 158
        The industry of Hummal 6b 160
        The site of Kaféine 160
        The Southern Caucasus: The Djruchula-Koudaro complex 161
      Technical characteristics of Phases 1 and 2 161
      Third phase 162
      Fourth phase 163
      Fifth phase 164
    The blade products 164
      The debut of the blade phenomenon 164
        The Amudian and Hummalian blades 164
      The post-Hummalian 167
      Blade and bladelet products: from the Transition to the Neolithic 167
  The anthropological sense: at the crossroads of the
    chronological and evolutionary data 169
  A technical paleo-history of the modes of production and the
    tools produced 169

Contents ix

First phase: the Amudian from 300,000 to 200,000 years ago 169
  The structures of blade production and the tools
    produced 169
  The abstract stage of the tool 171
  The stage of the concretization of the support 171
Second phase: the Hummalian and the Blade Levallois,
  200,000–150,000 BP 173
  Blade production and associated tools 173
  Debitage of Type F1 and tools of Hummalian type. 174
Third phase: sporadic blade production—Levallois and
  non-Levallois, after 150,000 years ago 175
  Blade production and the associated tools 175
Fourth phase: the transition, 45,000/47,000–36,000 176
  The tools 176
  The exploitation of an energetic potential: an
    exteriorized transformative part 179
  Blade production 184
  The means of blade production 185
  The bladelet phenomenon: its tools and
    production 185
  Summary of the fourth phase 189
The fifth phase 189
  The modes of production 190
  The exploitation of an energetic potential:
    a transmitting part of the artifact that is
    individualized 190
  The phenomenon of exteriorization 191

4   Conclusion   198

The space-time of daily life 200
The space-time of a past daily life 201
The memory of the other 204
The production of new facts 205
  The ontology of lineages 205
The variety in situations 206
  Situation 1 207
  Situation 2 208
  Situation 3 209
  Situation 4 210

Bibliography   *212*
Index   *229*

Figures

Frontespiece: Etching by Marcel Duchamp based on the bottom panel of the work entitled The Bride Stripped Bare by Her Bachelors, Even. Yale University Art Gallery ii

1.1 Yabrudian, El Masloukh, Lebanon. The typological analysis classifies this object as a Yabrudian-type sidescraper with steep Quina-type (scalariform) retouch, while the techno-functional analysis makes it clear that there are two distinct types of cutting edges, of which one is adjacent to a backed edge. In effect, the object is the integration of two tools with different modes of prehension and functioning. 6

1.2 Early Yabrudian, Umm el Tlel, Syria. The techno-functional analysis shows that these two pieces, while both are classified as Yabrudian sidescrapers, are conceived as a matrix onto which are grafted either: (1) Two identical techno-functional units (both a). (2) Three techno-functional units (one a and two b). 7

1.3 Acheulean, Umm el Tlel, Syria. These bifaces are grouped together based on a morphological classification as lanceolates that appear similar. However, the techno-functional analysis shows that these are actually two different objects. The biface A possesses two different tools: a point/edge and an *avoyage*. (The *avoyage* consists of a series of notches created in such a fashion as to shift "teeth" created by the convergence of notches alternatively to the left or to the right.) In plain view, one has the impression of a denticulated edge. However, in sagittal view, one clearly observes picks that are offset in relation to the center. In transversal view, it appears in the form of a sinuous edge (Boëda, 2010). Biface B possesses two instances of the same tool: point/edge. 8

2.1 The three components of a tool. 21

2.2 A hafted Leilira (ethnographic unretouched point from Australia). 21

2.3 Hafted Leilira: (1) A triangular blade that was used for piercing and cutting (Noone, 1943, 1949). (2) A triangular blade held in

	a wrapping used for cutting and carving. (3) Pick (Spencer and Gillens, 1912). (4) Lance (Davidson, 1935).	22
2.4	The currently available data on the use of a Levallois point shows that it might be used for different manners of functioning, without a causal relationship with the type of worked material (Bonilauri, 2010).	23
2.5	The processes of instrumentalization and instrumentation.	24
2.6	The constraints of instrumentalization.	25
2.7	The constraints of instrumentation.	26
2.8	Structural breakdown of an incising artifact.	29
2.9	The transformative part always possesses *a priori* the characteristic of a sharp edge regardless of how variable this might be. The prehensile part on the other hand is completely variable.	30
2.10	The incising characteristic is normalized through its production. The prehensile characteristics are aleatory.	31
2.11	Barbas 1, Couche 7—Dordogne, France. Sidescrapers on fragments produced by natural processes (gelifraction of Bergerac flint) that present identical volumetric and technical characteristics.	32
2.12	Integrated structure: the different subunits interact in synergy.	32
2.13	The Acheulean industry of Umm el Tlel, Syria. The same silhouette, described as cordiform, serves as the support for a combination of different tools. Only a techno-functional analysis can reveal the different technical intentions.	36
2.14	El Meirah, Syria. Abstract structure. Mono-tool, a technically and functionally symmetrical structure on a bifacial piece.	37
2.15	Barbas C'3—Dordogne, France. Concrete structure. Asymmetric functional structure: mono-tool on a bifacial piece. Asymmetric functional structure: point/edge tool with a flat/flat (*plan/plan*) and flat/concave (*plan/concave*) cutting edge.	38
2.16	Barbas C'3—Dordogne, France. Concrete structure. Asymmetrical functional structure, multi-tool on a bifacial piece. Edge A—flat/convex (*plan/convex*) cutting edge with a convex plan view. Edge B—point/edge with a flat/flat (*plan/plan*) cutting edge.	39
2.17	El Meirah, Syria. Abstract structure. Asymmetrical functional structure. Multi-tools on a bifacial piece.	40
2.18	In this schema, one can distinguish the range of technical systems present in Europe between Oxygen Isotope stages 9 and 5e. The bifacial phenomenon is found in barely half the cases and is not homogeneous as there are clear disparities in the frequency of bifaces (Soriano, 2005).	41

xii *Figures*

2.19 In the case of the post-bifacial industries of the Middle East, the shaping of the flake (*confection*) plays a dominant role. With the shift to Levallois debitage, the supports for tools (flakes) are strongly predetermined and the shaping of the flake is limited to a functional role.   43

2.20 Terminology applied to the different parts of a tool. The tool can be differentiated into two parts: the mineral artifact and the non-mineral artifact, which is referred to as the haft (*porte-artefact*).   44

2.21 Umm el Tlel, Syria, couche VI 3, 75,000 years BP. Levallois blade, flakes, and points hafted with bitumen, which was used either as a binding or as a wrapping agent.   46

2.22 The specificity of the Levallois concept: a concept of debitage capable of producing a diversified range of tools for which the prehensile part remains stable regardless of the type of transformative part and regardless of the modality of hafting: (A) Oblique. (B) Along the axis. (C) Transversal.   47

2.23 Levallois debitage makes it possible to obtain predetermined supports that closely approach the form of the tool. The debitage (solid line) makes it possible to obtain almost all of the desired technical characteristics for the good functioning of the lithic artifact. The stage of shaping (*confection*, dashed line) makes it possible to put in place other technical characteristics if needed.   48

2.24 Umm el Tlel, Syria. Level overlying the last bifacial industries. In gray, normalization of the transformative part in anticipation of a specific form of hafting. The upper piece is latterly hafted following the preparation of opposed truncations. The lower piece shows the preparation for axial hafting (in relation to the axis of percussion and the morphological axis of the flake).   49

2.25 The case of the Umm el Tlelian. The debitage (solid line) makes it possible to obtain a certain number of technical characteristics that apply to the ensemble of parts of the artifact, but the functionalization of the artifact requires a significant stage of shaping (*confection*, dashed line), applied to the transformative and prehensile parts.   50

2.26 Lower Yabrudian, Umm el Tlel, Syria. Each piece is constructed based on the presence of a natural back (oblique edge). Pieces 1 and 2: based on a lateral parallel naturally backed edge and either an oblique or perpendicular naturally backed edge on the two extremities. Pieces 3 and 4: the naturally backed edges are present only at the extremities along the functional axis.   52

2.27 Lower Yabrudian, Umm el Tlel, Syria. Each piece is constructed to obtain a fan-shaped silhouette. The platform provides a technically backed edge.   53

Figures xiii

2.28 The case of the Yabrudian. The debitage (solid line) makes it possible to obtain certain technical characteristics that apply to the future prehensile part of the tool. The transformative part is the focus of a very significant stage of shaping (dashed line), which provides the tool with its characteristic silhouette with a suitable cross-section. 54

2.29 Hummalian, Umm el Tlel, Syria. The distal part of the laminar support is subject to a range of modification corresponding to different functions and functioning. (1) Convex lateral cutting edge, lateral cutting action. (2) Point/edge, action of penetration and longitudinal cutting. (3–4) Modification along an offset axis, action of penetration, and lateral cutting. The techno-functional analysis of the modification on these four artifacts shows very clearly that we should dissociate these into two distinct functional parts: (A) An apex formed by the convergence of the two edges and consisting of identical edge morphology (plano/convex) that corresponds to a modification of the silhouette of the penetrating part of the tool for an action of penetration along the axis. (B) A mesioproximal section with edges modified by flaking using a variable edge morphology that is distinct from the modification of the apex. The proximal part of the tool, which corresponds to the prehensile part, depending on its technical configuration, is either modified or unmodified to fit a haft. 56

2.30 Hummalian, Umm el Tlel, Syria. Pieces 1 and 3 present a modification of their transformative part of the type point/edge with plano-convex edge morphology. The prehensile part is also the subject of modification to fit a haft. It is the same for Pieces 2 and 4 except for the axial symmetry of their transformative part and the presence of two different edge morphologies: (2) Plano-convex edge morphology. (4) Plano-concave edge morphology. 57

2.31 The case of the Hummalian. The debitage (solid line) comes closer to the desired form of the prehensile and transformative parts. The stage of shaping (dashed line) is applied mostly to the transformative part. But if necessary, the prehensile part is also shaped. 58

2.32 Additional structure. The block to be knapped is composed of two volumetric subcomponents. One is designated as the useful volume or the core *sensu stricto*; the second is called the non-useful or residual volume. 61

2.33 Non-homothetic schema: The total volume varies and the useful volumes are identical. 61

2.34 Following the exploitation of an initial useful volume, the process of knapping leads to the morphological transformation of the block. 62

xiv *Figures*

2.35 Non-homothetic structure of additional knapping is found in the case where an identical successive series of removals result in residual volumes that are different (A, B), although the useful volumes are identical. 63

2.36 Integrated structure: the initial block is subject to a stage of initialization that makes the block to be knapped equivalent to the useful volume, which is thus designated as the core. 64

2.37 Debitage with an integrated structure. (1) The configured core integrates the criteria for reinitialization. (2) It is the recurrence of particular objectives that maintains the criteria of configuration. 64

2.38 An integrated homothetic structure interspersed with phases of reinitialization. 65

2.39 Continuous integrated homothetic structure. 66

2.40 Non-homothetic integrated structure. 67

2.41 The evolution of tools is made possible by the evolution of the modes of flake production and/or by the evolution of modes of shaping (*confection*). 68

2.42 The useful volume of Type A is chosen exclusively for its capacity to provide a surface for a striking platform adjacent to an undifferentiated debitage surface producing a flake removal with a cutting edge that takes any form. 70

2.43 The useful volume of Type B, maintained in a recurrent fashion, allows for the control of some technical characteristics of the transformative part of the flake removal or removals. 71

2.44 The useful volume of Type C, maintained in a recurrent fashion based on a useful volume that presents a naturally convex debitage surface. This double control—natural convexity and recurrence—allows for partial control over the transformative and prehensile parts of the flake removals. 72

2.45 The useful volume of Type D, maintained in a recurrent fashion based on a useful volume, is prepared by the establishment on the debitage surface of the collection of technical characteristics needed to achieve the functional objectives of the tool. The transformative and prehensile parts of flakes from a useful volume of Type D are therefore differentiated. 72

2.46 A single useful volume of Type C. On the left, the selection of a block possessing a useful volume (a) and a second non-useful volume (c). On the right, the useful volume (a1) is the core; the volume c remains unused. 75

2.47 Useful volume of Type C. Unipolar exploitation of three flakes from a similar usable volume (previously designated as C1). (1) The site of Oies à Wimereux-Pas de Calais (collection J. Louis). (2) The site of Gipo, Korea. (3–4) The site of Montsaugeon–Haute-Marne (Amiot, 1993). 76

Figures xv

2.48 Useful volume of Type C. Unidirectional exploitation of a series of five removals. The site of Guanyindong, China (after Li, 2014). 77

2.49 The multiple variants of the useful volume of Type C. At the left, the selected block offers useful volumes, a and b, and a non-useful volume, c. In the center, the first useful volume a1 is knapped without the volumes b and c intervening in any way whatsoever in the process of knapping. At the right, once the initial useful volume a1 is exploited, there is no possibility of producing a new series of removals from volume c, but this is possible using volume b1. 78

2.50 Type C1—High Lodge. The selected volumes offer multiple useful volumes of Type C1, which are exploited successively. The final appearance of the core can lead to confusion if one relies on the recognition of shape. However, technical analysis shows that multiple identical useful volumes have been exploited (after Ashton et al. 1992: 134, fig. 11.7). 78

2.51 A table of the potential variability in methods of initialization and production of a useful volume of Type C. 79

2.52 Knapping of Type C2. Barbas, Dordogne, France. Photo copyright S. Oboukhoff, CNRS photographic service, MAE Médiathèque, Nanterre. 79

2.53 Bidirectional laminar knapping of Type C2. Saint-Valéry-sur Somme (after Heinzelin and Haesaerts, 1983). 80

2.54 Knapping of Type C2, Kaféine, Syria. Following the knapping of an initial useful volume exploited for the production of at least four laminar removals per surface, a second opposed volume was utilized to produce a new series of blades, but as we will see later, this second volume was subject to a partial preparation which we designate as D2. 80

2.55 Unretouched blades derived from knapping of Type C2, Kaféine, Syria. Photo copyright E. Boëda. 82

2.56 Adjustment (*aménagement*) of the transformative part without modification of the prehensile part (Ashton et al., 1992). 83

2.57 The technical system of lithic production for the site of Guanyindong, Guizhou, China. Operational schemas of Type C. These schemas allow for a wide range of flakes, of which some with convergent edges are sought after to be transformed into specific tools. 84

2.58 Guanyindong, China. Tools with convergent edges made on flakes with a triangular transversal section. The stage of shaping reinforces the convergent form resulting in chamfered or pointed end. 85

2.59 Guanyindong, China. Tools with a chamfered end (after Li, 2014). 86

2.60 Conception of Type D. Left: the selected block. Center: the block is conceived as two subunits, the future useful volume (a) and a future

xvi *Figures*

non-useful volume (c). Right: the useful volume a1, designated as
the core prepared for knapping (a1), and the non-useful volume (c).   87

2.61 Table of the potential variability in the methods of initialization
and production of a useful volume of Type D.   88

2.62 Level C'3, Barbas, Dordogne, France. Cores of type D1,
Kombewa-type initialization.   89

2.63 Level C'3, Barbas, Dordogne, France. Kombewa flakes that
have served as the support for the fabrication of different tools.   90

2.64 Korolevo, Level C.II, Ukraine (Micoquian). Useful volume of
Type D1 with Kombewa initialization.   90

2.65 Level C.II, Korolevo, Ukraine (Micoquian). Modified Kombewa
flakes.   91

2.66 Fejej, Ethiopia, Type D3. A recurrent series of removals to
produce flakes with an adjacent or opposed back (de Lumley
et al., 2004).   92

2.67 Cagny-la-Garenne, France, Type D1 (Tuffreau, 2004).   93

2.68 Victoria West Cores, South Africa. Photo copyright Kathleen
Kuman.   94

2.69 Kaféine, Syria, Type D2. Preparation of a useful volume by
an anterior crest and a posterior crest. The useful volume,
which is extremely small, only allows for the controlled
production of two or three blades. Internal percussion with a
hard hammer.   95

2.70 Umm el Tlel, Syria, Type D2. Preparation of a useful volume
by one or two postero-lateral crests and through the integration
of a natural surface on one of the sides of the arch. Internal
percussion with a hard hammer.   96

2.71 Barbas III, Dordogne, France. Aurignacian core of Type D2.
Partial preparation of the carination. Photo copyright
S. Oboukhoff, CNRS photographic service, MAE-Nanterre
Médiathèque.   97

2.72 Barbas III, Dordogne, France. Aurignacian core of Type D2.
Partial preparation of the carination. Photo copyright
S. Oboukhoff, CNRS photographic service, MAE-Nanterre
Médiathèque.   97

2.73 Barbas II, Dordogne, France. The preparation covers the
entirety of the core, although the useful volume is limited to
only a part of the block. This volume is organized to obtain
large blades. Once these blades have been produced, the
useful volume is exhausted. The further pursuit of knapping is
impossible except for work aimed at the recreation of a new
useful volume regardless of the type of laminar objectives sought.   98

2.74 Umm el Tlel, Level II base, Syria. Different categories of
bladelet cores. The preparation of the useful volume in the case

Figures xvii

of Piece 1 is through an oblique truncation. In the case of Pieces 2, 5, and 6, the preparation is through overpassing cortical flake removals. In the case of Pieces 3 and 4, one observes several orthogonal flake scars that are difficult to interpret. The percussion is mixed, internal, and marginal.   99

2.75 Umm el Tlel, Level II base and III 2a, Syria. The gray zones represent the scars of bladelets intercalated within the knapping of laminar products.   100

2.76 Villiers-Adam, Val d'Oise, France. Production of Levallois typo-points (after Locht, 2003).   101

2.77 Villiers-Adam, Val d'Oise, France. Non-Levallois cores despite their morphological appearance of Type D3 with the production of Levallois typo-points (after Locht, 2003).   101

2.78 Villiers-Adam, Val d'Oise, France. A schematic representation of refit number 11. Type D3 with a Levallois typo-point with a unidirectional convergent initialization.   102

2.79 Villiers-Adam, Val d'Oise, France. A schematic representation of refit number 34 with two debitage surfaces (independent useful volumes). Type D2 with two Levallois typo-points obtained through the same method of initialization (Locht, 2003).   102

2.80 Villiers-Adam, Val d'Oise, France. A schematic representation of refit number 5 with four independent debitage surfaces (useful volumes). Type D3 with four Levallois typo-points obtained utilizing the same mode initialization.   103

2.81 A Levallois typo-point can be produced by three distinct types of volumetric structures: F2, E2, and D3.   104

2.82 Champ-Bossuet, Gironde, France. Pseudo-Levallois typo-point with Kombewa initialization (Bourguignon and Turq, 2003).   105

2.83 Table of the potential variability of the methods of initialization and production of a useful volume of Type E.   107

2.84 Queyssac, Dordogne, France. Core of Type E1. Photo copyright S. Oboukhoff, CNRS photographic service, MAE Médiathèque, Nanterre.   108

2.85 Külna, Czech Republic, Micoquian Level. Discoidal core with bifacial exploitation, with the production of four categories of flakes.   109

2.86 Kaféine, Syria, Anté-Mousterian industry. Core of Type E2.   109

2.87 Photo copyright S. Oboukhoff, CNRS photographic service, MAE Médiathèque, Nanterre.   110

2.88 Saint-Firmin-des Prés, Loir-et-Cher, France, Excavations of V. Lhomme. Core of Type E2 (Lhomme et al., 1999).   111

2.89 Saint-Firmin-des Prés, Loir-et-Cher, France, Excavations of V. Lhomme. Core of Type E2 (Lhomme et al., 1999).   112

xviii   *Figures*

2.90	Tabun, Israel—Unit XI, Amudian. Core of Type E2 (after Meignen, 1994).	113
2.91	Australian Leiliras (after McCarty, 1976).	114
2.92	Pyramidal core with its potential variants. (1) Quarter pyramidal. (2) Semi-pyramidal. (3) Pyramidal at the end of its potential.	114
2.93	Non-homothetic debitage of Type E1. The exploitation can take place through removals of one or two faces in succession or alternation. Regardless, the range of removals does not change. In Case 4, one can even see a change in axis as is observed archaeologically at the site of Beauvais (Locht, 2003).	115
2.94	Correlation between different types of useful volumes and the exploitation of volume versus surface. Black: Essential to the volumetric structure. Gray: Possible but not structurally essential, "whoever does the least, does the most."	116
2.95	Configured core of Type F obtained following a stage of initialization through alteration with or without a preliminary selection.	117
2.96	Villazette, Dordogne, France, Magdalenian. Configuration modifying the totality of the block with the goal of blade production.	118
2.97	The phase of initialization consists of finding the future core in a form that is already ready to be flaked.	119
2.98	Following this table, there is not a fit between the type of product and the volumetric structure of the core.	120
2.99	Core with a preferential flake removal of Type F1. The method of initialization is centripetal and the method of production is preferential. Syria, Palmyra Basin. Photo copyright S. Oboukhoff, CNRS photographic service, MAE Médiathèque, Nanterre.	121
2.100	Point core of Type F1. The method of initialization is bidirectional and the method of production is preferential. Photo copyright S. Oboukhoff, CNRS photographic service, MAE Médiathèque, Nanterre.	122
2.101	Core for production of a preferential triangular flake of Type F1. The method of initialization is centripetal at the distal end and unidirectional at the proximal end. The method of production is preferential. Syria, Palmyra Basin.	122
2.102	Preferential core for production of a Levallois point of Type F1. The method of initialization is centripetal and the method of production is preferential. Umm el Tlel, Level VI 3a', Syria.	123
2.103	Point Core of Type F1. The method of initialization is bidirectional and the method of production is preferential. Palmyra Basin, Syria.	123

Figures xix

2.104 Corbiac cavaille, Dordogne, France. Recurrent core of Type
F1. The method of initialization is centripetal and the method
of production is recurrent unidirectional parallel. Photo
copyright S. Oboukhoff, CNRS photographic service, MAE
Médiathèque, Nanterre. 124

2.105 Level C'4 Lower, Barbas I, Dordogne, France. Core with
recurrent removals of Type F1. The method of initialization
is centripetal and the method of production is recurrent
unidirectional parallel. 124

2.106 Bicheri, Syria. Recurrent core of Type F1. The method of
initialization is centripetal and the method of production is
recurrent unidirectional parallel. 125

2.107 Biache-Saint-Vaast, Pas de Calais, France. Core with
recurrent removals of Type F1. The method of initialization
is centripetal and the method of production is recurrent
bidirectional parallel. 125

2.108 Palmyra Basin, Syria. Recurrent core for point and
convergent flake production of Type F1. The method of
initialization is mixed unidirectional parallel and centripetal.
The method of production is recurrent bidirectional. 126

2.109 Palmyra Basin, Syria. Recurrent Levallois point core of Type
F1. The method of initialization is unidirectional parallel and
the method of production is recurrent bidirectional. Photo
copyright S. Oboukhoff, CNRS photographic service, MAE
Médiathèque, Nanterre. 126

2.110 Palmyra Basin, Syria. Core for recurrent point and laminar
flake production of Type F1. The method of initialization is
unidirectional convergent, and the method of production is
recurrent unidirectional convergent. 127

2.111 La Bouloie, Crenay, Haute-Marne, France. Recurrent cores
of Type F1. The method of initialization is centripetal and the
method of production is preferential (Boëda, 1993; Amiot and
Etienne, 1977). 128

2.112 La Bouloie, Crenay, Haute-Marne, France. Recurrent
centripetal debitage of Type F1. Production includes
unretouched and retouched flakes with convergent edges
(after Amiot and Etienne, 1977). 129

2.113 Des Forêts, Dordogne, France. Recurrent centripetal debitage
of Type F1. Production includes unretouched and retouched
flakes with convergent edges (after Brenet and Folgado, 2003). 130

2.114 La Bouloie, Crenay, Haute-Marne, France. Centripetal Levallois
debitage of Type F1. The selection is based on the selection of a
naturally convex surface (the result of fracture from freeze-thaw)
that is partially altered. Depending on how the debitage evolves
the appearance could lead one to think that there are different

xx *Figures*

	types of debitage, but a technological analysis of the totality of the assemblage immediately eliminates this possibility.	131
2.115	Evolution of the modes of detachment by laminar types of useful volume.	132
2.116	Schema of the exploitation of a core of Type F1, presenting the characteristic of "auto-correlation."	133
2.117	The criteria that define debitage of Type F1/Levallois.	135
2.118	Schemas of the initialization and exploitation of a core of Type F2, which present that characteristic of "autocorrelation." Initialization 1: An anterior crest and two lateral posterior crests. Initialization 2: Two anterior and posterior crests. The percussion is direct marginal and requires phases of a partial reinitialization of the debitage surface and striking platform surface. This is made possible as a result of the integrated structure of the core. Initialization 3: Marginal indirect percussion initialization 4: As the yield and productivity increase, the initialization reaches its peak with pressure flaking.	136
2.119	Villazette III, Dordogne, France. Magdalenian laminar core of Type F2. Photo copyright S. Oboukhoff, CNRS photographic service, MAE Médiathèque, Nanterre.	137
2.120	Queyssac, Dordogne, France. Perigordian laminar core of Type F2. Photo copyright S. Oboukhoff, CNRS photographic service, MAE Médiathèque, Nanterre.	138
2.121	Chalcolithic, Susa, Iran. Core of Type F2, pressure flaking. Collection of Macquenem (after Dauvois, 1976).	139
2.122	Suyaggye, Chungcheongbuk Province, Korea. Upper Paleolithic Yubetsu core. (Yonsei University Press, 2001).	139
2.123	Bladelet cores of Type F2, pressure flaking. Northern China. Photo copyright S. Oboukhoff, CNRS photographic service, MAE Médiathèque, Nanterre.	140
2.124	Maomaodong, Guizhou Province, China. *Splits* transformed into tools. Drawing copyright H. Forestier.	142
2.125	*Splits* transformed into tools. Only debitage of Type C will be used to produce flakes with only slightly regularized shapes, as at the site of Maomaodong, Guizhou Province, China. Photo copyright E. Boëda.	143
3.1	Chronological table of the industries of Phases 1 and 2.	159
3.2	The structures of blade production and types of tools (in the classic typological sense in the Near East).	166
3.3	The evolution of the structures of production in the Near East.	169
3.4	The evolution of the ensemble of structures of production in the Near East.	170
3.5	The modalities for normalizing supports according to the different technical facies. Acheulean: shaping and confection; Yabrudian: debitage and confection; Amudian: debitage.	172

Figures xxi

3.6 Modalities of normalizing supports according to the different technical facies. Amudian: debitage. Hummalian: debitage and confection. 174

3.7 Umm el Tlel, central Syria. Level III2b: First level of the transition phase between 42,000 and 35,000 years. 176

3.8 The phenomenon of the exteriorization of the transformative part in relation to the prehensile part. 180

3.9 The Hummalian of Umm el Tlel: 1–3: tools with lateral retouch; 4–6: convergent tools. 181

3.10 The laminar volumetric structures represent the initial evolutionary stages (C2 and D2) in contrast to debitage of type F1/Levallois, which is the last evolutionary stage of the lineage of the production of diverse flakes. There thus exists a discontinuity in the structures of production that is not found in the structures of the tools where one sees a structural evolution of supports. 183

3.11 Umm el Tlel, Syria. 1–4: Hummalian convergent pieces; 5–7: Levallois-Mousterian pieces of Tabun D facies. 184

3.12 Umm el Tlel, central Syria. Bladelets from Level c.II base. 186

3.13 Umm el Tlel, central Syria—traces of hafting. a–h: hafting along the morphological axis of the bladelet; i–k: lateral hafting (Boëda and Bonilauri, 2006). 187

3.14 Bladelet cores. Umm el Tlel, Syria, level c.II base: 1, 3. Type D2 on a flake, and Type E2. 3. Type C2 on a fragment of block 4. Qualta, Syria: Type D2 on a flake. 188

3.15 Substitution of the prehensile part through the phenomenon of exteriorization and elongation of the part that transmits energy. 191

3.16 New positioning of the prehensile part in relation to the length and the part that transmits energy. 192

3.17 Modification of the qualitative characteristics of the part for the transmission of energy and modification of the implantation of the transformative part. 192

4.1 Representation of the interaction object/subject. 199

4.2 Spatial representation of a technical system consisting of multiple objects. 200

4.3 The different memories at which we arrive. The fragmentary memory is still shared by us, which is not the case for the forgotten memory. The object thus harbors a memory that no longer has an echo for us. 201

4.4 On the basis of ethnoarchaeology the partial memory is capable of being partially reconstituted. 202

4.5 Situation 1: 1. The ontological and genesic (of lineages) perspective. 2. The historic perspective. 207

4.6 The different historical situations of Lineage α. 207

4.7 Situation 2: 1. The ontological and genesic (of lineages) perspective. 2. The historic perspective. 208

xxii *Figures*

4.8 The different historical situations of Lineage β. 209
4.9 Situation 3: 1. The ontological and genesic (of lineages) perspective. 2. The historic perspective. 210
4.10 Situation 4: 1. The ontological and genesic (of lineages) perspective. 2. The historic perspective. 210

Preface

A Conversation

Michael Chazan and Éric Boëda

MC: There is a stark disparity between the highly developed analytical apparatus deployed in the study of stone tools and the seemingly simple technology that is the apparent subject of this inquiry. When I first arrived at the University of Toronto, over 20 years ago, my proposal for a graduate course in Lithic Analysis was met with some skepticism by the Graduate Dean, after all what could be so complicated about studying the products of bashing stones together? In recent years I have engaged in making pottery as a daily practice. Here again I have a similar experience of endless complexity hiding behind seeming simplicity. The fashioning of a footed tea bowl, the form known as a yunomi, holds a fascination that can sustain potters for decades. Within the shaping and integration of the body, foot, and rim, there are seemingly endless possibilities.

Hiding behind the technical minutiae of lithic analysis lurks an enterprise of staggering ambition. Our goal in studying stone tools is to engage with generations of people using and making these objects, stretching millions of years back into the past. Like a potter shaping a yunomi, our subject is simple—the results of the application of fracture on brittle materials to produce objects that extend the human body—and endless.

For the most part, lithic analysts shy away from theoretical ambition. A lithic analyst often engages in a kind of reverse craft, where challenges remain grounded in a particular material engagement and the "raw material" is an archaeological assemblage rather than a rock or ball of clay. By contrast, this book is a work of philosophical ambition that has much to contribute not only to prehistory but also to theories of technology and materiality. It is a work that presents a perspective that grows out of a lifetime of experience. In translating I was greatly helped by my years of conversations with the author, it was in a sense easy for me to understand where this book is "coming from." This interview provides the reader with a similar orientation before plunging into a text that challenges some of our xxiv *Preface*

most basic assumptions about technology. What follows is a slightly edited email conversation.

I met Éric Boëda in 1992 as a postdoctoral student in the URA 28 of the Centre Nationale de la Recherche Scientifique, a unit under the direction of Catherine Perlès dedicated to the study of prehistoric technology. Coming from the American university system, I was surprised to find that several researchers, including Éric, had medical training. It was hard for me to imagine abandoning a career in medicine for prehistory, but I always believed that there was some connection between this medical background and the approach of the French-speaking school to stone tools. As a point of departure, I asked Éric to explain how he came to study medicine and his decision to move from medicine to archaeology. Moreover, I think it would be helpful to understand whether there are overlaps between these two seemingly disparate domains.

EB: On the anecdotal level, the reality is that I wanted to become a geologist. With the support of a Zellidja grant I was able to spend three months at the age of sixteen, working in the mines in Mauritania and Senegal. The Quaternary came to fascinate me all the more as these countries were rich in prehistoric and historical archaeology. On returning to France, I was determined to become a geologist, with prehistory as a hobby. But life is unpredictable, and a family crisis ruptured this dream.

I chose to pursue medicine because it would help me become independent through my studies, which I could pay for by working as a nurse's aide, and later as a nurse, among other things. I did not have the calling (*Je n'avais pas la vocation*). In a way I found this situation so "unjust" that while I was enrolled in medical studies at Paris VII, I also enrolled myself at Paris I and Paris VI to take courses in prehistory and geology.

Even if medicine is not a calling, it can still pull you in because it brings you in contact with remarkable human qualities. Those of the patients, who quite often provide you with life lessons, and those of some great medical authorities, who teach you humility, engagement and honest expression, all of which can be transformative. In brief, the perspectives one is exposed to in a hospital, around the sickbed, in the operation theater, at a debriefing.

Because medicine demands lengthy training and considerable knowledge, I was academically unable to seriously pursue my other interest. Nonetheless, during all these first years, I always kept contact with the prehistoric milieu thanks to one person, Professor Brezillon, who enjoyed sharing his knowledge and passion with the amateur that I was.

It was only much later, in the fifth year of medical studies, that I decided to resume an academic course in prehistory at the Paris Nanterre University. At this point, I was able to actively pursue these different activities. In medicine, I made the choice of resuscitation, first aid, and emergency care, which subsequently took me far from the university hospital to a wide range of settings where I had the chance, or rather the opportunity, to encounter other human realities including both the good and the horrific. Archaeology then became a time of refuge, a time without temporality, an interval between past and present, the perception of an otherness (*altérité*) of the present that must extend back to the past.

In reality, I did not make a spelled-out decision between medicine and pre-history. It was the interactions with particular women and men that gave me the opportunity to make prehistory my profession. As I finished my PhD dissertation in medicine, I began another degree in prehistory under the direction of Jacques Tixier. This work, given my academic career, should logically have been a mixture of physical anthropology and archaeology. However, recovering the living inter-ested me far more than studying the dead. Objects are the products of intelligence, while bodies are only the outcome of a biological evolution.

Objects harbor the otherness that is *a priori* hidden from our eyes. They are the material proof of a living memory, to which the traces on each object bears witness. The practice of knapping hard rocks has greatly helped me to submerge myself in this ocean of memory.

Now, can one say that I deliberately made a choice between medicine and re-search in prehistory? Professionally, yes, because I undertook the process of apply-ing for a position in the Centre National de la Recherche Scientifique (CNRS), but the path to reach this point is so much the outcome of unfathomable factors, that it is not really you who actually determines the future path.

However, even though the scale has tipped to the side of archaeology, I have never forgotten my Hippocratic Oath, and wherever I go to conduct excavations, usually in areas that are a medical desert, I open a small clinic when we are not excavating. I never do this out of a desire to make myself useful but rather as an obligation imposed by an oath. My Masters tell us: you have received, you must give, medicine is not a title but a responsibility.

It would be a lie to say that one can move from one domain to another without there being anything but a historical connection, because my research in prehistory is profoundly imprinted by my medical training.

First and foremost, I would emphasize the sense of obligation implicit in spoken language. Obviously, one can easily understand that one cannot speak carelessly in front of a patient. We have the responsibility to say what we know, and that what we know and say makes us aware of our responsibility toward the other. Our engagement rests on arguments, which one hopes are pertinent. This is the opposite of an opinion, a belief, a judgement or a certainty. One knows this posi-tion can change, and that makes us responsible to the other. In archaeology we can make errors without serious consequences other than for our ego, nothing terribly serious. In other terms, one can allow oneself to say anything as well as its oppo-site, all under the pretext of the right to hypothesize. In the reality of medical life, faced with a patient, our speech is listened to and anticipated. We are responsible for what we say because it can affect the life of the other. This sense of commit-ment and of the consequences of this commitment can leave me resolute, as when I set out a diagnosis and an effective treatment, but these factors might also push me to be uncompromising towards those of my colleagues who do not have, in my opinion, what I consider to underly the word "ethical." The commitment is to know what one knows and what one does not know, and it is to know one's

xxvi *Preface*

potential and limits. From my experience, a doctor knows his limits better than an archaeologist. Secondly, I would point to the semiological basis of reasoning. A systemic semiology. My medical training took place during a period of change in the history of medicine, during which the semiology of perception by our own sensory abilities was enriched by mechanization capable of seeing what one could only have suspected. It is not our purpose to place these two approaches, which permitted medicine to advance rapidly, in opposition. However, since you point out that there is a connection between the medical training of some researchers and the manner in which the French school approaches stone tools, I think you have perfectly sensed the essence of a particular French school, which is demanding and systematic. This school has freed itself from external perception, to which the notion of form had been reduced. The exterior manifestation of the symptom does not define its cause, it is only one of the expressions of the cause. For knapped stone, it is the same thing. The form is what we are able to see. However, an illness is a structural disturbance that is manifest through signs. Situating these signs within a system allows me access to the structure. It is the same for knapped stone. This is first and foremost an object made of traces (signs) that signify a structured memory. From this flows a register of inquiry capable of grasping structure—who, what, how, why, and what is it done for. However, this is without forgetting the essential, the existence in the background of self-doubt, that which in the case of prehistory take the form of a different inquiry, that of "of what?" Of what is the history that I recount a history? I embed the researcher, or the doctor, in an awareness of epistemological engagement. This awareness does not question the real, but rather its place within a system.

MC: It is very striking that in your discussion of the responsibility of the medical worker you walk a fine line between certainty and speculation. In my reading of the archaeological literature, particularly some of Ian Hodder's writing, this is the quality of interpretation as opposed to explanation. Whereas some have argued that scientific knowledge implies certainty in one's conclusions, I think the opposite is the case; a scientific approach abandons certainty for a judicious and responsible effort to bring together the available data. As you imply, in archaeology the immediate stakes of interpretation are lower than in providing medical care, yet it is striking that we often feel ourselves to be involved in a venture where error is perilous, resulting in inflated claims of certainty and an aversion to interpretive innovation. I want to continue to follow the path of your engagement with prehistory and particularly the way that semiology, imported from your medical experience, transposed itself into archaeological insight. My sense is that a key moment in your thought about stone tools took place during your analysis of the stone tool assemblage from the site of Biache St. Vaast in Northern France. Biache St. Vaast is a site where a productive salvage operation took place under the direction of Alain Touffreau, if I remember correctly in response to the construction of a mayonnaise factory. Finds included fragmentary Neanderthal fossils, among the earliest evidence for fully evolved

Neanderthals, together with a large collection of stone tools from a broad exposure. You took on the technological analysis of this assemblage, resulting in one of the key publications of the emerging French *chaîne opératoire* approach. My sense is that it was in this study that you found a way to link your experience as a flint knapper with the study of prehistoric artifacts. Could you describe how your analysis of the Biache St. Vaast assemblage unfolded and how this project fits into your development of an approach to studying stone tools?

EB: At the beginning of my career there was obviously no conscious, reflexive, connection between the semiological method and archaeological method. It is difficult for me to explain the "why" of my life history, or of what history my own life history is the history. I prefer to remain factual. If we want to trace the connection between medical semiology and archaeological semiology, I would say that in my case it came out of the archaeological objects which I initially collected in the fields beginning when I was 13-year-old, and subsequently those that I collected during my first responsibility for an archaeological sounding, when I was in my second year of medical studies. By chance these were Levallois, or to be more precise, Levallois points. Of course, the literature available at that time did not provide a means of explaining what I held in my hands. It was at this moment that I grasped the need to understand through replication (I prefer the word replicate or copy over experimentation, which in the case of prehistory is trite). I only had available the observations I could make of morphology and the manual experience that allowed me to understand the technical consequences of my gestures. Hundreds of kilos of flint, if not more, passed through my hands without my being able to master, and above all to organize, the logic of production. It was at this moment that I for the first time understood the function of flakes that come off the edge of the core (*l'éclat débordant*). The simple flake opened up to me the voice of the Levallois point. This was also the moment when I understood that the two faces of a core constitute a singularity, that the core is a single structure that integrates the two faces and not the summing of two faces to form a structure. But what I was reproducing in reality was limited to the material from my sounding.

When I began my thesis on Biache Saint Vaast, a range of different forms were designated as Levallois. It was at this moment that I realized that my flint knapping experience did not enable me to understand what I had before my eyes. In reality, I did not yet have a holistic vision of the Levallois "problem." This holistic vision was all the more difficult to grasp because there were objects that everybody considered to be Levallois, but nobody was able to classify typologically due to the extent of diversity.

It is like working with a patient: you never have the totality of the symptoms, and even the same symptom might vary in intensity, however you know that this is nonetheless sufficient to propose a diagnosis; you have the cause of the symptoms, which does not mean that you have the cause of the illness. In the case of

xxviii *Preface*

Biache, I had only a semiologic diversity that one could intuitively connect to a singular cause, but this was not sufficient to explain the reasons for such variability (symptomology). At this stage, it was my knapping errors that were most enlightening, not the efforts at reproduction. This makes it sound like experimental practice is similar to a therapeutic intervention; but in reality, this is a trap. It is not the principle of trial and error that makes it possible to reach an ultimate conclusion. Copying does not enable the copyist to discover and formulate the truths that the objects contain. This is neither maieutically nor dialectically possible. For the story at hand, by hanging the ensemble of the diacritical drawings of the cores from Biache Saint Vaast on a wall and engaging in a reflection like that of a chess player trying to anticipate the moves of his adversary, I was able to get out of this bind. It is the semiologic organization of the variable expressions of a singular cause that allowed me to connect the totality to the notion of the Levallois concept. That day, I remember very well, I rearranged each drawing in its place, as though you predict in advance the moves of your adversary's strategy.

From this moment, I understood that our hylomorphic manner of assessing objects only by their form was a trap and that it was necessary to return to a comprehension of the underlying structure which manages the variability, of which the form is only one expression. In medical terms, if the semiology leads to a diagnosis, it does not lead to the cause of the illness. This is the source of my research, which rests on the principles of holism (that is only interested in its object in its totality) and on methods capable of restoring life to the traces of which we do not retain memory. Toward this end, these methods are based on the totality of the object such as it is, in the sense of physical properties, environment, and so on. But this totality itself is contained in a larger totality which is the world of objects within which our object exists: an object does not have existence except among its own.

MC: I want to pick up on your discussion of your experience when you were studying the Levallois method. You describe the importance of realizing the integration of structure at the level of a single object, in the case of the Levallois core that the two surfaces are integrated as part of a whole. In this book you take matters a step further as you develop an argument, inspired by Simondon, that the structure of a core or tool exists not only at the level of the internal integration of an object but also in the integration of an object into a lineage, which is in a sense an autonomous entity (although perhaps it is less a static entity than a process of emergence). I can see the logical continuity in the development of your thinking that situates an observable reality within expanding scales of integration. However, I think it is very likely that many of your readers may object to the idea of technical lineages as in some sense autonomous actors. This problematic recapitulates debates about culture that animated North American anthropology for the early part of the twentieth century. For example, Leslie White wrote of the "autonomy of culture" and its "logical independence of its human carriers." Obviously, your own work comes out of a French tradition reaching back to Durkheim and Mauss, and there are clear divergences between French and North American intellectual traditions. But for much of the twentieth-century anthropologists on both side of the Atlantic were engaged with the question of the existence of culture or technology as an entity with a trajectory independent of human intentionality. Leroi-Gourhan's discussion of the "tendance" comes to mind as an example of French conceptualization of the autonomy of technology. Yet if I look at the anthropological landscape today, it seems that few people are engaged with this issue. The project of decolonization, which often rejects the concept of culture, is dominant, and even within archaeology, or at least the archaeology of human origins, the emphasis seems to be heavily on aspects of adaptation to the environment and cognitive evolution. Your book seems an exception as you develop the concept of technical lineages, and how this concept applies not only to modern technology but also to the deep past. But I am left with questions about why you think that this idea is critical at this moment. Is this simply a tool toward improving our understanding of the archaeological record (already a valid goal), or is there a more general significance in our current intellectual/historical moment?

EB: The more the world is technical, the less we are interested in the technical. Because we have become consumers. One speaks of technique and of technology, confounding these words. One has lost the meaning of the words. I believe that we do not even pose the question: of what? Of what history is the history that one recounts as history? In the domain of lithic artifacts, it is only necessary to see the evolution of the representation of artifacts and by extension the place one grants to human perception. It is very rare to see anymore drawings of the traits of a tool, such as diacritical diagrams. We see photos, because it is said that this is more objective!

It is necessary to have never made photos to understand the degree to which this approach is aberrant.

In brief, this is to say that the object in its representation has almost completely disappeared from most journals, with the exception of *Lithic Technology*, and for good reason, the word "lithic" is in its title. Not to speak of explanatory diagrams which have practically disappeared.

These developments are only the reflection of the questions asked by prehistorians. The tendency is to pontificate about the ideas one has about an object or a group of objects (as though it is by chance that these are the ones of which we still have a memory). For example, in the Americas one talks about only one object: the projectile point and nothing else. Or, in Asia the hunting season for bifaces is open!!! Or for the Levallois!!! It is as though the unconscious of the prehistorian having created markers of a universal (globalist thinking) sets off on the hunt. . . . Thus when an author begins to talk about technique, it is "a pain in the neck." Because one expects hypotheses no matter how far-fetched they might be. The key is to produce a discourse. It is a little bit like "The Voice," we have five pages to explain something complex. I do not know of any book of philosophy that is less than five pages long.

xxx *Preface*

All of this is to say that research in prehistory has been globalized with the imposition of canons of thought. Is this still science . . .

To return to your question, I think that what I can say cannot be heard because the world of science has become the world of the videosphere, of the image.

If people are truly interested in artifacts, one must at the very least engage in an interrogation of the memory of which the traces are the expression that is accessible to our eyes. Thus, to do this kind of analysis one must at the very least directly confront the objects. On the other hand, if one combines a lack of interest in the technical and a prehistory that is becoming more and more sociological, everything will come to be linked to the present. It will become self-evident to you that regardless of the age of the objects that you are working with, one poses the same question. However, the further one goes back in time the memory of traces becomes fainter and less informative because they are less numerous. And this is without considering the alterity that is mowed down by globalization. As a result, although by any logic we should be seeing a growing interest in objects and the techniques from which they are derived, because these are the only vestiges that transcend time . . . but, no.

Believing one has found a way out of the apory, one will talk about the "cognitive," focusing on temporal recovery. As though this would be enough.

Thus, every modified cobble is Oldowan. After this object one should find bifaces, so it is the hunt for bifaces as in East Asia. And obviously one will assume that the biface is the equivalent of the Acheulean. One even speaks of a civilization. . . . The words no longer have any meaning. Subsequently it is Levallois, with which one breaks through a barrier, it is the quest for the Holy Grail. Is there not an outpouring of articles claiming to discover Levallois, where it had never been described, and for good reason?

Thus, this long diatribe is to say to you that people are not prepared to take an interest in artifacts. The preconceived ideas are sufficient, and this eliminates the subject. One limits oneself to thinking about factors such as the cognitive capacity of production.

For myself I am focused on a single question: what am I to talk about when I have an object for which the traces that it carries do not awaken in me any memory. To the extent that I do not have the means to respond, I no longer have the impetus to carry out research in prehistory. I was ready many times to return to medicine, because I did not see the point of repeating the same thing a thousand times and I did not have the tools for comprehension. When I finished my PhD dissertation, I always said that I knew that producing a Levallois flake depended on a core that was also called Levallois, but in reality, I still did not know what a Levallois flake was. It took me 30 years to finally provide a response in my 2021 book. I arrived at this answer having seen tens of thousands of artifacts from the four corners of the world, the majority of which were previously unfamiliar to me. Instead of seeking to organize them by their cross-section or outline, or a part thereof, I asked myself questions that came back to objects of our daily life.

My own life experience has given me the opportunity to see the transformation of objects that had not yet become black boxes. Today, as we are consumers, we are confronted by black boxes.

Preface xxxi

The idea is simple.

A black box can only be defined by its external appearance. Its internal structure is invisible to us. It is necessary to access the interior in order to comprehend the mode of functioning. If I do this for all objects, I can compare them, compare their particular structure and thus see their potential linkages. It is the same for artifacts. One must have at hand a method of reading that allows us to reconstruct the techno-functional intentions of each one of the gestures, which allows us to see their synergy or lack of synergy. It is as simple as that.

Now, the history of techniques from antiquity to our own time shows us that in structural terms certain initial structures have the potential for transformation that allows them to maintain the same functioning principles and the same objectives and thus belong to the same technical lineage. Take, for example, the automobile. We falsely group together under the same term technical objects that do not have the same functioning principles. It is true that an electric automobile and an automobile with internal combustion permit you to go from point A to point B. These objects might even have the same external configuration, but these are not objects that belong to the same technical lineage.

But everybody will recognize that based on each of these functioning principles one has seen transformations and will see transformations in the future.

The entire challenge for a prehistorian is to determine the functioning principle and the objective. One sees immediately that beyond the objects of which we still have a memory, it becomes very complex. We must therefore have the humility to say that we must re-examine our definitions. It is essential to be capable of reaching this stage of reading. It is not a deconstruction that is needed, it is a new perception.

Now, to say that artifacts are autonomous is absolutely ridiculous. I know that we have always had the myth of automaton, but an artifact is not an automaton . . .

An object is a human production as is its transformation. Now, once one analyzes an object on a structural level one becomes aware that particular structures are "improvable" (I do not like this term, but it is the most easily understood) while others are not. Now, instead of fighting over belief or skepticism concerning the existence of lineages of lithic artifacts, it would be better to explore the principles of invention, and the driving forces of transformation that can only be social. But to arrive at this level of questioning it is essential to know what one is talking about. Technology is a science of techniques, and like all sciences, this requires knowledge. You speak of adaptation. But before addressing this question I would want to know what the preceding lithic structures were.

Because as a function of the potential these structures have for adaptation the potential responses are multiple.

Adaptation can result in a structural transformation, or not. Adaptation has nothing to do with lithics unless this is possible. We see that with this type of approach we truly encounter a social realm with the potential for multiple responses. The ethnology of Marcel Mauss showed us the genius of humanity. It is up to us to find the traces of this genius in the temporal depths using all means at our disposition. I often have my student read Mauss' manual of ethnography. I realize that this is a bit old fashioned, but this book has the distinction of opening our eyes to a dynamic xxxii *Preface*

humanity, for whom technique plays a fundamental role, which is not to say isolated or exclusive.

I think that prehistory is dead. There are now prehistories that draw together disparate methodologies, even though they are not responding to the same questions. Can one imagine posing the same questions of objects of greater and greater age, that are more and more unknown?

This is not to say that the goal is not to comprehend the human. Quite the contrary. This allows us to perceive that we as humans have the need to control the history that we recount of our humanity.

Who, what, how, why, and for what reason are excellent, universal, questions, but what memories do we have access to in order to be able to respond?

There is thus undeniably a need for both an epistemological and a philosophical inquiry. But these words have little place in a discipline that delegates these questions and their response to machines and allows little place for reflection. And yet, all of our questions are those with which every generation engages. Think for a moment about the information that we produce . . .

I do not think that a philosopher worries about Google Scholar and their h score.

MC: In choosing an illustration for the frontispiece of this book it felt appropriate to choose an image that reflects a philosophical engagement, and, also, an iconoclastic perspective, rather than a simple icon of prehistory. The work of Marcel Duchamp provides this combination. Duchamp challenged our ideas about the boundary between artifact and art—installing a snow shovel, a bicycle wheel, along with the celebrated signed urinal. Much of his work also expresses an interest in dynamics and movement, both of which are central to the ideas presented in this book. The image selected here is an etching based on the bottom panel of the work entitled The Bride Stripped Bare by Her Bachelors, Even. This image represents the enigmatic relationships underlying the technological world we inhabit, a relationship that this book explores in deep time. This work of Duchamp's, in its original format, was etched on a large glass panel that was broken accidentally, an accident Duchamp chose to incorporate into his work. This is thus one of the few works of modern art to incorporate fracture, the physical transformation at the root of the emergence of the techno-logic presented here.

We would like to thank Antonio Pérez Balarezo for editorial assistance.

Introduction

Since the 1970s, what we could qualify as a French-speaking school, has made major advances in the analysis of prehistoric objects. These advances are based on recognition of the relationship between these objects and the people who produced and used them. The object is seen as both external (an inanimate vestige) and indirectly as a simple intermediary in terms of its functional reason for being in the world. However, this functional logic is possibly not the *raison d'être* of the object (Simondon, 1958). Experience has shown that the relationship between people and technical objects, the relationship that, as archaeologists, we strive to comprehend by studying the way these objects were manufactured and functioned, is not adequate to the task of understanding the changes we observe through time. Essentially, for the past 20 years, we have been cataloging our knowledge the way that an entomologist classifies insects, stumbling on the understanding of the reasons for the patterns of change. It is as though we have been waiting for the accumulation of information to transform itself into insight. Certainly, our current way of approaching prehistoric objects is one of the reasons for this blockage.

Before pursuing this point, it is essential to rethink the choice of an indirect perception of the object, focusing on the phenomena of convergences. How can we explain that the same object can be made and used in an identical way in different places (as is demonstrated by ethnology[1]) or at different points in time (as is demonstrated by archaeology)?

We have chosen to use the term "archaeology"[2] rather than "prehistory" intentionally to emphasize that while the phenomenon of convergence is largely accepted for recent time periods, the possibility of convergence in the study of the distant past is rarely accepted, and in fact usually rejected. This refusal to acknowledge the role of convergence is buttressed by ubiquitous scenarios for population dispersals and migrations throughout the Pleistocene. From reading the archaeological literature, one would think that early humans existed in a condition of Brownian motion that only came to mysteriously subside over time. In fact, we are asked to accept a prehistory of motion, consisting of phases of expansion and stasis where cognitive capacity and environmental pressure play the deterministic role until the appearance of *Homo sapiens*, that is to say, ourselves. In the context of such scenarios the concept of convergence, evidence of potential entropy, cannot exist. The concept of convergence stands in contradiction to the vision of prehistory that is gradual,

DOI: 10.4324/9781003359081-1

2 Introduction

linear, and expansionist, a doctrine that claims to provide a universal vision of human origins, predicting the process of becoming to better explain the present.

The place of *technique* in this discussion is minimal. The *technique* is treated as the exterior trace of modifications in the relationship between humans and the environment and in the development of human cognitive capacity. Changes in *technique* are relegated to serving as the extrinsic proof of this intimate systematic relationship between humanity and nature.

By giving artifacts a human aspect Technology (in the sense of the study of technical systems and technique) offers the potential of escaping this circularity. The use of experimentation has played a particularly important role in this processs of humanizing artifacts. However, within technology there has not been adequate attention to questions of an epistemological nature. From our point of view, in striving to use experimentation to arrive at a positivist approach that aspires to objectivity, technology has ended up confounding the means with the ends and has narrowed its interest to the identification of facts. Technology has become an archival science that accumulates data about the knowledge and know-how (*savoir faire*) needed to manufacture and make objects function, but it remains stuck in the perspective of the indirect relationship between humans and their environment. Current paradigms cannot accommodate the observations of convergence that are emerging from rigorous and well-dated excavations.

A second observation should not be overlooked. Since the beginning of the twentieth century, it has been noted that there is a development from a so-called primitive technical state to an "evolved" technical state. This dynamic plays itself out in every case of technical novelty,[3] like a repeating cycle, wherever one is in the world. It is as though there is a law[4] of the technical that is the result of a techno-logic.

But instead of understanding this "phenomenon" and its cyclicity, the tendency is to speak about progress and to consistently explain these transformations as the consequences of biological evolution.[5] And yet, these "universals"—convergence, change, and cyclicity—cannot be ignored. To fully take this observation into account, it is necessary to change our analytic perspective, to extricate ourselves from the way we conceive of the technical object. Does this dynamic not suggest a reality that is unique to artifacts? This single idea is viewed with dread, suspected of cloaking a determinism of objects, of giving artifacts a kind of independent humanity—the products of an evolutionary phylogeny—ignoring the socio-historic reality that is seen as the only determinant of the evolution of technique (Flichy, 1995; Bensaude Vincent, 1998)!

The long term of prehistory allows us to go beyond these antinomical positions by showing that certain aspects of objects can evolve because of their structural potential, and thus respond to new functional constraints, while other objects do not evolve but rather retain the same functional register regardless of the type of hominin or environmental context. This temporal transcendence, which is thus "a-cultural," indicates that certain structures of objects have an evolutionary potential that comes into being by a cycle regulated by "laws." Nonetheless, the tempo of evolution, its rhythm and frequency, is a uniquely human phenomenon.

In accordance with the constraints that societies impose or are subject to, humans invent, innovate, and diffuse their techniques.

Therefore, the analysis of the world of objects takes place in a double linkage, a double coevolution: humans and the environment, humans and the technique. The relation of the technique to humans takes place in the context of the capacity to respond to new cultural and environmental constraints. The objects, as a result of their own structural potential, are thus a cofactor in evolution, thus in a direct linkage with humans. This "transductive"[6] structural potential, once present, requires an ontological perspective that is capable of considering the connections between different stages of transformation. In fact, the object must be perceived through its structural dynamic, which is what makes it come into being, and not as what it is at a given moment, that is, its form.

Notes

1 "Alongside biological convergence there exists technical convergence, which has provided from the beginning of ethnology an element in the refutation of theories of contact" (translated from Leroi-Gourhan, 1945/1973: 338).
2 On a semantic level, the term "archaeology" signifies for us the study of ancient civilizations. The term "civilization" applies to the totality of the social element of a society, a totality that is obviously not possible to observe for Pleistocene human groups due to the lack of evidence, and the same is true for the early Holocene. This is why we use the term "prehistory," which signifies that we study the evidence and the events of a past without writing. But it is true that the current practice has lost the primary meaning in favor of a term, archaeology, which has become generic and is applied to all that is before the present. Do we not talk of an industrial archaeology? What then is the difference with the word history: A difference of method and data?
3 One thus finds the qualifications and prefixes such as "proto" and "pre" indicating the beginning of a technical process, and the terms "evolved," "well-made," and "masterful" to indicate the culmination of a technical process. It is in this vein that one can read such terms as pre-Oldowan, pre- or proto-Achelean, and proto-Levallois.
4 The term "law" is used here in its metaphorical sense.
5 Insidiously linked to the development of each type of hominin.
6 Capacity to pass from one state to another.

1 An epistemological perspective

From typology to technique, from technique to technology

Typology and technology are hybrid concepts that provide us with bits of information that we strive to decipher. Yet the fact is that our advances are modest and only provide a fragmentary perspective on the daily lives of the people of the Pleistocene. In most cases we accumulate data without going much further.

We have committed ourselves to far-reaching hypotheses lacking any real heuristic value, without stopping to consider why it is so difficult to go beyond the stage of accumulating data. Is this perhaps because we have mishandled our analytical tools? On reflection, it appears unlikely that the problem can simply be attributed to methodological deficiencies. Could it be that our perception is distorted by our conceptual framework? Could it be that we need to rethink our fundamental ideas underlying the methodological tools offered by typology and technology?

Over the past 20 years, technology, perceived as an analytical improvement, has come to replace typology as the method for archaeological analysis of artifacts. But this perspective on objects, in the way that it is practiced, always harkens back to a hylomorphic dualism, which follows the Platonic tradition in opposing form and material, dissociating *logos* and *techné*. From this perspective, technology is a simple analytical tool, like a manual that makes it possible to understand an unknown object, but without understanding its purpose. Neither the history nor the potential destiny of the object (individuality) is apprehended, except perhaps its operating mode (specificity), but alas this operating mode of the object is largely hypothetical as it is based on intuitive reasoning, which is speculative and never comparative.[1] Under these conditions how can we understand anything about early prehistory when the only witness we possess is the artifacts that are made, in the great majority of cases, from a single type of material: minerals?

Technology, as applied by archaeologists, leads us to a double contradiction. In an effort to restore the humanity of the object, we naturalize[2] it by altering its *raison d'être* in the world, that is, its utilitarian and sign functions (Deforge, 1985).

We must return *logos*[3] to *techné*.[4] This requires rethinking the relationship between technique and human. Technique is too often experienced as an instrument dedicated to satisfying objectives whose establishment is foreign to itself.

DOI: 10.4324/9781003359081-2

In a sense, no technical object exists for itself, but rather it exists through and in relation to a milieu. As Simondon (1958) pointed out, in creating a technology,[5] in the sense of the study of technique, it is necessary to integrate the technical reality into the universal elements of culture. Technique should stand on the same footing as magic religion etc. as a mode of being in the world. But this recognition of the cultural value of technique requires an investigation of the technical nature of the object. The object must be reconceptualized in a structural coupling with humanity, itself in a process of becoming. This idea of coupling necessarily implies a coevolution of humanity and technique, the latter of which is regulated by the "laws of evolution."[6]

Our goal is to rethink the object in the process of becoming rather than from a naturalistic perspective. To do this, we begin by considering typology and technology as they are currently experienced and used before launching a proposal for a new analytic approach: a techno-logic and a genesis of the technical object.

Typology: a necessity with limited utility

Typology was developed in the first part of the twentieth century to put order into a jumble of taxonomies.[7] Typologies made differences apparent by taking into account a limited number of characters and groupings. For this task typology was an effective tool.

Difficulties began once researchers tried to determine how to interpret these differences (Bateson, 1977, 1980). Even though this effort was logical and necessary, it actually required taking a step back to consider the actual informational content of the criteria used in typologies. Following the initial stumbling blocks and the polemics that followed—the most renowned of which is the debate between Lewis Binford (Binford, 1973; Binford and Binford, 1966) and François Bordes (Bordes, 1953, 1961a, 1981)—the need for such introspection should have been clear. Two questions can thus be posed:

1 Why are there such disparities in the ability of typologies to make distinctions among the industries of the Upper Paleolithic in comparison to the industries of the Middle Paleolithic?
2 Are typologies capable of making sense of the differences that they make apparent?

In response to the first question, the apparent differences between the Middle and Upper Paleolithic are an illusion created by using a single method for the two periods. If it is the case that in the Upper Paleolithic one can differentiate macroscale chrono-chronological entities while the same is not possible for the Middle Paleolithic this indicates that the criteria used to define types in each of these periods are different or not of the same kind.

If the morphological, or rather technical, characters of artifacts are similar from one period to another, then the name they are given, for example, sidescraper, endscraper, and burin, is not neutral. In referring to entities in this way we are making reference to tools with a precise function and mode of functioning. Put in other terms, one associates descriptive characters with techno-functional characters that, if they turn out to be correct, become diagnostic. When one talks of a projectile

6 An epistemological perspective

point, even if we do not know the precise method of hafting, it is nonetheless a projectile point. The same is true for an endscraper, a burin, a borer, an axe, an adze, etc. The types thus created are based on both descriptive and functional criteria.

But we are on less certain terrain for periods earlier than Oxygen Isotope Stage 3 (Last Glacial Period, 57–29,000 years ago). Even if we are certain that these tools served for cutting, scraping, slicing, piercing, or other similar action, it is less clear what techno-morphological characteristics we should be using to identify which function was served by a particular tool. If we take, for example, the Yabrudian sidescraper (Figures 1.1 and 1.2), it is difficult to say based on the form alone whether the retouch on this artifact was created as a transformative part of the tool (for tasks such as scrapping and/or cutting and/or slicing) or whether this retouch actually served to fit the tool to the user's hand (prehensile part). In the same manner, it is far from clear that the designation "hand axe" does not include a variety of differently functioning tools (Figure 1.3). Use wear analysis has convincingly

Figure 1.1 Yabrudian, El Masloukh, Lebanon. The typological analysis classifies this object as a Yabrudian-type sidescraper with steep Quina-type (scalariform) retouch, while the techno-functional analysis makes it clear that there are two distinct types of cutting edges, of which one is adjacent to a backed edge. In effect, the object is the integration of two tools with different modes of prehension and functioning.

An epistemological perspective 7

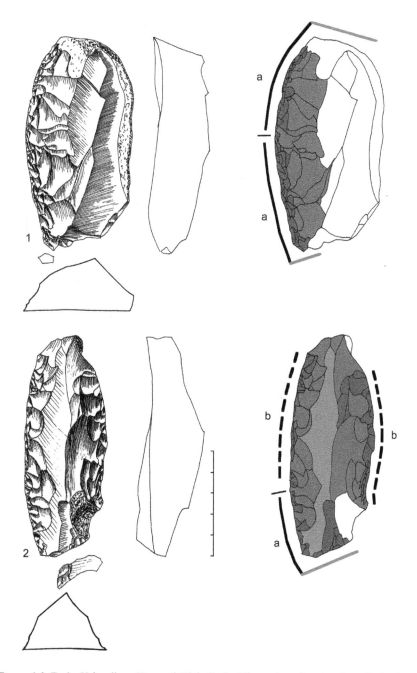

Figure 1.2 Early Yabrudian, Umm el Tlel, Syria. The techno-functional analysis shows that these two pieces, while both are classified as Yabrudian sidescrapers, are conceived as a matrix onto which are grafted either: (1) Two identical techno-functional units (both a). (2) Three techno-functional units (one a and two b).

8 *An epistemological perspective*

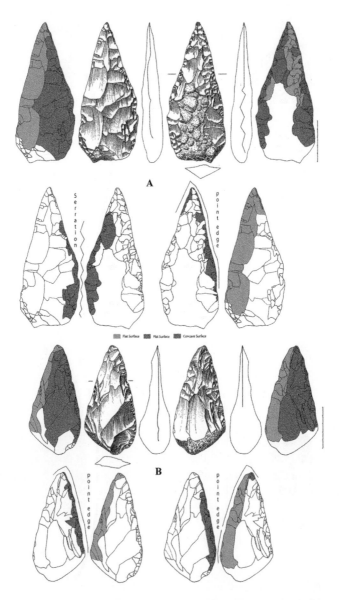

Figure 1.3 Acheulean, Umm el Tlel, Syria. These bifaces are grouped together based on a morphological classification as lanceolates that appear similar. However, the techno-functional analysis shows that these are actually two different objects. The biface A possesses two different tools: a point/edge and an *avoyage*. (The *avoyage* consists of a series of notches created in such a fashion as to shift "teeth" created by the convergence of notches alternatively to the left or to the right.) In plain view, one has the impression of a denticulated edge. However, in sagittal view, one clearly observes picks that are offset in relation to the center. In transversal view, it appears in the form of a sinuous edge (Boëda and Al Sakhel, 2010). Biface B possesses two instances of the same tool: point/edge.

shown that during the Mousterian, there is not an equivalence between a type, following the typology created by Bordes (1953), and a function (Anderson, 1981; Beyries, 1987a).

Moreover, most stone tool typologies only include retouched pieces. What are we to do with unretouched flakes that do not fit under the category of Levallois flakes[8]? Even supposing that we are able to pick out the other predetermined flakes, could we be certain that these flakes in fact corresponded to the knapper's goal?

Recognizing a flake derived from what is called a Levallois debitage is one thing but knowing whether or not it is "successful," that is to say that it conforms to the goal of the knapper or the potential user of the flake, is a different problem (Boëda, 1982). What is the fit between the intention and process of production on the one hand and the functional intention on the other (Bonilauri, 2010)?

The same problems are found in the study of bifacial pieces. If distinctions are based strictly on morphological criteria, we will never make progress. The same form might conceal different tools, while morphological diversity might obscure a single type of tool.

From all available evidence, typology is incapable of taking into account the reality of a tool that is beyond all memory.

It is important to stress the consequences of employing "types" that bear the imprint of a fanciful functionality when one then tries to interpret the resulting groupings. But even if we accept that these types are capable of classifying variability, what can they possibly do other than differentiate? Typology is not a tool for giving meaning, rather it is meant to bring out differences. In the case of typology, as we practice it, the objects are *naturalized*. As such, typology is an essentially hylomorphic approach. A paradox emerges. Rather than trying to understand the particular meaning of different assemblages, one endeavors to show that differences are in a sense natural because they are in essence anthropological/biological and/or environmental. It is as though the assemblages have become inert, passive, and without any dynamic, to be explained based on factors that are external to the assemblages, which have become *naturalized* objects. This line of reasoning continuously negates the *hyle*, the material, in favor of the *morphe*, the form. The form and the material are considered in exteriority.

In such conditions how can we possibly understand anything about technical worlds that are beyond memory? Does typology not lead us into a double contradiction, that in our desire to endow the object with its human element we do the contrary by naturalizing it as an instrument in the service of a goal and, moreover, by distorting its actual reason for existence in the world: its function for use and/or its function as sign?

Techné without logos

The goal of technology, as developed by its founding figures—Marcel Mauss (1947) and André Leroi-Gourhan (1943, 1945, 1964, 1965, 1983)—was to put humans back at the heart of the debate based on what is accessible to us: our technical reality. This was not the technique of a technician who takes a perspective from

10   *An epistemological perspective*

"the interior of the object." Rather this is a technique that encompasses people and their external milieu within a symbiotic relationship where culture serves as the mediator, thus creating what Leroi-Gourhan called the "exterior milieu" (Leroi-Gourhan, 1943, 1945).

The technology of Leroi-Gourhan opens a double perspective on the reality of prehistoric people. The first is a synchronic perspective capable of reconstructing a temporal and spatial understanding of daily life through the concept of the *chaîne opératoire*. The second is a diachronic perspective that rests on the concepts of *tendance* and evolution of technique. According to Leroi-Gourhan, *tendance* is a kind of general evolutionary process regulated by functional determinism. The interior and external environments of each society are inherent in the object, without necessarily modifying its functional essence. Each "lineage"[9] of objects evolves toward increased effectiveness. As research on prehistory has developed, the different perspectives found in Leroi-Gourhan's writings on technology have led to divergent intellectual paths. The idea of the existence of a logic in the evolution of tools has held much greater interest for researchers from domains outside of prehistory, while prehistorians have focused on the synchronic observation of technical facts. To a certain extent, the approach taken by prehistorians leads back to a view of technique that lacks temporality. From this perspective, technique has a role of instrumental complementarity that exists at a particular moment and place. As a result, there is no reason to explore the essential connection between different times and places because evolution is in the capable hands of the anthropologico/environmental dyad. Technique is reduced to an accumulation of knowledge and skill that has only operational consequences. If we follow this reasoning, there would not be a technical culture with all of its imbricated implications that are manifest before the expression of symbolic activity and thus of thought that uses language. Of course, this extreme position is not held unanimously, but it is nonetheless dominant (Tattersall, 1997, 1999).

The refusal to deploy the diachronic dimension as an essential component of technique rests on the same principles.

Despite these fundamental hurdles to a comprehensive understanding of technique, the application of the *chaîne opératoire*, together with experimentation, has made it possible to approximate the knowledge (*connaissance*) and skill (*savoir faire*) required to achieve particular objectives. The results have shed new light on the means and modes of production, shaping (*façonnage*) and flaking (*debitage*), that have clarified the systematics of Paleolithic stone tool assemblages such as Clactonian, Levallois, Discoid, and Quina (Boëda, 1993, 1994, 1995b; Bourguignon, 1997; Forestier, 1993; Soriano, 2000, 2001), using a new system built around techno-types (Boëda, 1997).

However, it is imperative to recognize, as I have argued above, that the resulting technological approach has gradually diminished in scope to the most technical aspects while abandoning the goal of a comprehensive perception of technique, as envisioned by Mauss and Leroi-Gourhan. In a way we find ourselves making diacritical diagrams of cores or bifacial pieces without a goal beyond showing similarity and difference. The methods of technological analysis have simply replaced the cumulative graphs of François Bordes without fundamentally changing the goals of analysis. The absence of a synthesizing perspective has led to a practice that focuses obsessively on the mode of production at the cost of a broader goal of the technical analysis of the objectives—the actual tools. The result is to indirectly validate the goals of typology, the approach the technological analysis was meant to replace. Does one not end up with an analytic approach that joins together the identification of the technical modes of production with a typological approach to the tools? This dichotomy in analysis leads "naturally" to a rupture between the production of supports and the tools they are used to make, and that are their reason for manufacture in the first place! It is as though the production was a finality in and of itself without a relation to the objective of production. Of course, in principle, nobody would support such a vision, but in reality, this is the nature of our practice!

The focus on identifying modes of production can be considered a positivist approach that aims to add scientific knowledge through the establishment of facts. However, what this approach gains in rigor it loses in terms of its *raison d'être*. The absence of a diachronic perspective in technological analyses that goes beyond the dynamics of a particular production sequence has the end result, like typological analyses, of *naturalizing* the objects.

On the necessity of a technology of change

The notion of tendance

In introducing the term "tendance" (Leroi-Gourhan, 1945/1973: 336) Leroi-Gourhan drew attention to the technical object as the result of an evolutionary process that follows a functional logic. In other words, the technical *tendance*[10] was a unique means of gaining objective knowledge of a tool but without proposing an explanatory model.

The functional logic that Leroi-Gourhan sought was based on the conception of a tool as at once material and gesture—the form implies the grip, which implies the use. The *tendance*[11] draws on both the object itself and the operational scheme through which it was made. Leroi-Gourhan distinguishes three principal lineages of gestures—thrusting percussion (*percussion lancée*, where the tool held in the hand is projected toward the material to be worked as in the case of a hammer), resting percussion (*percussion posée*, where the tool is applied to the material through the direct application of muscular force as in the case of a knife, scraper or saw), and resting percussion with a hammerstone, which is in a sense a combination of the previous two types of gesture.[12] Each of these lineages is served by a succession of tools technically adapted to the task. Because the lineage is defined based on a gesture rather than a physical object, the physical object does not define the lineage and it can therefore change form which is to say structure. The evolution of tools is thus regulated by a technical determinism related to the properties of the material worked using one gesture or another. For Leroi-Gourhan, there are no lineages particular to objects. The objects transform themselves to optimally respond, according to the law of determinism, to their purpose.

12   *An epistemological perspective*

If we adhere strictly to this idea of techno-genesis, which shows that tools are the product of transformations, it becomes apparent that to understand the adaptation of the tool to its function, it is first necessary to examine the tool itself as a locus of evolution. But we must initially take into account Simondon's statement that "no fixed structure corresponds to a specific usage. The same result may be obtained through very different operations and structures" (translated from Simondon, 1958: 19). As a result, the notion of determinism becomes null and void and can only be applied in a very general fashion that provides little insight. However, situating the tool as the locus of evolution, which manifests itself through a succession of tools, assumes two preconditions that we are far from having achieved. We must first be capable of truly identifying the function and the functioning of each prehistoric tool, and both function and functioning must not vary across either time or space.

In essence, if one should apply the idea of *tendance* to the tool in action how can we observe *tendance* over the course of millions of years, for tools that we know nothing about, that are beyond memory, except for an epi-phylogenetic memory (Stiegler, 1994)?[13]

We must also consider another scale of analysis: the technical ensemble, or ensembles. No technical object can be understood outside of the milieu within which it is embodied. This associated milieu[14] (Simondon, 1958) develops from the combination of the geographical environment (physical and human) and technical environment (formed by the totality of the technical objects and systems present at a given moment) within the framework of a reciprocal relationship with the object. Thus, for the Paleolithic, we find that we have an additional problem. If there is no culture without space, how can we have access to this interactive construction? This is all the more significant if the cultural element, whatever it may be, escapes us. If Leroi-Gourhan's goal was to develop a classification based on the knowledge of the particular object through its contextualization within a process of evolution, it is nevertheless the case that we have no method available that allows us access to the objective of the tool or the system of objects within which it was situated. Developing a comparative approach to give sense to differences is one thing, but what are we comparing?

In the case of lithic analysis, does typological or technological analysis—such as they are currently practiced—allow us to determine that two assemblages are similar? On what basis can we talk about a *tendance* over long periods of time? What connects the elements of the *tendance*? In fact, it is not our perception of that object that is at fault (even though it is clearly insufficient), but rather the error is to imagine that the laws of becoming correspond to this perception, since the individuality and specificity of objects are unstable.

In summary, to extend the ideas of Leroi-Gourhan, the understanding of a tool is only possible to the extent that it can be situated within a *tendance* that is expressed by the existence of a lineage. But there are two problems:

- The access to the objectivity of the tool remains unresolved. The exception is those tools for which the essential elements are still present in our memory, where there remains an agreement between the epi-phylogenetic memory carried by the tool and our own memory of this same tool[15]; however, objects older than 40,000 years are completely unknown to us.

- It is not clear what type of objectivity we are talking about. If one takes the concept of *tendance* as defined by Leroi-Gourhan, then the function creates the object, thus resulting in the creation of a limited range of tools through time. Nonetheless, he qualified his ideas by recognizing that one must allow for a limited *tendance* that is grafted onto a general *tendance*, because many ethnographic examples show the use of different objects for the same action.

This problem is, in our opinion, derived from the rule according to which the function creates the object. The introduction by Simondon of the concept of structure as a replacement for form[16] shifts the foundations for the understanding of the tool, of its objectivity, and opens an unexpected analytic perspective.

From form to structure, from *tendance* to individuation

Leroi-Gourhan sought to classify tools based on their mode of operation, but the equivalence he made between function and form led automatically back to a classification of objects according to their form. For Simondon, the structure, disassociated from a particular use, took priority over form, the latter being only an element (as in a part of a system). These concepts of form and structure evoke the classic Aristotelian definition of the object (being) known under the rubric of hylomorphism, according to which each object is the product of the impression of a form *(morphe)* in matter *(hyle)*. Form is thus the source of qualitative properties and matter is the source of quantitative properties. This perspective gave rise to a disequilibrium in that matter, viewed as amorphous and inert, has a passive and non-creative role in contrast to the desired form that is the result of creation. Hottois correctly emphasizes that "the relation between form and matter is considered from the exterior, without consideration for the reality which is active and determinant" (translated from Hottois, 1993: 35).

But to truly grasp the technical object does it suffice to rethink the relation between form and matter from a systemic approach that allows matter its constructive role and form its place as one of the elements that structure matter? Certainly, this approach enhances the understanding of the object, but it does not fundamentally reorient our perspective. We continue to think of the object as an established entity. Understanding of tools has certainly increased, whether in terms of their realization or their mode of functioning, but this does not alter in any way their mode of perception, which is that of the artisan producer/consumer.

It is the same for the concept of *tendance*. Is this not simply a succession of states, without explanatory linkages? Evolution becomes just the sum of successive states punctuated by the hazards of life. The *tendance*, just like the technical object, is experienced from the exterior. In fact, even if one succeeds in perceiving the changes, it is impossible for us to understand them. Because understanding change requires us to discern the processes that lead to change. These processes are of the order of ontogenesis and not simply ontology. Simondon

14   *An epistemological perspective*

designates these processes as individuation (Simondon, 1958). The individual—the constituted object—can only be apprehended through its genesis: not of its material existence but of its existence in becoming. Every technical object is thus at once the result of individuation, meaning a particular individuality, and a becoming, that is, individualizing. Thus, understanding a technical object must be based on "criteria of genesis for defining the individuality and the specificity of the technical object: the individual technical object is not one thing or another in the here and now, but that for which there is a genesis" (translated from Simondon, 1958: 20). This comes back to objectivizing every technical object by the place it occupies in a lineage. Each object on the same lineage is also a new form of equilibrium that calls out to be superseded and transformed. Each state is a metastable state and not a stable state without a becoming, as was claimed based on hylomorphic perception.

At the same time, we must also emphasize that these states of successive metastability are not in any sense steps of improvement toward perfection, as suggested by Leroi-Gourhan to explain the concept of *tendance*. On the contrary, it suggests the successive integration of anterior states, with each state having the potential for restructuring and being capable of responding to new functional demands. The notion of improvement toward perfection is an external view of the technical object, exterior and subjective. It is similar to the perception of the fit between the integrated milieu of the object and the object itself. In other words, improvement toward perfection is a means of assessment on the side of the one who manipulates, while the recognition of the changing object is "in the object." One could suggest that the notion of improvement toward perfection is experienced in an ambivalent fashion. It involves an exterior appreciation reflecting the continual innovative change of an invention, but this, in turn, takes us back to an internal dimension of the object that is never explored. This situation is the result of the concept of progress, the primary cause of improvement toward perfection, which in prehistory is experienced entirely on the exterior of the object. The driving forces of this exteriority are the cognitive capacity of different hominids and/or environmental change. This determinist model limits the tool to an instrumental role, detached from the human, without a distinctive becoming.

However, if we think of every technical object as an object potentially in a process of becoming, thus in transformation, this implies that the transformation is inherent in the potential for becoming that we have called a lineage. The object possesses its distinctive becoming, its genesis having been inscribed in itself. This requires an evolution of technique to develop through an inorganic exteriorization that mediates between the living organism and the environment. Change is thus the outcome of positive feedback effects between the human and the internal structure of the technical object, the only "location" capable of their integration. The capacity to integrate new input depends on the evolutionary potential of the structure of the technical object and its stage of evolution. One can thus observe an additive process that creates the conditions for a dynamic of the renewal of the objects, with all the potential social consequences. One can then talk of coevolution between humans and technique. To become real, these

An epistemological perspective 15

structural exigencies need the human, which is at the center of the evolutionary mechanism. It is the human who produces, induces, modifies, orients, and halts. It is the human that allows them to be.

From structure to lineage

To get beyond a descriptive and comparative study of technology, it is not only a matter of looking beyond a synchronic perspective to a technology of "genesis." We must approach technical objects in terms of structure rather than morphology.[17] Although form is visually apparent, this does not mean that the technical object can be reduced to form. Form is only one of the structuring characteristics, which has variable consequences. However, the search for structuring characteristics takes place within the framework of a diachronic perspective. The analytical tools must consider the structuring elements of the technical object and the evolutionary stage to which this structure corresponds. This amounts to recognizing the existence of lineages. Understanding technological change takes place through recognition of the phylogenetic lineages to which technical objects belong.

A technical object is not this or that particular object at a given place and time, produced by spontaneous generation. Rather it is the product of an evolution that responds to functional exigencies and more importantly to structural exigencies (distinct and irreducible) that must be considered because they are the condition for the becoming of objects. This becoming constitutes, across time, a lineage. Thus, a lineage groups together the ensemble of technical objects that evolve serving the same function based on a stable principle of functioning, according to the structural exigencies that respond to distinct laws, to which the non-technical considerations (social, economic, etc.) are foreign (Deforge, 1985).

The direction of evolution: from abstract to concrete

The classic "law of evolution"[18] in technology is the trend, leading from the abstract object to the concrete object (Simondon, 1958). By abstract we mean technical objects that can be disassembled into several components that are functionally independent of one another.[19] This can involve the simple juxtaposition of elementary functions. The abstract technical object is different from the concrete technical object, which is characterized by a series of components that must interrelate in order to be operational.[20] In other words, a concrete object is an object in which none of the parts can be separated without the object losing its sense. The concrete object is the result of an evolution that, through a sort of internal convergence of adaptation to itself, culminates in the creation of a synergy between the various components. This synergy results in an increase in structural and functional complexity.

This "law of evolution," as we will see, is perfectly applicable to archaeological objects of study. It has already been the object of synthesis by our predecessors in the study of the transition from primitive to evolved industry. The problem is that the labels "primitive" and "evolved" mask a conceptual deprecation of the former and valorization of the latter. But this is in no way the case in our situation. The

16 *An epistemological perspective*

concrete object is a technical object that has evolved by convergence and adaptation to itself and is thus not necessarily more effective than an earlier technical object in the same lineage. What is involved is an augmentation of the functional synergy of the collection of different elements that make up the object. One can talk of an internal autocorrelation of the different functions of the object culminating in an internal perfecting, but not of a better adaptation to function.

From this principal "law" several laws can be derived, which we qualify as correlative, that make further statements about the evolution of objects in a lineage (Simondon, 1958):

- Technical objects in a lineage evolve toward reduced volume and/or weight. This is what we observe in all periods, and we denominate this as microlithization. This phenomenon can be observed in both the Acheulean and the Mousterian.
- Technical objects in a lineage evolve toward a quasi-autocorrelation illustrated by the case of cores flaked by pressure,[21] and also by "split" type bipolar debitage.[22]
- Technical objects in a lineage evolve toward an extreme specialization (*hypertélie*) that leaves the object nonadaptive once there is a change, even if minor, in the external environmental and cultural milieu.

It is essential to test these propositions on the archaeological material that provides access to very long time periods. If the analysis of prehistoric technical objects reveals that they follow the same laws as contemporary technical objects, it would confirm the existence of a structural evolution that is distinctive to technique, which transcends time and space. This would demonstrate the existence of a single and unique history of techniques, consisting of contemporary and/or successive independent technical lineages, with each lineage undergoing a cycle of transformation that obeys the same laws of evolution!

Through this approach, which we describe as "genetic" in the metaphoric sense of the term, the study of technology becomes an inductive science of operational schemes. This science aims to comprehend technical objects through their geneses, structures, dynamics, and interactions (Hottois, 1993).

The technicity of objects is controlled by the "laws" of evolution, which is particular to the structure of technical objects, but with a necessary interaction between the human and technique. We can thus conceive of a coevolution between humanity and technique. Humans create the technical, and the technical, controlled by the "laws" of evolution particular to the structure of technical objects, makes apparent its potential to become.

In the course of evolution, the interaction between humans and\technique has become increasingly fraught. We have reached the point where these issues have become particularly tangible to modern society. Today, in effect, the lineages of modern technical objects can be perceived at the scale of a single generation or even an individual. This was never the case during prehistory where the scale of a lineage was of the order of a millennium if not more. It is thus remarkably interesting to inquire into the causes of this acceleration. The capacity for memory

An epistemological perspective 17

and communication is certainly essential. Memory is the locus of storage, capitalization, and of reorganization of input, which provides the sources of invention. Communication, from individual to individual through apprenticeship and between groups through contacts and exchange, would have a cumulative effect and would most certainly be amplified by demographic growth.

The place of the human

Recognizing the distinctive role of technical objects in evolution, based on their internal potential dynamic, does not signify that humans are outside the course of this development, quite to the contrary. As stated earlier, in order to become real, the structural exigencies need humanity, which is at the center of the evolutionary process. It is humans who produce, induce, modify, orient, and halt.[23] It is a person that allows the technical object to be. However, several particular points are worth emphasizing. In the first place, there is a process of invention, independent of these modalities. The "absolute" point of departure is a human creation. But a creation made from recombination articulated around a memory, a heritage. The process of the individuation of the technical object is therefore exterior to itself. But its genesis, that which leads toward individuation is bound to its particular structural potential, from which is derived the concept of coevolution between humans and technique. In the second place, and deriving from what has just been stated, the structural potential cannot be revealed unless humans appropriate it. This appropriation can only take place in the context of a technical culture (Simondon, 1958, 1964). Technical culture in turn transforms humans and leads them to evolve (Hottois, 2004).

But can one speak of a technical culture for periods dating back two million years? Given the omnipresent underlying ontological questions, for these early periods, technique is reduced to only its instrumental condition: an ensemble of means with particular ends. The *longue durée* of the evolutions of techniques, the phenomenon of convergence, and the use life of certain technical objects are among the many factors that come together to create a biological/environmental paradigm that excludes the technique as a factor of coevolution.

But if we change the perspective of analysis, every technical object conceived as a stage in a phylogenetic lineage and no longer as an object fixed in a given time and place, we can revive an analysis of technology. If technological analysis is capable of taking into account these lineages, and the evolutionary cycles distinctive to each lineage, then we can clearly grasp the "locus" of interaction between humans and technique.

In place of a linear and gradual vision where every change is attributed to the biological/environmental duo, through the recognition of technical culture, we restore to humanity its capacity to produce alterity (otherness).

Notes

1 We will see later that the memory carried by the object varies by chronological period.
2 Much as we do to conserve a plant or animal by mounting it. One only conserves its exterior envelope!

18 *An epistemological perspective*

3 This is a term that has taken on multiple meanings over time. We use it here as a synonym for a mode of speech, a language capable of expressing in the case of technology the knowledge of a discipline.

4 The *technè (tekhne)* for the Greeks designated the knowledge and skill (*savoir faire*) of the artisanal professionals or artists. It combines experience and doctrine, such that the knowledge can be applied and thus demonstrate its real existence (Charles, 1984).

5 The word "technology" has multiple meanings and it would be futile and useless to attempt a synthesis. This word has evolved as a function of the development of techniques. To paraphrase the famous title of the book by Simondon, we would say that technological knowledge allows us to arrive at the "mode of existence of technical objects." In other words, technology should allow us a more objective perspective on the process of technical evolution by becoming increasingly operative and not more narrowly anthropocentric, that is to say, an instrumental vision of tools as viewed by the human: "The process of technical evolution is the process through which the relationship to nature becomes objective and is formalized in the form of an ensemble of increasingly well-coordinated operations" (translated from Guchet, 2008).

6 Taken in the metaphorical sense of the term.

7 The most influential works for the Middle and Lower Paleolithic are Breuil, 1923, Leakey, 1951; Movius, 1957; Tixier, 1957, 1958–1959; Bordes, 1953, 1961a; Heinzelin de Brancourt, 1960, 1962; Bosinski, 1967.

8 As only the classic forms are incorporated in the typological classification, only a small number of the intentional Levallois artifacts are taken into consideration.

9 Leroi-Gourhan does not actually use the term "lineage," but his notion of the "evolutionary series" can be assimilated to the notion of lineage borrowed from Deforge (1985).

10 The notion of *tendance* is taken in its philosophical sense as was recognized by Leroi-Gourhan (1945: 338) to bring together the Bergsonian concept of "*elan vital*" (Bergson 1959, 2009) and the concept of "convergent evolution" of P. Teilhard de Chardin (1955, 1956).

11 For Leroi-Gourhan, if the *tendance* is a generalized trajectory then technical convergence is completely possible, and is in and of itself the proof of the existence of the *tendance* (Leroi-Gourhan, 1945: 338). There is thus not simply a convergence of objects but a convergence of *tendances*, which is the same saying that there is thus only a single tendency: a method of use corresponds to the same object.

12 Translator note: The description of the three types of percussion is drawn from the discussion of Leroi-Gourhan in L. Febvre (1944). Techniques: coment classifier les techniques. *Melanges d'Histoire Sociale* 5(5): 71–74.

13 Epiphylogenetic memory (techno-logic) follows an epigenetic memory (of the nervous system), which is evidence of the increasing corticalization of "flint" (Stiegler, 1994, 1998a). "Epiphylogenesis designates the appearance of a new relationship between the organism and its environment, a new relationship which is also a new state of the material: if the individual is organic matter and thus organized, its relationship to the environment (to the material world in general, both organic and inorganic) is mediated by this organized material that is however inorganic which is the *organon*, the tool with its instructive role (its role as an instrument). Of course, the epiphylogenetic reality, which constitutes in and of itself a new form of drift in a transductive relationship with genetic drift, is animated in a new way after the achievement of corticalization—that is to say after Neanderthal man. The transductive relationship is then no longer between the evolution of chipped flint and the evolution of the cortex (which has stabilized, having entered into the conservation of the supersaturated being), but rather a transduction of technique and the ethnic or social (that is to say the psychic and collective individuation), which demands its own specific method of analysis" (translated from Stiegler 1998b: 251). For Stiegler, epiphylogenetic memory is evidence of a parallel differentiation between the knapped flint and the brain, which reaches an end with the

appearance of Neanderthals. But this barrier, however real it actually is, is not based on any real scientific data, but rather on a classic evolutionary paradigm. On the contrary, the currently available technological data indicate that epiphylogenetic memory appears with the first knapped objects.

14 Simondon's associated milieu is an environment (geographic or other) that becomes, as a distinctive characteristic, one of the functional elements of a system. This is different from Leroi-Gourhan's external milieu that is defined as "a natural inert milieu, consisting of rocks, the wind, trees, and animals, but also the bearer of the objects and ideas of different human groups. The inert milieu provides the basic consumable materials, and the technical envelope of a perfectly enclosed group would be such that it would, as the bearer of object and ideas of human groups, allow for the maximum use of the aptitudes of the internal milieu" (translated from Leroi-Gourhan, 1945/1973: 334). This environment thus plays a deterministic role, the engine of the tendency as indicated by the technosphere—the elementary means of action on material, which is an interface between humanity and the environment. While for Simondon, the associated environment is a constitutive element of the technical object. The technical object and the associated environment create a system on the basis of strong interactions and retroactive effects.

15 This is the case for the material studied by Leroi-Gourhan, which he published in his thesis in 1946: *Archéologie du Pacifique-Nord*.

16 "No fixed structure corresponds to a defined function (*usage*). The same result can be obtained through very different operations and structures" (translated from Simondon, 1958: 19).

17 Explanation of the appearance of bifaces is one of the best examples. Is this object not explained on the basis of the appearance of symmetry without any attention to what is covered by this new structure? And what happens if we apply this reasoning to the Eiffel Tower? This would be to forget the structural properties specific to the material employed. The proof is that at the end of the twentieth century, due to the utilization of new materials, some structures could be built in asymmetrical fashion.

18 Of course, the concept of "law" must be taken in tis metaphorical sense and at the level of generalization.

19 The entomology of "*abs-trait*" signifies outside of, separated from.

20 Concrete is derived from *concrescere, concretum*, which signifies growing together and relates to a common development to engender something new.

21 The relationship between the knapper and the core, which results from the mode of detachment and the structure of the core, are such that one can imagine a system that only terminates with the disappearance of the raw material.

22 This conception of knapping, which is discussed in detail in Chapter 2, sees the replacement of the cobble core by two identical flakes. There is not a residual volume that has not been transformed. This mode of knapping, which is unique, is the quintessential expression of structural rationality because the "core" disappears to the benefit of the objectives.

23 When we speak of humans (*l'homme*), we are thinking in a general universal sense. But this convention introduces an apory, because each human or group of humans has its own grasp of the reality of the world and lives this reality as unique, as *the* world (Husserl, 1988). For us as prehistorians, as opposed to ethnologists or historians, it is impossible to elucidate these different representations of the world. On the other hand, we seek, by looking at long periods of time to make a correlation between humans and their techniques (through the objects) as a process of social construction (de Villers, 2010), in order not to *naturalize* the objects, or to reduce them to an ensemble of data whether obtained through experimentation or not, nor to limit them to a causal relationship that unifies humans and the object so that we can bring out the universals, the "laws" that elucidate an element of the evolutionary potential of objects.

2 The techno-logic of evolution

A key to understanding human technicity

Tools

The contribution of a techno-functional approach

Our objective is to promote a holistic technical analysis capable of taking into account the long history of incising[1] tools from prehistory until our own time. As the capacity to incise is an intrinsic potential property of all hard rocks, this then allows us to develop a structural analysis capable of making evident the dynamic evolutionary potential of this material, mediated by humans.

By first making apparent the existence of lineages of technical objects and/or of production schema that are controlled by the "laws of evolution," it is subsequently possible for us, taking into account the spatial dimension that is constitutive of every culture, to arrive at the phenomena of invention, innovation, diffusion, migration, and/or convergence. This is, and must remain, our objective. Even if the theoretical reflection leads to methodological innovation, we must nonetheless resist having methodology become an end in and of itself, as has happened every time there has been a methodological contribution to lithic technology, confounding the means with the ends.

The necessity of theorizing the tool

Every technical gesture is conditioned by the realization of a goal, by means of an object, while respecting the learned way of making. The technical investment is oriented toward the objective, the tool is the means, and the production is its condition of existence.

As a result, the ultimate goal of every technological analysis should be the determination of the objectives through an understanding of the tools used and their means of production. It is this relationship between the tool and the means of production that, in many cases, provides the basis for the possibility of observing the evolution of tools.

In a sense, any evolution (change, modification) of tools has a feedback effect on the mode of production. The latter, depending on its structure and its evolutionary stage, will or will not be able to respond. Thus, there exists a coevolution between the technical object and its method of production, in the same way that there is a

DOI: 10.4324/9781003359081-3

coevolution between technique and humans. The evolution of tools is dependent on the responsive capacity of modes of production. Modes of production will not evolve except as a function of the evolution of the sought-after means to respond to goals, in other terms, new goals that require new means. However, here again, only humanity, through the desire to make a change, is at the center of the mechanism.

What is a tool?

A tool only exists in action (Leroi-Gourhan, 1964). We must consider the tool as a mixed entity consisting of three components: the object itself designated as an artifact, the utilization scheme (Rabardel, 1995), and the energy that sets it in action[2] (Figure 2.1). In typological analysis, in the way this is still practiced, these three concepts are confounded.

In a typology, the utilization scheme is suggested through the name given to an artifact (e.g., endscraper and axe). Of course, this "functional" attribution flows from the technical memory that persists around every object. This attribution might have some merit, in the case of a tool such as an axe, an arrowhead, or an endscraper, or it might be completely subjective and erroneous, as in the case of sidescrapers and bifaces. This problem is all the more pressing when the object has not been shaped through retouch as for example in the case of the Leiliras of Australia (Figures 2.2, 2.3; Spencer and Gillens, 1912; Noone, 1943, 1949; Davidson, 1935), or in the study of Levallois points (Figure 2.4; Bonilauri, 2010). In both of these cases, the same triangular object corresponds to different functions and functioning.

The concept of energy, in and of itself, is never evoked directly.[3] One speaks of maintenance, hafting, and/or gesture without discussing the type of energy input. There are two interrelated reasons for this lack of attention.

The behavioral approach to ancient periods is the primary reason for the lack of attention to the concept of energy. Behavioral approaches are based largely on

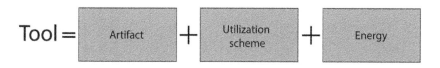

Figure 2.1 The three components of a tool.

Figure 2.2 A hafted Leilira (ethnographic unretouched point from Australia).

22   *The techno-logic of evolution*

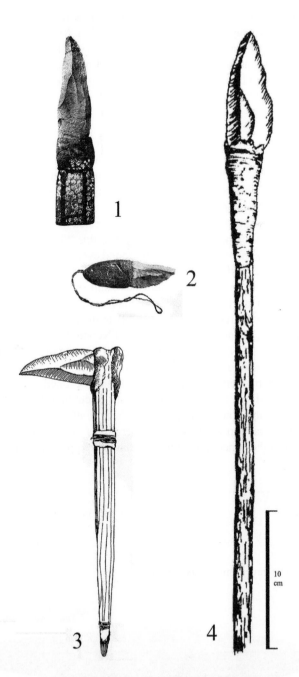

Figure 2.3 Hafted Leilira: (1) A triangular blade that was used for piercing and cutting (Noone, 1943, 1949). (2) A triangular blade held in a wrapping used for cutting and carving. (3) Pick (Spencer and Gillens, 1912). (4) Lance (Davidson, 1935).

The techno-logic of evolution 23

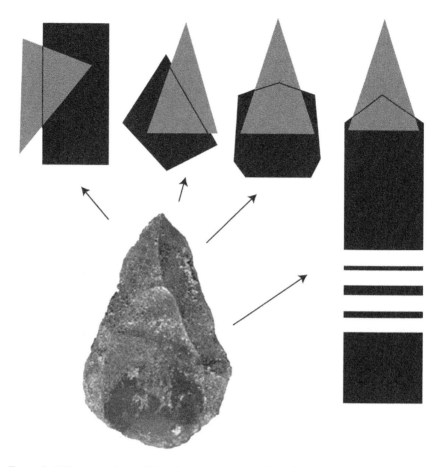

Figure 2.4 The currently available data on the use of a Levallois point shows that it might be used for different manners of functioning, without a causal relationship with the type of worked material (Bonilauri, 2010).

models derived from ethology. On this basis, manual prehension, the way in which an object is gripped and the quality or efficiency of the gesture that follows, is presented as pieces of evidence of an evolutionary process, when, in fact, this is a purely speculative opinion that is not based on any scientific data.[4]

The second reason is the result of an implicit general law, accepted since Condorcet, according to which the principal role of technique is 'the infinite improvement of our species' and that sees in *Homo sapiens* (us), *Homo faber* (man the toolmaker).[5] There flows from this an unexamined assumption according to which tools are gripped directly in the palm of the hand until the Upper Paleolithic, or slightly earlier. There are a small number of studies that convincingly demonstrate hafting in the Lower and Middle Paleolithic[6] (Anderson-Gerfaud, 1981; Keeley, 1982; Anderson-Gerfaud and Helmer, 1987; Beyries, 1987a and b); however, this is a domain of research that is only beginning to be explored[7] (Bonilauri, 2010).

We must conceive of every tool as possessing the functional and cultural particularities held by the operator, which are evident in the artifact and/or the operational scheme. This pair can result in a high level of variability that nullifies any attempt at generalization: the same artifact can be associated with multiple utilization schemes, in the same way that the same utilization scheme may be realized using different artifacts. Similarly, we must take into account the phenomenon of catachresis, where the function of the object is completely diverted from that which justified its existence. In other words, one uses a tool by conferring on it a function that is different from the one for which it was initially destined.

In fact, speaking about a tool without knowledge of its epi-phylogenetic[8] memory is an apory.

To eventually reach an understanding of the content of this memory, we must rethink the genesis, in the sense of that which structures the tool and that is structured with it. The artifact is an element of a system where the subject (the actor), the matter that is to be worked, and the social and natural milieu are all structuring elements. However, to be operational, in the sense of being able to produce the desired effects, the artifact must also be structured according to the scheme that is adopted. To define these two levels of structuring, we borrow from ergonomics (Rabardel, 1995) the terms instrumentalization and instrumentation. The perception of the object is referred to as the process of instrumentalization and the scheme(s) of utilization are subsumed under the processes of instrumentation (Figure 2.5).

The process of instrumentalization: a techno-centric approach

Within the framework of the triad of subject/object/worked material, one can readily understate the degree to which the artifact is subject to a broad range of restrictions, flowing from the relationship between humans and the worked material. These relationships translate into constraints that are at once technical (inherent to

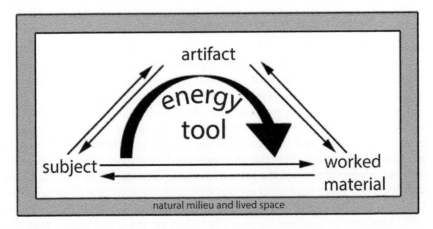

Figure 2.5 The processes of instrumentalization and instrumentation.

The techno-logic of evolution 25

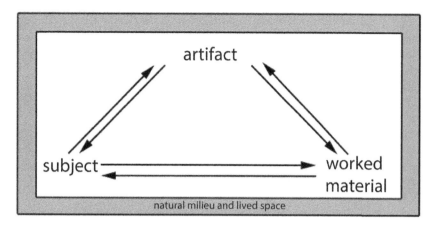

Figure 2.6 The constraints of instrumentalization.

the material) and cultural, which will combine to structure the object (Figure 2.6). One can distinguish two categories of constraints: extrinsic and intrinsic.

We consider four inherent extrinsic constraints:

1 *The material that is to be transformed.* It is obvious that achieving the expected result and the manner of proceeding to reach this result requires a synergy between the physical properties of the material that is to be worked and the technical characteristic of the part of the tool that will be in contact with this material. For example, the hardness of a material will have implications for the technical character of the cutting wedge (the cross-section of a cutting edge), which in turn have consequences that affect the angle of attack used with the tool and thus on the various aspects of the gesture (maintenance and transmission of energy).
2 *The natural milieu in which the action takes place.* This context exercises a potential "constraint" in terms of the quality, availability, and accessibility of the raw material with which the tool is made.[9]
3 *The lived space.* Lived space is interiorized on both the material and the symbolic level: the territory.[10]
4 *The technical memory.* Technical memory is inherited by every member of a group. It is this factor that explains why in a given period and place one produces distinctive objects that are made to function in a particular fashion.[11]

The intrinsic constraints are those that are inherent in the structure of the object used by a group. The blade, the Levallois flake, the biface, or the bifacial piece are objects that despite having different volumes functions or does not, in the same fashion: cutting, engraving, scraping, piercing, and so on. To comprehend each object, it is necessary to analyze it as a technical "individual" structured by an ensemble of technical criteria and interaction, organized as the function of a goal. The interactions between elements can take more or less complex forms, as in the flake and the Levallois point. These relationships are themselves subject to the functional rules that determine the anticipated effect, but other rules could be adopted, producing different effects, as can be observed by comparing a flake held in the hand versus a flake grasped through the intermediary of a haft or grip.

These intrinsic constraints are also the reflection of the evolutionary stage that is distinctive to each lineage. Every development within the lineage is at the same time the reflection of the evolutionary potential of the structural principle of the lineage and a new response to novel constraints. If one accepts the principle that the functions of tools remained the same across millions of years, then the evolution of each lineage will play out on the part of the tool that receives energy and as a result on the part that transmits energy.

The process of instrumentation: an anthropo-centric approach

If, as we have seen, the technical object integrates constraints in relation to the person and the worked material, shifting perspective to the technical object in action leads us to consider another level of constraints linked to the utilization schemas. This consists of a four-way relationship of structuring constraints that must be integrated into the conception of the tool (Figure 2.7).

1 *The constraining relationship of the artifact and the worked material.* These are multiple constraints that are analyzed in terms of effectiveness and know-how. The achievement of an objective requires an effective gesture that can be executed by the tool. It is the gesture utilized that constrains the tool to possess particular technical criteria. It is because I want to realize a particular action that I have need of a particular tool. If I do not respect this condition, I place myself in a situation of catachresis (the use of a tool in place of another for a function that is not its own).

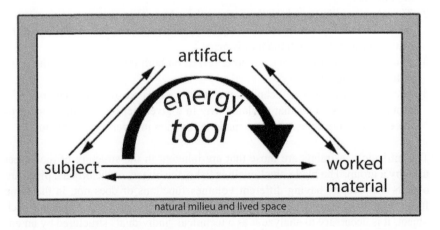

Figure 2.7 The constraints of instrumentation.

2 *The constraining relation of the artifact with the person.* The constituent (structural) properties of artifacts determine the range of gestures and movements. In other words, a flake, a blade, or a bifacial piece offers a range of possible gestures that are particular to each, although they might partially overlap. For example, the same retouch on the edge of a rectangular Levallois flake, the edge of a blade, or even of a biface will have distinctive schemas of prehension and utilization because of the characteristics of the supports.

3 *The constraining relation of the energy transmitted by the person on the artifact.* The success of the task depends on a fit between the energy needed to accomplish the gesture, the reception of the energy, and its transmission. Depending on the exterior cultural constraints, the artifact will be the object of an internal reconstruction of its elements, the evolution of an additional structure (abstract) toward an integrated structure (concrete), as we will see for bifacial pieces, which were replaced by flakes that are artifacts with a more efficient structure. This restructuring or new structure can be a direct response to an improved utilization of energy, as in the shift from flakes to shaped pieces (a worked cobble or biface)—or it can be the result of a modification of the required energy through the creation of an intermediary object—handle or grip—between the hand and the artifact, as in the transition from shaped pieces to Levallois flakes.

4 *The constraint of the person, the artifact, and the worked material in a spatial relationship.* The setting where an activity takes place in some cases will create constraints that require an adaptation of the gesture.

The techno-functional approach

Every crystalline substance can be used for at least two of its properties: its mass and the cutting edge(s). These properties exist naturally or as the result of natural fracture. These two properties can be utilized to transform a worked material using either stationary percussion or throwing (Leroi-Gourhan, 1943/1971). These actions are known from primatological ethology. In a sense, the chimpanzees of West Africa, the macaques of Thailand, and even the capuchins of Brazil utilize the mass of particular rocks as hammers for breaking nuts, fruit, and wood. For the capuchins (*Cebus libidinosus*), some distinctive rocks are used like a hoe for digging out roots and arthropods (Mannu and Ottoni, 2008). This mode of utilization provides indisputable evidence of the selection of rocks for "incising," in this case incising dirt.

Even if the use of rocks for "incising" is generalized among the primates, nonhuman primates do not carry out any transformation of artifacts. Among primates, there is only a selection, whereas among hominins the selection of an object possessing more or less the required technical criteria creates a second artifact. This new artifact can be the outcome of four operational schemes of production and confection.

Scheme 1: Selection[12] of a natural support that has the general volumetric characteristics of the future tool and preparation of a cutting edge.

28   *The techno-logic of evolution*

Scheme 2: Selection or not of a block, shaping, and confection of a cutting edge.

Scheme 3: Selection or not of a block, debitage (flaking, in the sense of producing flakes as supports), and preparation of a cutting edge.

Scheme 4: Mixed scheme with selection/partial shaping/confection of a cutting edge or debitage/partial shaping/confection.

These different schemes appear in succession over time in order to respond to the production of new tools to accomplish the same or different functions and to novel cultural constraints. To understand these transformations, we must adopt a structural framework of analysis, focused on the structural aspect of a tool. We must determine the technical intentions (criteria) required and judged necessary for the the tool to function well. These techno-functional criteria can be completely established during the production stage or be partially present requiring a supplementary step of confection that can vary in length. Therefore, it is necessary in the framework of a techno-functional analysis to combine the production stage with the confection phase.

As was stated previously, an artifact is not defined by what it is at a given moment but by what it is in the process of becoming. It is the determination of the place of the artifact in its lineage that allows us a true understanding. It is essential therefore to choose the criteria capable of taking into account the artifact as it is, as it was, and, eventually, if we are not at the end of a lineage, as it will be. Put in other words, "We must consider the technical object itself both in terms of the internal relations that structure it and in terms of its relationship with anterior forms of the lineage, within the extension of which it is inscribed" (translated from Tinland, 2006: 23).

The internal structural relationship of incising artifacts

An incising artifact[13] can be defined as a material object that can be broken down into a minimum of two techno-functional units (Boëda, 1991, 1997): a prehensile part and a transformative part (Figure 2.8) (Lepot, 1993).

One can distinguish a third intermediary part that, although always present, will play a more or less important role depending on the type of support used[14] and the corresponding function(s). This is the part that transmits energy.[15]

The processes of individuation of the lineage of incising artifacts

The absolute beginning: a naturally incising object

Fragments of hard rock, due to the way the material fractures, have characteristics that form a cutting edge independent of any conscious scheme.[16] Natural processes such as thermal shock, compression, or fracturing can produce effective cutting edges. In fact, the cutting edge is a predetermined trait inherent in the crystalline structure of a mineral material. On the other hand, there is no aspect of predetermination whatsoever that affects the prehensile part. The prehensile part can have

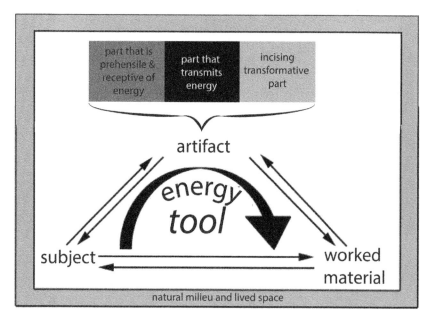

Figure 2.8 Structural breakdown of an incising artifact.

any form, size, or technical criteria that it is possible for chance to produce. Put in another way, if as the result of a natural process a flake possesses at the very least a cutting transformative part, the potential prehensile part will have, in this case, random technical criteria.

This aspect of predetermination that is inherent to mineral material is an intrinsic cause capable of giving rise to lineages of tools. In other words, the lineages of cutting tools did not appear with the imperative to cut, it is the cutting edge that made it possible for the action of cutting to exist. This interior contingency possessed by mineral material does not exclude in any way the influence of extrinsic factors (social, environmental, cognitive), but the absence of a multitude of technical solutions at a given moment is a fundamental proof that these extrinsic factors are not all powerful. In other words, it is the small number of technical solutions that have appeared in the world that are undeniable evidence of an internal technical imperative that results from the specificity and constraints of mineral material.

Thus, the first cutting tools[17] can be defined on a structural level as an entity composed of two independent sub-units, of which the first—the transformative part—spontaneously possesses the operational characteristics, while the second—the prehensile part—can take any form whatsoever (Figure 2.9).

From the perspective of the archaeologist, we must ask how one can be sure that this mode of production is evidence of a human appropriation (recuperation). In a sense, we are in the worst possible situation because the potential indicators of human activity are exterior to objects. How does one move from the status of

30   *The techno-logic of evolution*

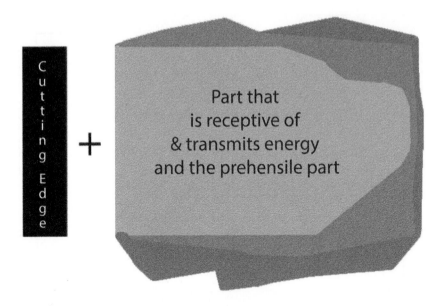

Figure 2.9 The transformative part always possesses *a priori* the characteristic of a sharp edge regardless of how variable this might be. The prehensile part on the other hand is completely variable.

an object to that of an artifact? The answer rests on an integrated analysis of data derived from multiple fields of research: stratigraphy, taphonomy (postdepositional processes), techno-functional analysis, spatial analysis, and so on.

As a result, it will only be possible to identify such objects under extraordinary circumstances. It will be practically impossible for us to recover the time zero of the evolution of incising artifacts. We will grasp the story along the route.

Abstract or additional anthropic structure

The first incising artifact produced by human action (through percussion) can be broken down structurally into component elements in the same manner as those objects that are the result of natural processes. The two functional sub-units, the transformative and prehensile parts, are independent. The entity of the artifact can be conceived as the sum of the two independent sub-units. These sub-units are independent because the technical criteria of the prehensile part do not in any way interfere with the operational characteristics of the cutting edge. In the same way, the transformative part (the cutting edge) does not require particular characteristics in the prehensile part in order to be operational. In fact, with the exception of the capability of at least one edge of a systematically obtained flake to incise, the remainder of the volume can take any characteristics taking any possible "form" (Figure 2.10).

The techno-logic of evolution 31

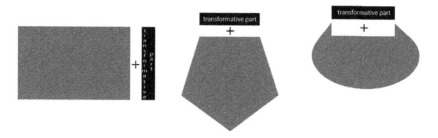

Figure 2.10 The incising characteristic is normalized through its production. The prehensile characteristics are aleatory.

In this situation, each of the two subunits can evolve independently without having any effect on this noninterference. The cutting edge can become regularized across one or more of its criteria—length, cutting angle, cross-section—through the adoption of different concepts of knapping without being associated with any evolution of the prehensile part. The latter might also be the subject of an evolution. Rather than being random, as described earlier, the prehensile part can become the object of a particular predetermination. In this case we can distinguish two approaches.

The first approach consists of selecting an object that naturally possesses the required technical criteria (Figure 2.11). This selection corresponds to an act of predetermination, even though it does not involve acts of volumetric transformation (debitage or shaping).

The second approach corresponds to an act of transformation—debitage, shaping, and preparation. In the case of debitage, the required criteria can be present on the debitage surface of a core. This is the case when the goal is to have a backed flake (an oblique angle along one edge).

Concrete or integrated anthropic structure

As the result of novel functional exigencies—that are in a sense the new constraints to which the technical system must respond through adaptation, modification, or disappearance—the different structural components will trend toward an increasing synergy, which leads them to become dependent.

If the different structural components were at first juxtaposed, they will move to becoming interrelated, merging into one another. Over time, the emerging synergy of the structuring components leads to an object with an increased structural and functional complementarity (Figure 2.12). The concretization develops, synergy by synergy, an integration (organization) of the functional subunits into a unified functioning.

This structural evolution can be observed across long periods of time. But what is the cause? The phenomenon of concretization is evidence of a potential structural adaptation in response to novel individual and societal constraints.

32   *The techno-logic of evolution*

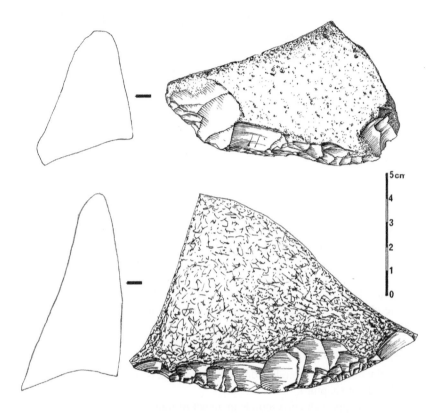

Figure 2.11 Barbas 1, Couche 7—Dordogne, France. Sidescrapers on fragments produced by natural processes (gelifraction of Bergerac flint) that present identical volumetric and technical characteristics.

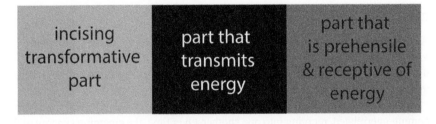

Figure 2.12 Integrated structure: the different subunits interact in synergy.

Modalities of structural evolution: confection, debitage, shaping

The achievement of any particular new concrete structure is directly reliant on confection and/or the modes of production—shaping and debitage.

The process of confection makes it possible to restructure an artifact. This involves putting into place missing structural elements. The extent of the retouch depends on the gap between the technical elements naturally present on the artifact and those elements needed to result in a tool.

The modes of production—shaping or debitage—produce an artifact that can be immediately functional—according to the criteria judged to be necessary and sufficient by the user—or require a secondary stage of confection. In the case of debitage, where the analysis is easier, one can identify a degree of fit between the structural functional evolution of the artifact and the evolution of the structure of production. However, every new structure of an artifact is not synonymous with a new structure of production. In effect, depending on the structural capacity of a mode of debitage (the structure of the core) it will or will not be able to respond to new constraints. For example, the persistence over time and the generalization in space of Levallois debitage can be explained by the capacity of this method to qualitatively and quantitatively diversify its production. This potential for diversification results in variability and thus in the differentiation of one group from another, even though they have the same operational capacity. On the other hand, the disappearance of the bifacial and its replacement by Levallois debitage—as well as the disappearance of the latter and its replacement by blade production—is evidence of new technical exigencies that cannot be satisfied by adapting the available structures for debitage and shaping. In fact, from these two modalities of structural evolution, two tempos can be disassociated: the tempo for modes of production and the tempo for tools.

The tempo of production

From a structural perspective, changes in the mode of production are linked to the capacity of each mode to respond to technical demands. At this stage of analysis, it is useful to contrast the two major modes of lithic production: shaping and debitage. The adoption of these modes over time takes the form of a parabola. In the initial stages of tool production[18] there is debitage,[19] and shaping only develops much later, only to be supplanted by the readoption of debitage. This schema must of course be refined depending on the continent or specific region.[20]

The passage from debitage to shaping

We are interested in the movement from an exclusive focus on debitage to an exclusive focus on shaping. Put in other terms, at a structural level, what is the contribution of shaping to tools?

To clarify this point, we can distinguish three periods:

Period 1: Exclusive debitage
Period 2: Dominant debitage with a bit of shaping
Period 3: Exclusive or dominant shaping

At first glance, this division into three major periods evokes a progressive and linear evolution of technical systems. In fact, this is not the case at all as the techno-functional status of the shaped pieces of Periods 2 and 3 are not identical. One is

34   *The techno-logic of evolution*

not the precursor of the other. It is essential to consider the entirety of the technical system rather than adopting a study focused on one type of object to the detriment of the rest. Every object takes on its sense only in relation to its context. It is necessary to take into account the technical system in its entirety, what Simondon (1958) referred to as the *associated milieu*. An exclusive focus on a single category of object extracts the object from its context. In this approach each type of tool is given an arbitrary status of equivalence from one industry to another, and the result is to combine under the same terminology ensembles that, strictly speaking, have nothing to do with one another.

We find an example of this problem of excessive focus on individual artifact types in attempts to define the Oldowan based on a particular typological composition. Oldowan industries are characterized by production of flakes that are mostly made through phases of debitage. There is variability among sites in the frequency of shaped objects, such as choppers or chopping tools, which make up between 5% and 20% of the tools. Despite this reality, the widespread representation of the Oldowan is as a "homogenous culture" of choppers and chopping tools.[21] Why isolate one type of object and extract it from the other aspects of the assemblage? This diversion is the result of our methods that are essentially naturalist. I would even dare to say that these methods are essentially morphological. Put in other terms, we highlight that which we are able to see.[22] In Oldowan industries the diversity of flakes is such that a morphological analysis is incapable of discerning any trace of techno-functional repetition. There also exists an anthropological dimension to our selective vision. In effect, choppers and chopping tools are often linked to cognitive development. With such a bias, could one possibly have an accurate vision of such ancient industries?

Understanding this distortion in the analysis is crucial because it allows us to see how a change in perspective can bring a different reality to light. If the choppers or chopping tools draw our attention, it is because they possess a structural level that is more organized than the flakes which, in their diversity, provide evidence of a primary abstract structure.

Change of perspective: from morphology to structure, from the object to the ensemble

The chopper and the chopping tool in the case of the Oldowan, and later the biface in the Acheulean, must be read as an effort to achieve a particular volume and/or mass that is different from most of the flakes produced. The volume and mass allow for the establishment of one or more transformative parts and a specific prehensile part. Thus, these objects only make sense within the technical ensemble to which they belong. They are thus not "thinkable" outside the context within which they take on their signification as an artifact[23,24].

When we consider the third period, where shaping is dominant,[25] the analysis of the technical system sheds a different light on the role of the shaped object. This object may still be a chopper/chopping tool[26] (linear cutting edge), as in certain African or Asian industries, or it may present a different form such as the convergence

The techno-logic of evolution   35

of two edges, known in some African and Near Eastern industries under the term "biface."

In these two cases, chopper/chopping tool or biface, the shaped piece substitutes for the flake as a unique support and becomes a matrix whose structure imposes new technical demands (exigencies) not possible in the associated flakes. The term "matrix" (*matrice*) does not signify that these are already concrete structures. Quite to the contrary, we will observe a complete cycle of evolution from the abstract toward the concrete[27] in most of the industries with bifacial pieces in Africa, Europe, and West Asia.

In the case of the chopper/chopping tool or biface, the matrix carries with it new exigencies imposed through the creation of a volume by shaping. Does this mean that debitage does not provide the potential to obtain this type of volume and form? The answer is no. It is possible to produce flakes of an identical volume and to retouch (confection) the edges. But the modes of production of Period 2 do not correspond to the stage of evolution necessary for producing flakes that approximate the desired volume. Therefore, instead of observing this solution as a mode of production, one sees shaping substituted for debitage. The use of shaping was adopted to produce supports that are as close as possible to the eventual volume of the tools, limiting confection to the role of simple adjustment of the cutting edges. We think that shaping was an efficient solution that allowed the resolution of two problems: obtaining a precisely reproducible volumetric structure and allowing for the development of the three parts that are constitutive of every stone tool: transformative, prehensile, and receptive of energy. But is it necessary to have a trigger mechanism?

We have said many times that a tool is not a tool except in action; however, we only rarely insist on the role of energy in the evolution of techniques. In this case why do we not introduce energy as a factor in the structural dynamic? Energy and the gesture that follows intervene in the process of invention. The passage from Periods 1 and 2 (all or dominant flakes) to Period 3 (all or dominantly shaping) becomes a question of configuration and controlling of manual energy and thus of the gestural. To push this hypothesis further, if we compare technical actions across time, we see that there are always the same actions of cutting, slicing, carving, piercing, grating, and scraping. Then, what has changed? Perhaps it is the structural capacity of the artifacts to better adapt to the energy that they receive in order to develop new actions and new gestures. Shaped artifacts become novel supports for tools, while tools on flakes—since they persist—also have a new techno-functional status. It will therefore be very interesting to see the new structure of these flake tools. But, to date, a technological analysis on this theme has not been carried out.

For the shaped component, we observe a cycle of structural evolution that the first prehistorians had already identified using descriptions of archaic and evolved pieces. Is this cycle of structural evolution the evidence of a new energy, a new gesture? We do not think this is the case. Rather it is a case of classic structural evolution where we see in operation the integration of different sub-ensembles, leading to an object in which the functions of different parts are integrated into the functioning of an ensemble.

36 *The techno-logic of evolution*

To better understand the role of shaped pieces in a lithic ensemble, we must employ three degrees of analysis.

The first degree of analysis is the technical ensemble. As we have already said, the object makes sense only within its context. The object is both a constitutive and constituent element of the exterior milieu. Two situations are thus possible:

- The bifacial piece is a predetermined support for a specific tool within a realm of flakes, which requires—contrary to the requirements placed on flakes—a defined mode of production, in this case shaping. The modes of production for the associated and dominant flakes can be varied and can be more or less strongly predetermined.[28]
- The bifacial piece is the predetermined support (matrix) capable of integrating one or more identical or different tools (Figure 2.13). In this case the bifacial piece is quantitatively dominant. The associated flakes are the result of a weakly predetermined mode of production where only the transformative part is the subject of technical investments, or alternatively the result of a mode of production that shows an elevated degree of predetermination, which in some industries is completely absent.

The second degree of analysis relates to situating the structural development within its evolutionary cycle, its lineage. The determination of the evolutionary

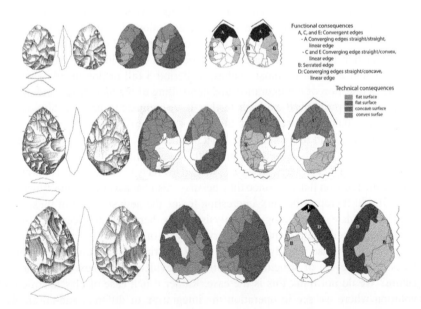

Figure 2.13 The Acheulean industry of Umm el Tlel, Syria. The same silhouette, described as cordiform, serves as the support for a combination of different tools. Only a techno-functional analysis can reveal the different technical intentions.

The techno-logic of evolution 37

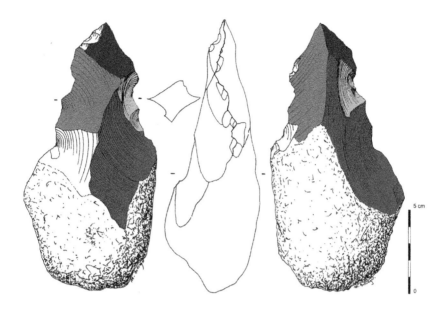

Figure 2.14 El Meirah, Syria. Abstract structure. Mono-tool, a technically and functionally symmetrical structure on a bifacial piece.

stage within a lineage is based on the same principle of study that we have already proposed, which rests on the degree of integration of the three functional parts of a tool: transformative, transmitting, and prehensile. There is evidence of potential independence in production between the transformative and prehensile parts, as is the case for tools on flakes (Figures 2.14 and 2.17). Each of these parts can develop independently without interfering with the functioning of the other. On the other hand, the integrated stage of a shaped piece is based on a global conception of the object (Figures 2.13, 2.15, and 2.16). This globalized conception is expressed by the development of more "standardized" volumes. This standardization takes into account the technical connection between each of the elements, which does not leave much room for flexibility in terms of structural variability. Pieces that show a degree of integration resulting in standardization define the Middle and Upper Acheulean. Like every terminal technical stage, this standardization signifies the final form of a lineage, the end of the cycle of shaping.

The third and final degree of analysis relates to the function and functionality—single tool or multiple tool—of bifacial pieces and the type(s) of tool(s) that they support. Globally, every bifacial structure is organized based on the convergence of two edges, which produces a pseudo-symmetrical plan view. However, as many techno-functional studies have shown, the use of the circumference of the tools is asymmetrical, as in the case that we designate as point/edge, which leaves one of the edges free of any functionalization (Figures 1.3, 2.14, and 2.15). The distinction between single and multiple functionality is *a priori* independent of evolutionary stage. Therefore, we can find mono-functional or multifunctional tools with

38 The techno-logic of evolution

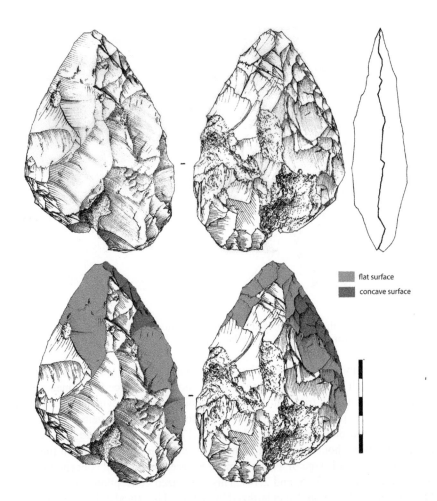

Figure 2.15 Barbas C'3—Dordogne, France. Concrete structure. Asymmetric functional structure: mono-tool on a bifacial piece. Asymmetric functional structure: point/edge tool with a flat/flat (*plan/plan*) and flat/concave (*plan/concave*) cutting edge.

an abstract structure (Figures 2.14 and 2.17) or a concrete structure (Figures 2.14 and 2.15) in the same way that concrete structures can be the support of a single (Figure 2.15) or of multiple tools (Figures 1.3, 2.13, and 2.16). Whoever can make more, can also make less.

The tempo of the bifacial phenomenon

Two observations must be taken into account in considering the preceding discussion. The first is that the bifacial phenomenon appeared multiple times and the second is that the tempo of each developmental cycle is not identical.

The techno-logic of evolution 39

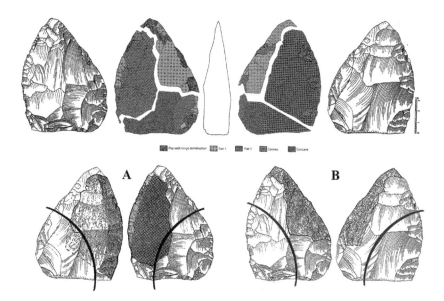

Figure 2.16 Barbas C'3—Dordogne, France. Concrete structure. Asymmetrical functional structure, multi-tool on a bifacial piece. Edge A—flat/convex (*plan/convex*) cutting edge with a convex plan view. Edge B—point/edge with a flat/flat (*plan/plan*) cutting edge.

The phenomenon of shaping, and in particular the bifacial phenomenon, appears in its abstract form in distant locations and disparate times—1.7 million years ago in Africa, 1.2 million years ago in the Middle East, and 0.7 million years ago in Europe.[29] But, each time, in each of these three regions, when bifaces first appear, it is in an abstract form. This is a strong indication that the reappearance of the bifacial phenomenon—each time in its initial "abstract" form—signifies that this is undoubtedly the result of a process of convergence and not a "migrating" technical phenomenon that can be labeled "Mode 2," as we read in some articles. The appearance of "Mode 2" assemblages has been linked to the spread out of Africa of populations of *Homo erectus* (or *Home ergaster*) conquering the world. If this was indeed the case, should we not expect to find the bifacial phenomenon in its developed form from its first appearance in Europe given that there is a delay of almost one million years before the initial appearance of bifaces in Africa and the earliest bifaces in Europe? But in fact, the technique of biface manufacture during the Early Acheulean[30] of Western Europe "remains primitive (usually hard hammerstone), the forms being still in general poorly defined" (translated from Bordes, 1984, Tome II: 15). Nonetheless, the migratory view of evolution, although marked by a surprising lack of scientific argumentation, is dragged from book to book, from scientific article to scientific article, in the most prestigious journals.[31]

In our opinion, it is only if the bifacial form that first appears in a region corresponds to a developed stage in the lineage, without the presence of the entirety of

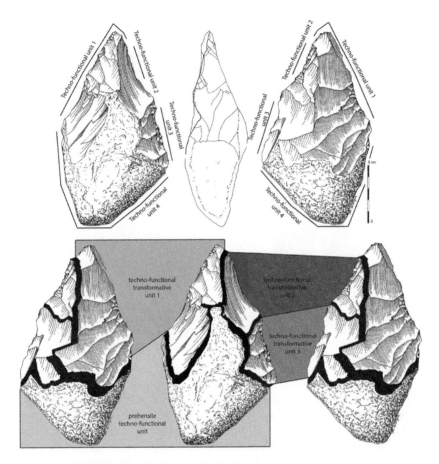

Figure 2.17 El Meirah, Syria. Abstract structure. Asymmetrical functional structure. Multi-tools on a bifacial piece.

anterior stages, beginning with the initial abstract forms, that we can talk in terms of borrowing ideas from migrating populations. If a population at a technical level x departs from point A toward point B, we should at the very least find a technical level x at point B and not a new anterior level u, v, or w.

On the other hand, one can also observe cases where the evolution of bifacial pieces does not proceed through its stages, as is the case in all of East Asia and very surely in eastern India, where one does not observe the evolution toward the concrete forms found in Africa and the Near East. This phenomenon is far from ephemeral and is manifest across an entire continent. How can this be explained?

The analysis of the tempo of the cycles of development from the abstract to the concrete must be treated distinctly in each continent. While in Africa and the Near East,[32] the tempo is very gradual, extending across more than 1.5 million years, in Western Europe the cycle is very rapid, covering less than 300,000 years, and is apparently relatively constant without periods of stasis or disequilibrium in the unfolding of the cycle.[33] On the other hand, in the Near East, it seems that the concrete stages are relatively precocious and last a long time. The African data is too preliminary to make large-scale observations.

It is evident that only well-developed studies can make evident the tempo characteristic of a specific region. This is logical *a priori* because the realization of cycles of development is the work of societies. Nonetheless, if we enlarge our approach to encompass non-bifacial technical systems that are roughly contemporaneous, we can observe a difference between Western Europe and the Near East. As Sylvain Soriano (2005) has shown in an analysis of the technical systems of Western Europe, between Oxygen Isotope Stages 10/9 and 5 (Figure 2.18), the bifacial

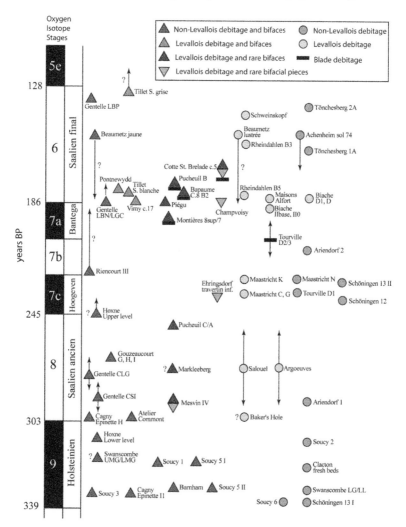

Figure 2.18 In this schema, one can distinguish the range of technical systems present in Europe between Oxygen Isotope stages 9 and 5e. The bifacial phenomenon is found in barely half the cases and is not homogeneous as there are clear disparities in the frequency of bifaces (Soriano, 2005).

42   *The techno-logic of evolution*

system is far from the only technical system present. There is a multitude of contemporary technical systems, evidence of a much greater techno-cultural variability than had been previously described. However, in the Near East and along the Levantine Coast, a sharper rupture exists between the bifacial industries included under the Acheulean and the industries made essentially on flakes and blades that follow. It seems that there is a bifacial period that lasts more than 500,000 years.

*The tempo of the post-bifacial phenomenon: from partial
to full debitage*

As in the case of shaping, where we have discerned several periods, we can create similar divisions for the industries made on flakes:

- Period 4: Almost exclusively debitage (in the generic sense of the term) and a little bit of shaping
- Period 5: Exclusively debitage

Shaping changes its status and reverts to the same situation as before its position of dominance. Making up a minor element in the industry, shaping is used to construct particular tools that the dominant system/s of debitage do not make it possible to produce. This is the case for the so-called Late Acheulean industries of Western Europe or the Yabrudian in the Middle East. In these two cases, the bifacial material makes up less than 5% of the assemblage and often consists of only two or three pieces. These low frequencies are a classic epiphenomenon that in other circumstances would not be noticed because the object found in low frequency might be less remarkable than the biface. However, the crucial element is the system for the production of flakes with which the bifaces are associated. Because debitage has again become dominant, and will later become exclusive, this is indicative of a radical change in the conception of the matrix/support of tool/s. It is the return of full debitage!

But it is not just generic debitage, but rather Levallois debitage that is characteristic of Western Europe and is also found around the periphery of the Mediterranean and throughout Africa (Figure 2.19). In general terms, Levallois debitage is a technical system of production that is capable of producing flakes (so-called Levallois flakes) that approach the form of tools. A supplementary stage of confection (retouch) may be needed to adjust the transformative part but is rarely required to alter the silhouette.

In the Middle East, a completely different technical solution is invented (Figure 2.19). The technical criteria of the tools are obtained following a stage of confection (retouch) that is much more significant because the technical criteria are lacking on the utilized support/flake. In other words, confection is an important stage in the volumetric construction of the tool and the creation of functional cutting edges.

This technical solution is present in three successive industries found in one of the major sites of the Middle East—Umm el Tlel. These industries are designated,

Figure 2.19 In the case of the post-bifacial industries of the Middle East, the shaping of the flake (*confection*) plays a dominant role. With the shift to Levallois debitage, the supports for tools (flakes) are strongly predetermined and the shaping of the flake is limited to a functional role.

from the earliest to the most recent, Umm el Tlelian, Yabrudian, and Hummalian (Boëda and Al Sakhel, 2009). And after the Hummalian we will see the appearance of Levallois debitage.[34]

The observations made at Umm el Tlel raise many questions. Why was there a return to flakes, or in other words, why was the exclusive use of bifaces abandoned? Why are there different technical options? What sense can be given to these differences? Why does the Levallois debitage emerge at the end of the sequence?

To respond to the first question, we must return to energy and pursue our line of reasoning in this regard. We have put forward the hypothesis that shaping, through its capacity to produce all sorts of forms and volumes, was one of the ways to optimize manual energy. So then, why would there be a return to flakes regardless of how predetermined they might be? It suggests once again a problem of energy! We are interested here in the mode of transfer of energy through the flint tool. Is the mode for this transfer of energy always direct or can it become indirect? Could we be faced with the first indication of systematic hafting? Whatever the technical system, both direct and indirect transfer of energy result in regularized tools in which the prehensile part is as significant as the transformative part. Hafting in and of itself does not suffice to explain this investment in the prehensile part. Remember that although the predetermined character of the first tools applied only to the cutting edge (the transformative part), these tools could be hafted, despite the diversity in their prehensile part. In reality, we need to distinguish between two ways of thinking about the relationship between the prehensile part of the tool and the prehensile part of the non-mineral element that we will call the haft (*porte artefact*) (Figure 2.20).

Either it is the tool that adapts to the prehensile part of the haft, or it is the inverse—that the prehensile part of the haft must adapt to the prehensile part of the

44 The techno-logic of evolution

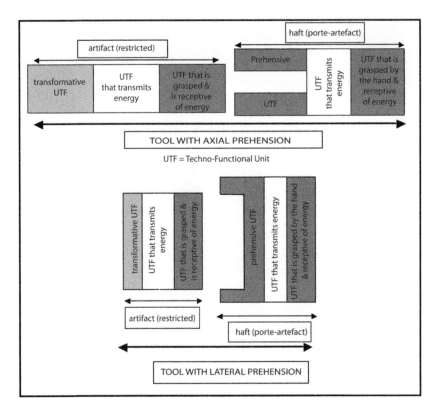

Figure 2.20 Terminology applied to the different parts of a tool. The tool can be differentiated into two parts: the mineral artifact and the non-mineral artifact, which is referred to as the haft (*porte-artefact*).

tool. With the help of this distinction, it becomes clear that if it is the prehensile part of the tool that must adapt, there exist only two possibilities. The first consists of using the stage of *confection* to modify this part of the tool. This is the case for example with the artifacts of the Umm el Tlelien, Yabroudien, and Hummalian industries, as well as with those of other industries from other continents.

The second possibility consists of producing a flake for which the morphological criteria of the prehensile part are always the same. This normalization is made possible as a result of the specificity of Levallois debitage. The systematic debitage of blades is also a potential normalization of the prehensile part, but Levallois debitage possesses a unique specificity that makes it the ultimate stage of development in the lineage of the modes of production of flakes and what we consider to be the terminal stage. It follows that unlike Levallois debitage, which is an ultimate concrete stage, we observe all along the laminar (blade production) lineage successive modes of production leading toward an increased normalization in the production of blades. The Hummalian, the case of blade production that is relevant here, is situated at the very first stages of the lineage of blade production. As a result,

The techno-logic of evolution   45

confection plays a particularly important role in the Hummalian industry, a point we return to later.

The "circum-Mediterranean" Levallois option

Levallois production has, among other characteristics, the particularity of being limited to the production of a range of differentiated flakes that can be placed into categories based on form, including quadrangular, oval, triangular, laminar, and laminar convergent. However, despite this variability in the forms that can be produced, there is very little diversity in the prehensile part. From the production stage, Levallois debitage integrates within its predetermined criteria, a prehensile part that is normalized (two or three techno-types) and an adaptable transformative part. The transformative part can take on different technical characters to fit with the requirements needed to carry out the desired action. The prehensile and transformative parts are in complete synergy, which is the very essence of concretization. The different functions proper to each element are integrated into the functioning of the ensemble.

In the case of Umm el Tlel, Syria, the use of natural bitumen makes it easy to identify this aspect of Levallois debitage (Figure 2.21, Boëda et al., 1996, 2008a, 2008b, Bonilauri, 2010). However, the discoveries made at Umm el Tlel were the result of extraordinary taphonomic conditions and in general direct evidence of hafts and hafting is quite rare. Unfortunately, this rarity has often been treated as a synonym for absence. As is often the case in prehistory, the raw data trumps analysis.

This leads us back to the question of our ability to grasp technical reality. In the case of hafts and hafting, this reality has disappeared,[35] but is seeing really necessary to envision its existence? We arrive here at the problem of the use and working of other materials—such as those derived from animals and plants—as raw material alongside the stone tools that make up the bulk of the archaeological record. How can we think about the invisible? The techno-functional analysis of stone tools situated within the framework of a techno-genetic approach allows us to think about the associated milieu (in the Simondonian sense) and thus the non-visible. Thus, rather than invoking a stage of cognitive evolution that might explain, for example, that the initial concept of hafting appeared with blade production in the context of the European Upper Paleolithic blade industries, the techno-functional analysis that we propose gives back to the invisible its material element and thus its existence. But this approach also provides an explication of the necessity of the existence of now invisible aspects of technical systems. The Levallois flake is the expression of the recombination of different functional elements, leading to a total synergy with certain external elements, such as the haft. The lithic artifact has become a sub-ensemble of an entity in combination with another sub-ensemble: the prehensile artifact.

The Levallois tool is above all an innovative concept that can be defined as (Figure 2.22) follows:

- A prehensile part that must respond to the norms of hafting, which requires a normalization of a certain number of technical characteristics that combine to make

46 *The techno-logic of evolution*

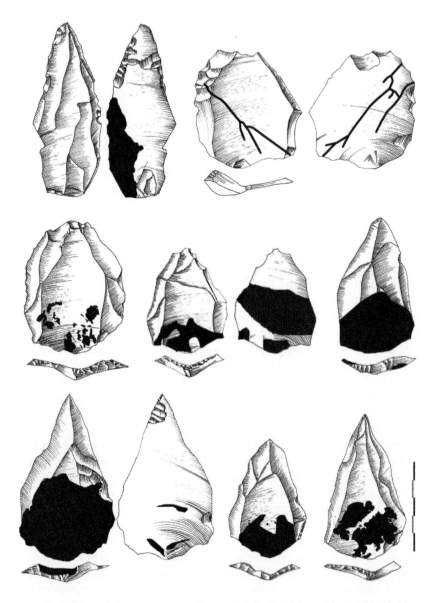

Figure 2.21 Umm el Tlel, Syria, couche VI 3, 75,000 years BP. Levallois blade, flakes, and points hafted with bitumen, which was used either as a binding or as a wrapping agent.

it relatively invariant. The prehensile part can be observed based on one of the technical elements: the striking platform. The striking platform has been the focus of debate in terms of the criteria used to identify Levallois products. In effect, it is often proposed that a faceted platform or the distinctive convex-faceted platform, known as "*chapeau de gendarme*," should be equated with Levallois.

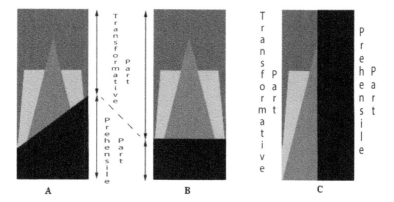

Figure 2.22 The specificity of the Levallois concept: a concept of debitage capable of producing a diversified range of tools for which the prehensile part remains stable regardless of the type of transformative part and regardless of the modality of hafting: (A) Oblique. (B) Along the axis. (C) Transversal.

- Depending on the type of action and gesture, the prehension will be parallel, oblique, or perpendicular to the morphological axis.
- A variable transformative part, which can be associated with different plan views (such as triangular, quadrangular, and elongated) and technical aspects (number and type of flake scars, type of edges, edge angles, and cross-sections).

The concept of the Levallois tool is made possible by the invention of a new mode of production that is itself the expression of a unique concept of debitage, which we return to later (Figure 2.23). There is thus a concept of the Levallois tool and a concept of Levallois debitage.[36]

The option of debitage and confection

As discussed earlier, the Levallois post-bifacial solution is not universal. In the Near East, other technological solutions follow the bifacial idea. We have already named three of these stages: Umm el Tlelian, Yabrudian, and Hummalian. These three stages, each clearly distinctive, precede the onset of the Levallois that becomes completely dominant in the Near East, as is the case in Europe.

Among these three stages, the first—the Umm el Tlelian—and the last—the Hummalian—confirm the rupture between the bifacial and the concepts of hafting and normalization of the transformative parts. The case of the Yabrudian, chronologically situated between the Umm el Tlelian and the Hummalian, seems anachronic, outside of any lineage, hypertelic.

THE CASE OF THE UMM EL TLELIAN

Within the stratigraphy of Umm el Tlel, this industry corresponds to the production of large flakes that are subject to a confection phase on both the transformative and

48 The techno-logic of evolution

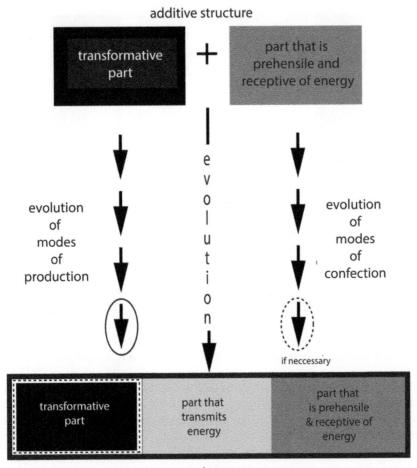

Figure 2.23 Levallois debitage makes it possible to obtain predetermined supports that closely approach the form of the tool. The debitage (solid line) makes it possible to obtain almost all of the desired technical characteristics for the good functioning of the lithic artifact. The stage of shaping (*confection*, dashed line) makes it possible to put in place other technical characteristics if needed.

prehensile parts. The adjustment of the prehensile part clearly indicates the use of a normalized haft, which is applied to a variety of flake types (Figure 2.24). The transformative parts are also subjected to considerable confection, which points to the disparity between the desired techno-functional criteria and those that are present on the unmodified flake. The need for significant adjustment through confection is evidence of a mode of production with limited predetermination.

The stage of confection overcomes the deficiency in predetermination and allows the integration of the two sub-ensembles of the artifact: transformative and

The techno-logic of evolution 49

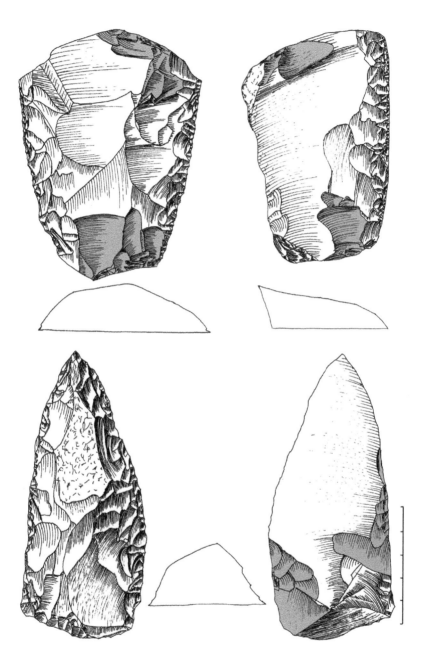

Figure 2.24 Umm el Tlel, Syria. Level overlying the last bifacial industries. In gray, normalization of the transformative part in anticipation of a specific form of hafting. The upper piece is latterly hafted following the preparation of opposed truncations. The lower piece shows the preparation for axial hafting (in relation to the axis of percussion and the morphological axis of the flake).

50 *The techno-logic of evolution*

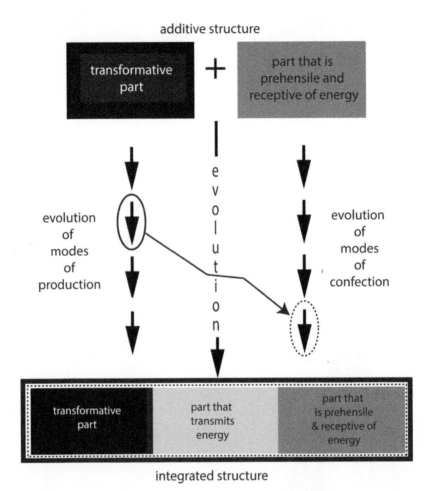

Figure 2.25 The case of the Umm el Tlelian. The debitage (solid line) makes it possible to obtain a certain number of technical characteristics that apply to the ensemble of parts of the artifact, but the functionalization of the artifact requires a significant stage of shaping (*confection*, dashed line), applied to the transformative and prehensile parts.

prehensile. The stage of confection is the means that makes it possible to also arrive at a concrete stage of the tool, without changing the structure of production (Figure 2.25). This original technical approach, clearly different from what is found in Western Europe, argues against large-scale population movements during these early periods and indicates that there were multiple technical solutions for identical inventions. Put in other terms, these technical solutions that take advantage of a new idea are convergent from one region to another but are also external manifestations of an internal contingency particular to mineral raw materials.

The techno-logic of evolution   51

THE CASE OF THE YABRUDIAN

In the stratigraphy of Umm el Tlel, following the Umm el Tlelian, we again observe a change in the system for the production of supports and tools. This industry is designated as Yabrudian. Without, for the moment, entering into the details of the different transformative parts that exhibit an undeniable diversity, we first note that the Yabrudian structures represent a rupture with preceding industries. The supports used for Yabrudian tools are thick, and narrow flakes with a plan view that is longer than it is wide (with the length along the axis of debitage, or perpendicular to this) that are shaped using scalariform retouch. Analysis of the production sequence indicates the pursuit of thick flakes but not of a plan-view morphology that is longer than it is wide. It is worth pointing out that the mode of production is not fixed between sites belonging to the Yabrudian period; these assemblages are only united by the thickness of the flakes used for the supports of tools and the scalariform retouch, which is omnipresent and unique. This retouch is used to shape the plan-view morphology of the tool and the techno-functional criteria of the edge.

As a result, the stage of confection is very important, perhaps even more significant than the debitage, because it has a double function: the creation of the volume of the tool and the functionalization of the elements of the tool (Figures 2.26 and 2.27). The stage of creating the volume could be categorized as shaping that is disassociated from the confection stage *sensu stricto*. The confusion, or more precisely the conflation of these two phases into one, under the single label of confection, is due to the use of the same mode of production of removals, known as "stepped scalariform retouch," throughout the process of transforming the support.

We can now turn to the technical significance of this particular approach to tool manufacture. A comparison with the preceding industries provides some guidance. The tools of the Umm el Tlelian are much larger (double or even triple the size) than the tools found in the Yabudian. In the Umm el Tlelian, the role of confection is limited to establishing the functional attributes necessary for the prehensile and transformative parts without the use of stepped scalariform retouch, even though the supports are quite thick. If we consider the combination found in the Yabrudian, a narrow plan view with a thick cross-section, what is the significance of these different characteristics? The techno-functional analysis of the transformative part provides information that is relevant for understanding the mode of functioning of these tools. The plan view—longer than it is wide— could correspond to an emphasis on distal or lateral-distal transformative parts, but this is not the case. The transformative part is most often on lateral edges, either a single edge (simple) or two edges (double). The location of the transformative part is indirectly related to the zone of prehension, which is narrow and thick. Assuming that our understanding of the location of the prehensile part is correct, then the use of the tools through a variety of movements requires a particular energy that the thickness of the flake makes more effective. A haft is equivalent to an increase in the size of the zone through which energy is transmitted, allowing for an augmentation in the energy. But there is no trace of preparation of the parts of the tool that are thought to be receptive of energy. Two technical hypotheses

52 *The techno-logic of evolution*

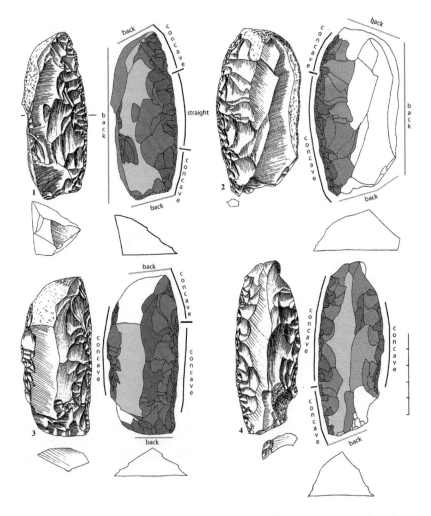

Figure 2.26 Lower Yabrudian, Umm el Tlel, Syria. Each piece is constructed based on the presence of a natural back (oblique edge). Pieces 1 and 2: based on a lateral parallel naturally backed edge and either an oblique or perpendicular naturally backed edge on the two extremities. Pieces 3 and 4: the naturally backed edges are present only at the extremities along the functional axis.

can be advanced. The first hypothesis favors the role of hafting, even though the prehensile part is not greatly altered by confection. The absence of confection on this part of the tool could simply indicate that an adequately regularized form was obtained through the process of flake production with the thickness of the flake being a trait that played a role in attachment to a haft. The second hypothesis discounts the role of hafting and focuses instead on the possibility that these tools were held directly in the hand. The thickness of the tool is an excellent

The techno-logic of evolution 53

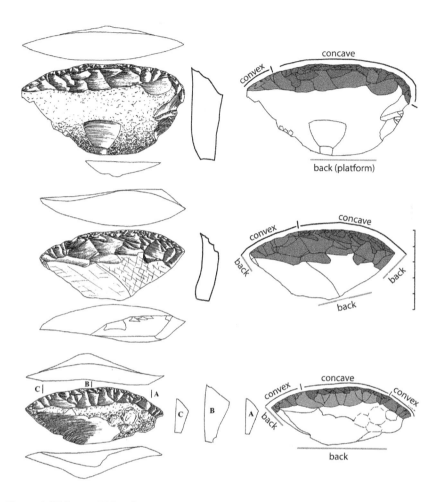

Figure 2.27 Lower Yabrudian, Umm el Tlel, Syria. Each piece is constructed to obtain a fan-shaped silhouette. The platform provides a technically backed edge.

stop-gap measure for fitting the tool to being directly gripped by the hand, the equivalent of simple hafting. Where there is an oblique edge (backing) this allows for an effective grip, and thus an element that efficiently receives the energy, and the thickness of the flake allows for a more expansive grasp in the hand.

The first hypothesis situates the Yabrudian as a rupture with the manual grip of bifaces and advances the idea that these tools were hafted. The second hypothesis views these tools as a continuity with bifaces, as tools that would be held in the hand with an ergonomic volume that is sufficient for ideal technical conditions to transmit energy to achieve the objectives. The thickness would thus be a criterion related to the functioning of the tool, and the stepped scalariform character of the final retouch would only be a consequence of the need to narrow the gap between the plan view of a thick flake and that of the desired tool, and thus to adjust the form of the cutting edge.

The study of the transformative part of Yabrudian tools indicates a diversity of cross-sections. Some of the tools, although not all identical, show the plan view, which could correspond to the regularization of the support in order to accommodate a haft. But other supports combine two identical or different tools, which fit with the use of tools gripped directly in the hand and allows for the employment of multiple transformative parts (Figure 2.28).

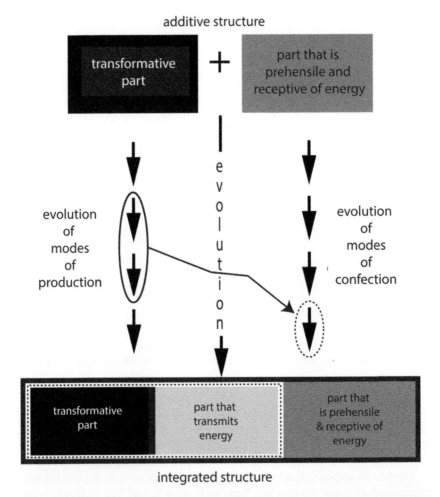

Figure 2.28 The case of the Yabrudian. The debitage (solid line) makes it possible to obtain certain technical characteristics that apply to the future prehensile part of the tool. The transformative part is the focus of a very significant stage of shaping (dashed line), which provides the tool with its characteristic silhouette with a suitable cross-section.

THE CASE OF THE HUMMALIAN

The Hummalian industry, which dates back 170,000 years, consists almost exclusively of retouched blades.[37] This is not the first blade production, as the Amudian blade industry is earlier (Jelinek, 1990; Barkai et al., 2005). But the Amudian, often interstratified with the Yabrudian, is characterized by the total absence of retouched blades. In contrast, the later Hummalian industry is characterized by the significant transformation of blades into retouched tools. Blades are the unique predetermined support found in the Hummalian and the only support used for retouched tools. The debitage itself is not elaborate (cf. Levallois type D2 laminar debitage) in the sense that there is a wide morphological and technical variability in the blades produced, and the unretouched blades do not correspond to the desired form of the tools.

The analysis of the Hummalian industry from Umm el Tel demonstrates that the confection can vary in intensity depending on the type of tool being manufactured (Figures 2.29 and 2.30). The choice of an exclusive focus on blade production and a significant diversity of tools, all of which are located on the distal end, indicates that the tools were grasped, either directly or with a haft, on the proximal end. The use of blades in the Hummalian has some similarity to the use of tanged tools, as is found for example in the Aterian of the Middle Stone Age of North Africa.

In the Hummalian system, the proximal part of a blade support can be the object of a confection stage with an intensity depending on the degree to which it fits the desired tool. The techno-functional analysis shows a high degree of homogeneity in the cross-section of the transformative part and a diversity of cross-sections for the prehensile part (Figure 2.31). When the prehensile part is of a form that fits the needs of hafting, it is not shaped (Figure 2.29: 1 and 3). The experimental reproduction of the Hummalian system of debitage has made it possible to demonstrate that although this system is effective in producing a normalized attachment for hafting and a generalized silhouette, the overall production is not very standardized, particularly at the distal end of blades. Therefore, a stage of confection is of fundamental importance with two objectives: the regularization of the silhouette towards the grip—whatever form it might take—and the specific configuration of the transformative contact. However, in the case of the most regularized blades produced in this system, the silhouettes show little evidence of retouch, and thus the alteration of the support is focused on configuration of the transformative part.

The Hummalian system of production, although normalized and stemming from an undeniable position in an evolutionary sequence, does not result in supports that are close to the form and volume required for the desired tools for which the demands of hafting are critical. As discussed earlier, blade production systems prior to the Hummalian are found in the Near East, although these are the product of a less evolved production system. As a result, in these cases there are few retouched blades, the unretouched blade being already a specific tool in and of itself, and not the support for a tool.

Should the Hummalian be considered an essential phase of the evolution of the lineage of blade production: the transition from the production of a combined support/tool to a blade matrix that can serve as the support for different tools? The

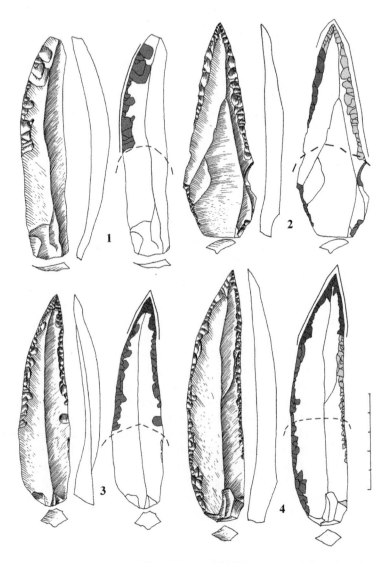

Figure 2.29 Hummalian, Umm el Tlel, Syria. The distal part of the laminar support is subject to a range of modification corresponding to different functions and functioning. (1) Convex lateral cutting edge, lateral cutting action. (2) Point/edge, action of penetration and longitudinal cutting. (3–4) Modification along an offset axis, action of penetration, and lateral cutting. The techno-functional analysis of the modification on these four artifacts shows very clearly that we should dissociate these into two distinct functional parts: (A) An apex formed by the convergence of the two edges and consisting of identical edge morphology (plano/convex) that corresponds to a modification of the silhouette of the penetrating part of the tool for an action of penetration along the axis. (B) A mesioproximal section with edges modified by debitage using a variable edge morphology that is distinct from the modification of the apex. The proximal part of the tool, which corresponds to the prehensile part, depending on its technical configuration, is either modified or unmodified to fit a haft.

The techno-logic of evolution 57

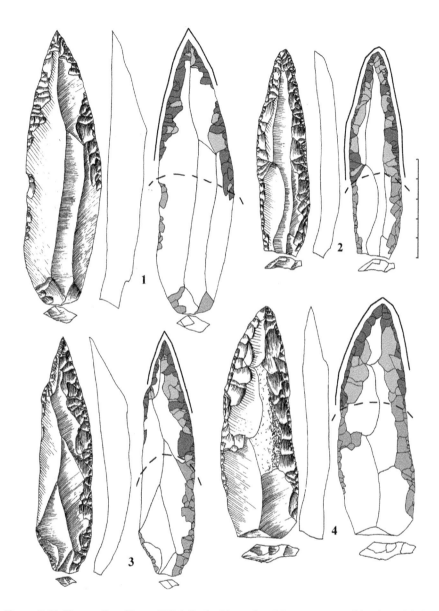

Figure 2.30 Hummalian, Umm el Tlel, Syria. Pieces 1 and 3 present a modification of their transformative part of the type point/edge with plano-convex edge morphology. The prehensile part is also the subject of modification to fit a haft. It is the same for Pieces 2 and 4 except for the axial symmetry of their transformative part and the presence of two different edge morphologies: (2) Plano-convex edge morphology. (4) Plano-concave edge morphology.

58 *The techno-logic of evolution*

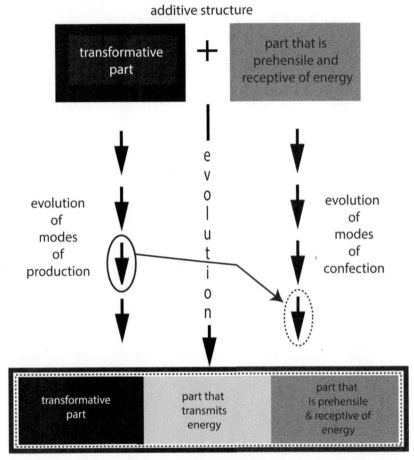

Figure 2.31 The case of the Hummalian. The debitage (solid line) comes closer to the desired form of the prehensile and transformative parts. The stage of shaping (dashed line) is applied mostly to the transformative part. But if necessary, the prehensile part is also shaped.

blade becomes in this case the exclusive predetermined support, in contrast to the blade that is in and of itself a tool and is one of the predetermined supports among others within the same lithic assemblage. The Hummalian is the last case of blade production in the Near East through the entire Mousterian. Blade production reappears in what we call the Intermediate (or Transitional) Paleolithic. At that point one finds all the steps of the evolution of the blade lineage in a very short time. However, the tools that appear in the Intermediate Paleolithic display elements not found in earlier periods. The innovation of the Intermediate Paleolithic is found not in the technical criteria of the supports or in their capacity for hafting, but rather in the novel functional registers: burin, endscraper, backed point, among others. These developments suggest a new range of tools for which the underlying structural conceptions had been discovered more than 300,000 years earlier.

Conclusions

The long duration of prehistory allows us to see that the structural evolution of artifacts takes place through the integration of different functional elements and that this process is not reducible to the developments that take place within a single part of the tool. This concretization can follow the path of the evolution of systems of production that have as an objective the integration of the techno-functional intentions from the onset of the stage of production. Alternatively, the same objective can be achieved by developing the stage of confection to obtain the totality of the techno-functional criteria.

These two rubrics of evolution are hierarchical. The ensemble of available data appears to show that confection is a means of adjusting between the production and the techno-functional intentions. Depending on the evolutionary stage of the type of production and the type of artifact produced, it will or will not be necessary to resort to a stage of confection. However, what is critical is that the evolution of the tool can be disassociated from the evolution of the support from which the tool is made. One can observe the use of a "concrete" tool that is possible as the result of the use of a stage of confection carried out on a "less evolved" support, meaning a support that does not possess directly (from the stage of production) the technical criteria required for the good functioning of the tool.

In the framework of the evolution of tools, two distinct temporalities can be observed. In the first, the evolution of tools toward a better integration of different parts takes place as a result of confection. The supports are poorly developed and distant from their eventual techno-functional criteria. In the second temporality the process is reversed. The supports as they are produced already are very close to the technical criteria required by the tools. The retouch serves to correct any absence in the technical criteria.

This evolution of tools is even more difficult to understand if we limit our analysis to the outcome of evolution: the diversity of cutting edges and/or prehensile parts! In the case of an abstract structure, the structural evolution can only apply to one of the two functional parts without having this interfere with the other part. This development may be the result of the stage of confection and/or the choice of a new type of support that can be produced by the same structure of debitage or by a newly developed structure. In the case of a concrete structure, these two functional elements are the result of the mode of production and/or confection.

To conclude we insist that the evolution of tools from an abstract structure toward a concrete structure can be accomplished independently of the type of support, and thus of the system of production, if a stage of confection is incorporated. On the other hand, this evolution might also be the result of the development of the production of supports. As a result, a techno-functional analysis must at the same time address the stage of evolution in which a tool is situated as well as the means of production employed: debitage and/or confection, exclusive or not.

60 *The techno-logic of evolution*

The structures of production

What is a core: an additional or integrated structure?

When working to identify systems of production, we tend to focus attention on one type of object: the core. The core is at the center of the production process because it yields the desired removals that will be used as is or after varying intensities of configuration. A core is defined as a block of raw material chosen to be reduced through fracture on which we can detect the traces of the technical stages of reduction, whether these are successful or not. To attain the desired objectives, the core must possess all the necessary technical criteria. Put in other terms, the core must be configured. This is to say that it must have three components: (a) a surface that serves as a striking platform; (b) a surface of flaking (debitage) that in relation to the striking platform forms an angle less than or equal to 90°; and (c) a volume related to the type and quantity of desired removals. The configuration of the core is established following a stage of initialization. The initialization stage can consist of finding blocks that naturally present the technical criteria considered operational for responding to objectives and/or a collection of technical gestures can be employed to artificially establish the same technical criteria.

This fashion of conceptualizing the core, regardless of its merits, nonetheless neglects an essential analytic step. Within the framework of a structural analysis, we should first revisit the question of what we actually mean by a core. Is the core actually the entire block of primary material held in its raw form at the time of debitage, or is it only a part of this block? In other words, does the configured volume or the useful volume include the totality or only part of the block? Remember that the configured volume is defined as a necessary and sufficient volume consisting of a surface of debitage, a surface of the striking platform, and mass.

Following this line of reasoning, the entirety of a block of raw material held in the hand cannot always be included within a structural analysis of a core. We can thus distinguish between two cases: an additional structure or an integrated structure.

An additional structure (abstract)

In the case of an additional structure, the flaked block consists of two independent sub-components: the useful volume, or the core (*sensu stricto*), and the remaining useless volume, which is not invested in because it is not necessary for the realization of objectives (Figure 2.32). The two sub-components are thus independent. The production phase of the useful volume does not require any alteration of the remaining volume to attain the objectives of production.

THE NON-HOMOTHETIC OR FALSELY HOMOTHETIC CHARACTER
OF ADDITIONAL STRUCTURES

In archaeological contexts, several variations may occur in the homothetic characteristics of additional structures.

The techno-logic of evolution 61

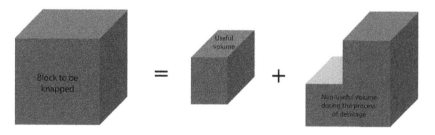

Figure 2.32 Additional structure. The block to be knapped is composed of two volumetric subcomponents. One is designated as the useful volume or the core *sensu stricto*; the second is called the non-useful or residual volume.

Figure 2.33 Non-homothetic schema: The total volume varies and the useful volumes are identical.

True non-homothety   The choice of blocks of different volumes for which the useful volume is identical may lead to a mistaken interpretation if we limit ourselves to a simple "naturalist" approach following the exploitation of these blocks (Figure 2.33). What can happen is that from a strictly morphological perspective, once the useful volume has been exploited, the remaining volume might vary considerably in morphology. This could lead us to say that there must therefore exist as many distinct conceptions of knapping as there are worked blocks/cores that are morphologically distinct. Isn't this what we often read of the earliest production, which is described as relatively anarchic? An anarchy that is often interpreted as the reflection of limited cognitive capacity.

However, the structural approach allows us to immediately recognize the similarity of the useful volumes and to deduce the use of a single and unified conception of knapping despite the use of blocks of varying volumes. On the other hand, if the analysis of the useful volume of an archaeological assemblage indicates different conceptions of knapping, regardless of the morphology of residual "useless volume," then this is evidence of differentiated technical concepts of production.

62   The techno-logic of evolution

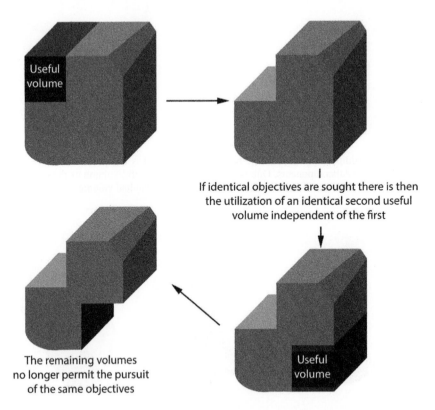

Figure 2.34 Following the exploitation of an initial useful volume, the process of knapping leads to the morphological transformation of the block.

Once the initial useful volume has been exploited, the block can be abandoned or be the object of a resumption of knapping. Thus, depending on the objectives—whether identical or different from the initial phase—the residual block may or may not be the object of further work. There are two possibilities at this stage (Figure 2.34). Either the block maintains a useful potential volume in addition to the volume exploited in the preceding stage or no such technical potential remains. In the latter case, the block is either abandoned or eventually made the object of further work—but this time with different objectives.

The corollary of this observation is that whether or not there is a series of successive stages of production, a structural analysis is critical because each exploitation phase of identical or different usable volumes is structurally independent of each other. As a result, if the knapper uses two blocks with the same morphology and the same type of useful volume but with a different number of series removed from each block, the result will be different residual blocks that are non-homothetic, even though they are of the outcome of the same additional conception (Figure 2.35).

The techno-logic of evolution 63

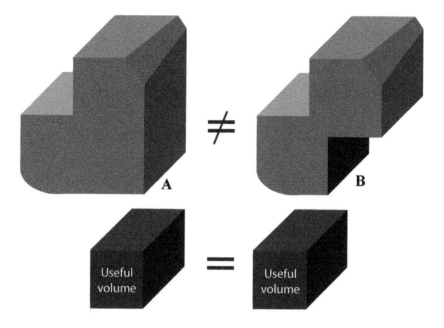

Figure 2.35 Non-homothetic structure of additional knapping is found in the case where an identical successive series of removals result in residual volumes that are different (A, B), although the useful volumes are identical.

A misleading homothety There is the possibility of misleading homothety in an archaeological context where the blocks of primary material are globally of a similar form. This is generally the case on sites where the raw material consists of cobbles. In such a circumstance the useless volume is identical from one cobble to another. The assemblage derived from this situation is homogenous and could be interpreted as the production of tools rather than cores. Refitting is then the only method to differentiate between cores and tools (Pereto et al., 1998). When there is no refitting, we often find these pieces designated as core/chopper.[80]

An integrated structure (concrete)

In the case of an integrated structure the useful volume is equal to the volume of the block before it is knapped. The block that is then held in the hand, ready to be flaked and to obtain objectives, is the core. This initial block is subsequently the object of a stage of initialization resulting in a new volume, the core.[38] The core is then a structure that encompasses and integrates the entirety of the technical criteria of configuration necessary for the realization of the objectives and, if necessary, the criteria that are integral to the reinitialization of the core. We call this type of core a "core with an integrated structure" (Figure 2.36).

64   The techno-logic of evolution

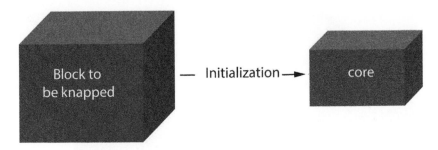

Figure 2.36 Integrated structure: the initial block is subject to a stage of initialization that makes the block to be knapped equivalent to the useful volume, which is thus designated as the core.

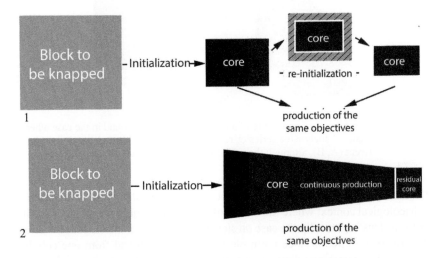

Figure 2.37 Debitage with an integrated structure. (1) The configured core integrates the criteria for reinitialization. (2) It is the recurrence of particular objectives that maintains the criteria of configuration.

Depending on the desired objective, and the integrated structure for which one has opted, a reinitialization of the core may or may not be necessary (Figure 2.37). The phases of reinitialization are inherent to the structure of the configured core itself. The configuration of the core thus integrates two constraints: those related to the functional objectives and those of its reinitialization for continuing to obtain the same range of objectives. Therefore, in general, the reinitialization is partial and only affects a minority of the criteria of configuration. This is the case, for example, with the Levallois debitage and the blade production found in the Gravettian, Solutrean, and Magdalenian.

In other cases, depending on the integrated structure utilized, the phase of reinitialization does not exist because the recurrence of one or several desired objectives serves to auto-maintain the configuration of the core (Figure 2.37). The essential element is the maintenance of the same objectives as is found in pyramidal or discoidal debitages. One can say that in such cases the mass of the predetermined products is equal to the mass of the volume. This situation is also observed in the structure of the blade or bladelet cores that are pressure flaked in the pre-Columbian industries or in some Neolithic contexts. The core has an integrated structure, and the use of pressure flaking serves to vastly improve the yield and standardization of the objectives.

THE HOMOTHETIC OR NON-HOMOTHETIC CHARACTER OF INTEGRATED STRUCTURES

If a particular conception of knapping is followed, the core will maintain its morphology regardless of the moment at which it is situated in the process of production of predetermined removals and regardless of the number of partial reconfigurations. In order to be operational, the structure of the core implies a necessary conservation of its "form."[39] This stability is at the structural level, and it will not be affected by the choice of method used to exploit the core. The morphology of the core will remain stable through the entire operational process, regardless of the method used or the moment that the core is situated in this process. As long as the structure of the core, that is, the synergy of the technical characters at play, is respected, the form of the core will not change. This is a homothetic process.

An integrated structure of homothetic character with a phase of reinitialization   Levallois debitage is the classic example of such a homothetic process. If one considers a Levallois core with preferential or recurrent flake removals and one observes its transformations following the production of a preferential removal or a recurrent series of flakes, regardless of the method utilized—unidirectional, centripetal, bidirectional—the general form remains the same from one core to another (Figure 2.38). The coherence of the Levallois volumetric structure resides in the non-transformation of the "morphological" criteria of the core through the debitage process (Boëda, 1994). When this coherence is lost, the use of the criteria of predetermination makes it possible to restore the coherence of the core and to restart a new series of removals. The residual core of this series will always present the same "morphology." The difference between stages will not be in form but in size, indicating the homothetic character of this process.

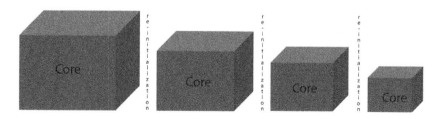

Figure 2.38 An integrated homothetic structure interspersed with phases of reinitialization.

66 *The techno-logic of evolution*

Figure 2.39 Continuous integrated homothetic structure.

An integrated structure of homothetic character with continuous debitage   In certain cases of blade and bladelet production dating to the end of the Upper Paleolithic through the Neolithic, the exploitable volume is equal to the volume of the core, to the extent that it is not necessary to re-prepare the debitage surface. The initial preparation allows for an auto-maintenance of the parameters necessary for the exploitation of the core (Figure 2.39). However, this is only possible by strictly maintaining the organization of the relationship between different types of blade/bladelets and, in some cases, the use of very particular techniques of fracture, such as pressure flaking and indirect percussion. Regardless of where debitage is halted, the description of the core is the same because the morphology will remain unchanged.

An integrated structure of non-homothetic character with continuous debitage   In contrast, in the case of discoidal-, pyramidal-, and Upper Paleolithic–type debitage,[40] even if the exploitable volume is equal to the volume of the core, it is the production of a broad diversity of products that allows for the auto-maintenance of the parameters necessary for the exploitation of the core (Boëda, 1988a, 1988b, 1988c).[41] In these cases, the morphology of the core can change during the process of debitage and will thus vary depending on when knapping is halted (Figure 2.40). A volumetric structure can thus change form without modifying its production. Perhaps we should say that the maintenance of a range of products through the entire exploitation of the block requires considering the "morphological" criterion as an adaptable rather than an invariant trait. The integrated character of the structures is therefore not equivalent to the notion of homothety, quite the contrary. Nonetheless, the integrated homothetic structures develop chronologically after the integrated non-homothetic structures.

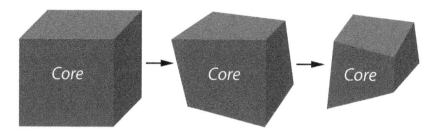

Figure 2.40 Non-homothetic integrated structure.

The process of concretization

The process of concretization for cores, as is the case for the tool, results in the emergence of what Yves Deforge (1985) called a "technical lineage." Recall that he defined a lineage as a group of objects "having the same use function and deploying the same principle" (Deforge, 1985: 72). According to him, the notion of principle was "a conceptual tool which one uses *a posteriori* with a degree of liberty to appraise the foundation of the lineage" (Deforge, 1985: 72). Transposed to prehistory, this can be a principle of production (debitage/shaping), a structural characteristic of the core (exclusive production of flakes or blades or a mixed production), a mode of functioning for the tools (held in the hand or a hafted), and so on.

It is thus that within each lineage of objects/cores we see a succession from cores for which the useful volume, in response to increasingly constraining functional demands, is restructured toward an increasing synergy among constituent elements. The long timespan of prehistory allows us to see cycles of transformation[42] that affect different lineages of objects. These cycles can be successive and/or contemporary.[43] However, to better understand the reality, we must adopt multiple perspectives at both the macro and micro scales (Deforge, 1985; de Rosnay, 1975).

At the macro scale, each lineage, if it reaches its culmination, proceeds from an abstract structure to a concrete structure. But the rhythm of this evolution is particular to each cycle. This lack of uniformity can be attributed to the fact that we have defined technical evolution as coevolution with humanity. The actual process of each cycle of evolution of a lineage is in human hands. Its rhythm, frequency, interruption, abandonment, and resurgence are the sociocultural expressions of a lineage, even if the lineage persists over many tens of millennia.[44] An environmental change could intervene in the evolution of a lineage by causing a bifurcation that leads to divergence. This would introduce a pseudo-determinism that cannot be causal because the human still is the actor, consciously or not. In the same way, the invention of the very first object of a lineage remains completely in the human domain even if the mechanism is complex or pluri-factorial.

STRUCTURAL STAGES OF EVOLUTION

We have established a scale comprising six levels of structuration of flaking (*debitage*), capable of responding to a need for supports for tools or tools that are increasingly structured. This structural evolution of conceptions of debitage is a response to the increase of the techno-functional constraints of use and the signs distinctive of each group, each culture.

Put in other terms, the structural evolution of cores is an adaptive response to the structural evolution of tools. There exist two processes of concretization: one operates on tools and the other on production. These two processes are not necessarily synchronized. Indeed, a new tool may be obtained by applying new ways of modifying blanks (confection, for example) without a new method of debitage being necessary (Figure 2.41).

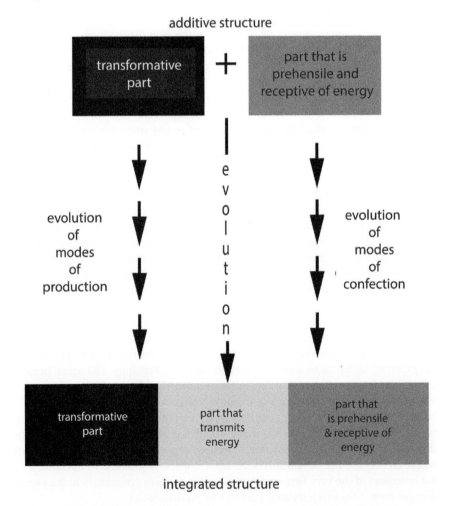

Figure 2.41 The evolution of tools is made possible by the evolution of the modes of flake production and/or by the evolution of modes of shaping (*confection*).

The techno-logic of evolution 69

The other solution is the transformation of the useful volume to be as close as possible to the required new technical criteria of the tool. One thing is certain: The evolution of tools[45] precedes the evolution of the modes of production. Various "interferences" may intervene. Nonetheless, the response to new constraints may follow the path of debitage or shaping without the interference of any technical logic, such as in the abandonment of debitage for shaping and then the return of debitage in the circum-Mediterranean.[46]

Characteristics of predetermination of the technical criteria of removals

The criteria of predetermination of removals are located on the surface of debitage or the surface of striking platforms. In terms of the surface of debitage, these characteristics are obtained in the course of the phase of initialization and/or production.

In the case of the phase of initialization, the procedure consists of putting in place, by removals from the surface of debitage, the technical criteria that furnish a part or the totality of the desired technical configuration. These characteristics can be grouped to form two categories. The first groups together the criteria of convexity that permit the control of the fracture along the edges and the distal extremities of removals. The second combines specific characteristics such as the dorsal scar ridges, the convergences, and the back.

In the case of the phase of the production of successive removals, it is the utilization of recurrence that reinforces the characteristics of predetermination. We introduced this notion for the first time with the Levallois concept (Boëda, 1994), but it is applicable to all conceptions of debitage. In effect, a so-called recurrent removal is one that, while utilizing the technical criteria put into place to produce a removal with the desired techno-functional attributes, also through its own extraction replaces the utilized technical criteria of the surface of debitage with a new or identical configuration of technical criteria. Thus, for example, an *éclat debodant* [a flake off the edge of the core] restores to the debitage surface a lateral convexity and a scar pattern (*errailure*) that serves as a guiding ridge for shock wave of the next removal. This guiding ridge replaces the initial lateral convexity.

For the surface of striking platforms, there are potentially multiple technical criteria of predetermination. The most classic involves the types of preparation of the impact surface that lead to obtaining varying platforms (flat, facetted, etc.). There are also other technical criteria associated with the type of hammer, the mode of percussion—tangential or internal—the percussion movement, and the angle formed between the plane of the detachment of removals and the axis of percussion, among others.

Although the "universal" means of control for the detachment of a removal—convexity and recurrence—are known and largely identified, there certainly exist others, for example, corresponding to gestures, for which generalization and recognition remain difficult.[47]

The assemblages with an abstract structure and the corresponding classes of removals

This first ensemble groups together the systems of production that are based on the exploitation of a useful part of the block/volume, which is designated as the core.

70   *The techno-logic of evolution*

The rest of the block does not have any technical role and is the residual volume that is not useful. The products will vary depending on the technical characteristics of the useful part of the volume.

Four types of useful volumes are identifiable, corresponding to the four classes of technical criteria present on the undifferentiated or predetermined removals. The distinction between each one of these classes is based on the predeterminations of the transformative and prehensile parts of the produced supports (unretouched removals). These levels of predetermination depend on the configuration of the useful volume.

Useful volume of Type A/undifferentiated flakes

A useful volume of Type A corresponds to the production of removals with technical criteria with a limited degree of predetermination.

Predetermination is limited to the production of a cutting edge (*tranchant*), while the other technical criteria of the removal are not constrained. The only predetermination is the presence of a cutting edge on all types of flakes (Figure 2.42). A single transformative part is sought, regardless of the form it takes. To achieve this goal, it is only necessary for a sub-volume of the block/volume to conform to the characteristics of a useful volume of Type A comprising the mass necessary to absorb the inertia of the impact, a striking platform surface either natural or prepared, and a natural debitage surface without any criteria of determination whatsoever.

Useful volume Type B/removals with a distinctive transformative part

A useful volume of Type B corresponds to the production of removals with a degree of predetermination applied to the transformative part of the removal.

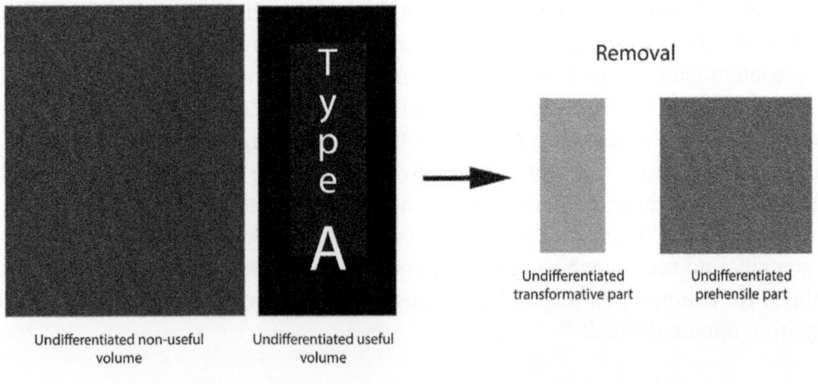

Figure 2.42 The useful volume of Type A is chosen exclusively for its capacity to provide a surface for a striking platform adjacent to an undifferentiated debitage surface producing a flake removal with a cutting edge that takes any form.

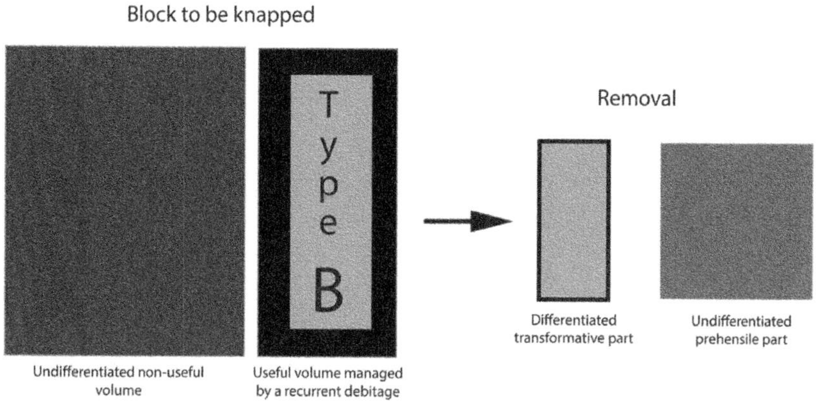

The techno-logic of evolution   71

Block to be knapped

Removal

T
y
p
e
B

Differentiated
transformative part

Undifferentiated
prehensile part

Undifferentiated non-useful
volume

Useful volume managed
by a recurrent debitage

Figure 2.43 The useful volume of Type B, maintained in a recurrent fashion, allows for the control of some technical characteristics of the transformative part of the flake removal or removals.

Control over the form of the transformative part of the removals is obtained through the notion of recurrence that allows for the enhancement of the criteria particular to the cutting edge: regularity and specific delineation. The absence of other criteria of predetermination on the useful volume limits any supplementary control over the cutting edge as well as the total control of the prehensile part (Figure 2.43).

Thus, the useful volume designated as Type B must possess, at minimum, a surface of striking platforms able to take multiple impacts and maintain a sufficient angle with the adjacent debitage surface.

Useful volume of Type C/removals with differentiated transformative and prehensile parts

A useful volume of Type C corresponds to a production of removals with criteria of predetermination evident in the transformative and prehensile parts.

This control over the morphology of removals is obtained by the adoption of a useful volume that naturally presents the technical criteria capable of controlling, to a certain extent, the transformative and prehensile parts of the removal or removals (Figure 2.44). The useful volume, designated as Type C, can be exploited to produce single or multiple removals. In the latter case, the notion of recurrence is introduced to exert an intensified control over the transformative and prehensile parts.

Useful volume of Type D/removals with differentiated transformative and prehensile parts

A useful volume of Type D corresponds to a production of removals with characteristics of predetermination evident on the transformative and prehensile parts.

72 *The techno-logic of evolution*

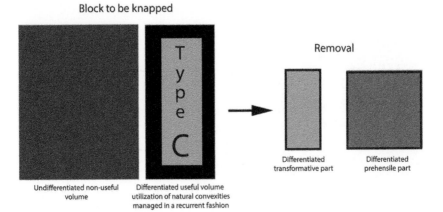

Figure 2.44 The useful volume of Type C, maintained in a recurrent fashion based on a useful volume that presents a naturally convex debitage surface. This double control—natural convexity and recurrence—allows for partial control over the transformative and prehensile parts of the flake removals.

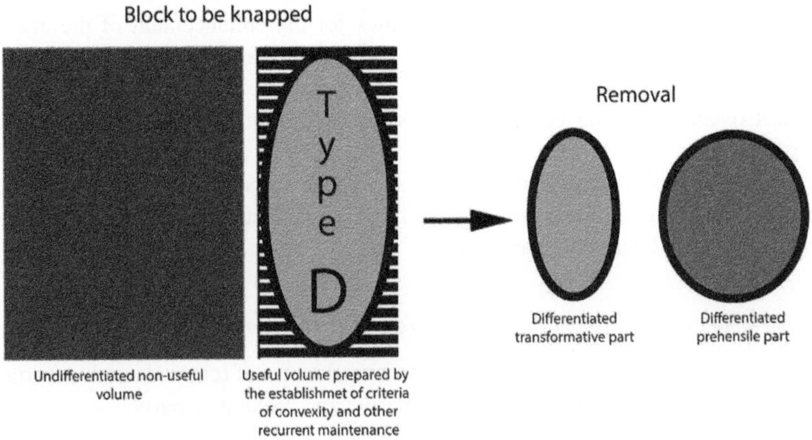

Figure 2.45 The useful volume of Type D, maintained in a recurrent fashion based on a useful volume, is prepared by the establishment on the debitage surface of the collection of technical characteristics needed to achieve the functional objectives of the tool. The transformative and prehensile parts of flakes from a useful volume of Type D are therefore differentiated.

However, in contrast to the useful volume of Type C, there is the production of single or multiple removals with a high degree of control and a greater latitude in the choice of technical criteria. To achieve this, a useful volume is first initiated and then used (Figure 2.45). The useful volume, designated as Type D, can be exploited to produce single or multiple removals. Those removals produced in the course of a recurrent series can be identical or differentiated depending on the operational scheme.

The techno-logic of evolution 73

Archaeological production structures

Abstract volumetric structures

A first ensemble groups together the technical systems of production that focus only on a part of the block to achieve their objective.

USEFUL VOLUME OF TYPE A

The useful volumes of Type A have as their only functional constraint the production of a cutting edge, regardless of the technical criteria of this cutting edge or the type of flake/support. The imperative is to create an incising edge, and this is the consequence of the detachment of a removal, which is the only predetermined criterion. To realize this objective, there exist two modalities of debitage. The first does not privilege any part of the block, and the production of a sharp removal is obtained by fracture that is technically minimally controlled or uncontrolled. The second corresponds to a simple operational scheme, organized on the basis of a striking platform surface and an adjacent surface of debitage that form an angle of less than 90°, on a block with the necessary mass. To realize this objective, it is not necessary to alter the totality of the block.

In the second case the block can be identified as a mixed entity composed of two independent components: the useful volume and the rest of the block. One part is inert and does not play a role in the current stage of exploitation. However, in the second stage, this "inert" part can be altered to realize a new scheme, a secondary configuration having no structural relationship with the first. This potential succession of schemes has no relation of cause and effect: they are independent. It is as though one is exploiting successive volumes. It is an addition of operational schemes from one to another.

The technical and morphological criteria of the removals produced as a result of this system are totally aleatory. It is only by pure chance if certain forms repeat, usually as the result of the utilization of blocks of the same morphology.

In an archaeological context, the identification of these technical systems is particularly difficult, even impossible, unless these are exceptionally well preserved and/or associated with a human-mediated faunal assemblage. It is perhaps for this reason that no regularized products are found in the earliest industries. This is also the reason that industries of this type are often the subject of heated debate. Nonetheless, it appears logical to find this type of production unless one believes in spontaneous technical generation. The problem is simply a lack of investigation of this material and, as a result, the methods capable of differentiating the first anthropic objects from eoliths, due to their great mopho-technique similarity: these two types of objects have only a cutting edge. Also, sites with this type of industry are often unreported due to a fear of becoming the object of ridicule, and if they are published, they are often mocked, and therefore never referenced, except in the case where they are associated with hominin remains.

What had been considered to be fantasy has become reality! This is in effect the reversal of a paradigm. While for Leroi-Gourhan "the only criteria for humanity

74 *The techno-logic of evolution*

that is biologically irrefutable is the presence of the tool" (Leroi-Gourhan, 1983), today one observes the inverse. Even given that the earliest technical vestiges are difficult to identify[48] and require a detailed technical knowledge, for some, even an in-depth morpho-technological still does not suffice as evidence of the anthropic character. This attitude is triply damaging because in the first place it devalues any technological approach, and it runs counter to a rigorous scientific process, believing falsely that the positive identification of a human artifact can only take place in the presence of its presumed maker. Moreover, this toolmaker must somehow be "judged" as an appropriate candidate for a being with ideas (*le concepteur*).[49]

USEFUL VOLUME OF TYPE B

The useful volume of Type B makes it possible to produce a series of recurrent removals without the surface of debitage, before flaking, possessing any criteria whatsoever that would lead to any morphological and/or technical regularization of the removal. Despite this, the use of recurrence during the process of production permits the normalization of certain attributes of the cutting edge: length, angle, and morphology. This procedure, because of the limited configuration of the debit-age surface and the weak predetermining criteria created by the recurrence in flake removals, results in numerous knapping accidents, including hinge fractures, along with flakes that are normalized but with a wide diversity of forms.

As with Type A, the volume of Type B is composed of two independent compo-nents: the useful volume and the non-useful volume. A second recurrent series is possible if the remaining volume presents a new useful volume that is exploitable. If this is the case, the second utilized volume has no relationship to the first. If there is no an adequate remaining useful volume, the knapper will use a different block and exploit a new useful volume.

Detecting archaeological cases of this type of system is challenging because it requires exceptional conditions of conservation. Nonetheless, when these condi-tions exist, such as the site of Lokalalei, thanks to the numerous refittings (De-lagnes and Roche, 2005; Roche et al., 1999), one can observe very clearly that the chosen surface does not present any technical characters of control and that it is only the recurrent debitage that allows a minimal degree of control. The exception-ally large number of accidents of knapping in the Lokalalei assemblage, mostly hinge fractures, is a clear indicator of a recurrent exploitation without criteria of convexity.

USEFUL VOLUME OF TYPE C

The useful knapping volume of Type C possesses a natural debitage surface with the technical criteria of predetermination, particularly the criteria of convexity (Figure 2.46). This useful volume is selected for its technical criteria of predeter-mination, which are naturally present on the unworked block. The initialization

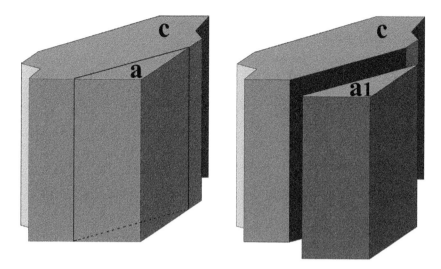

Figure 2.46 A single useful volume of Type C. On the left, the selection of a block possessing a useful volume (a) and a second non-useful volume (c). On the right, the useful volume (a1) is the core; the volume c remains unused.

thus consists of choosing a debitage surface that is favorable for the immediate production of the desired removals, without intervention, except on the surface of the striking platform. Once the surface of the striking platform, which can be a natural surface, is put in place, it is possible to obtain either a single removal or a recurrent series of two or three removals from the useful volume, although more removals than that are rare.

As a result of the association of natural criteria of convexity and the notion of recurrence, the removals are significantly more regularized than in the previously discussed systems (Figures 2.47 and 2.48). But this regularization is in a certain fashion constrained and without potential for variability. Thus, the counterpart to a better predetermination in certain criteria is a production that is limited in its diversity.

The utilized block, or usable volume, or core, corresponds only to one part of the block as a whole. Once this is exploited, the operator can subsequently seek out the presence of technical criteria that are naturally favorable to the pursuit of objectives on the part that until then had not been used. The knapper can thus exploit a new useful volume, completely independent from the first (Figure 2.49).

Multiple unrelated schemes of debitage can thus follow in succession. The second useful volume, if it is present, does not require the first in order to be operational. The schemas can be added on following the surfaces that are naturally favorable for achieving objectives. Based on refitting, this succession of useful volumes was identified in the Clactonian level of the site of High Lodge, (Ashton et al., 1992; Forestier, 1993, Figure 2.50).

76 *The techno-logic of evolution*

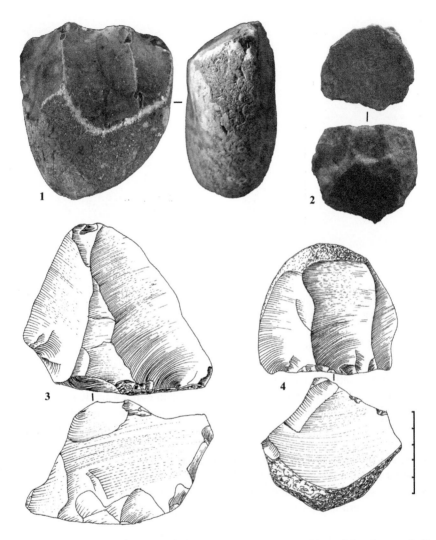

Figure 2.47 Useful volume of Type C. Unipolar exploitation of three flakes from a similar usable volume (previously designated as C1). (1) The site of Oies à Wimereux, Pas de Calais (collection J. Louis). (2) The site of Gipo, Korea. (3–4) The site of Montsaugeon, Haute-Marne (Amiot, 1993).

Variability of the modes of initialization, selection, and production   Despite a monotony in production, exploitation of a useful volume of Type C can present a degree of variability depending on the type of debitage surface used. This variability is expressed in the selection of the volume of exploitation and will therefore be more quantitative than qualitative.

On the qualitative level, there is variability in the number of removals per debitage surface. In effect, the exploitation of Type C permits the production of a single

The techno-logic of evolution 77

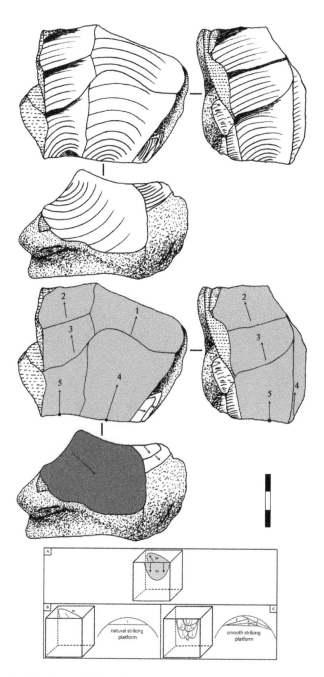

Figure 2.48 Useful volume of Type C. Unidirectional exploitation of a series of five removals. The site of Guanyindong, China (after Li, 2014).

78 The techno-logic of evolution

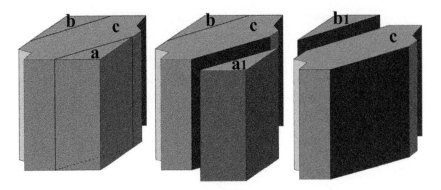

Figure 2.49 The multiple variants of the useful volume of Type C. At the left, the selected block offers useful volumes, a and b, and a non-useful volume, c. In the center, the first useful volume a1 is knapped without the volumes b and c intervening in any way whatsoever in the process of knapping. At the right, once the initial useful volume a1 is exploited, there is no possibility of producing a new series of removals from volume c, but this is possible using volume b1.

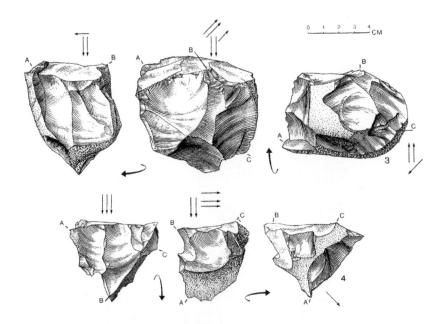

Figure 2.50 Type C1—High Lodge. The selected volumes offer multiple useful volumes of Type C1, which are exploited successively. The final appearance of the core can lead to confusion if one relies on the recognition of shape. However, technical analysis shows that multiple identical useful volumes have been exploited (after Ashton et al., 1992: 134, fig. 11.7).

			Type C	
			C1 flake	C2 laminar
methods	initialization	selection	+	+
		maintenance	-	-
	production	unidirectional	+	+
		bidirectional	+/-	+/-

Figure 2.51 A table of the potential variability in methods of initialization and production of a useful volume of Type C.

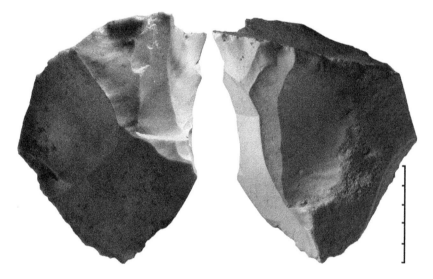

Figure 2.52 Knapping of Type C2. Barbas, Dordogne, France. Photo copyright S. Oboukhoff, CNRS photographic service, MAE Médiathèque, Nanterre.

preferential removal per chosen natural surface, or for the production of a recurrent series of removals. Moreover, it is possible to vary the length-to-width ratio of the useful volume and, to an extent, the morphology of flakes (Figure 2.51).

The exploitation of Type C when used to produce flakes is designated as C1, such as is found in the Clactonian of High Lodge (Figure 2.50) or the industries from Pointe aux Oies at Wimereux in the Pas-de-Calais, Monsaugeon in the Haute Marne, as well as at the sites of Gimpo in Korea and Guanyindong in China (Figures 2.47 and 2.48, Amiot, 1993; Li, 2014).

The exploitation of Type C when used for blade production[50] is designated as C2, such as is found at Barbas (Figure 2.52, Boëda, 1997) and at Saint-Valery-sur-Somme (Figure 2.53, Heinzelin and Haesaerts, 1983; Boëda, 1988c) in Europe as well as at Kaféine in Syria (Figure 2.54).

80 *The techno-logic of evolution*

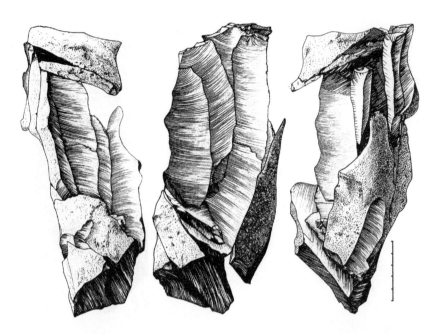

Figure 2.53 Bidirectional laminar knapping of Type C2. Saint-Valéry-sur Somme (after Heinzelin and Haesaerts, 1983).

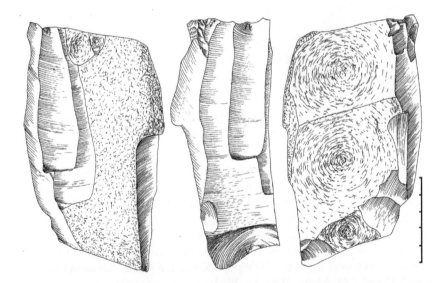

Figure 2.54 Knapping of Type C2, Kaféine, Syria. Following the knapping of an initial useful volume exploited for the production of at least four laminar removals per surface, a second opposed volume was utilized to produce a new series of blades, but as we will see later, this second volume was subject to a partial preparation which we designate as D2.

Method of initialization, method of production   There exists only a single method of initialization,[51] which consists of selecting a useful volume, whatever it might be, without preparing it in any particular way. Although the mode of initialization introduces only a small amount of variability in the flakes produced, this variability is nonetheless present. The schemes of production, on the other hand, can be diversified, although the unidirectional method is by far the most important. In several cases, bidirectional removals are present. But the presence of bidirectional removals can also be the result of the utilization of two successive useful volumes.

The resilience of the morphology of the blocks of raw material   To the extent that the selection of a block of raw material is the method of initialization, it is essential to consider the sources of the raw material that are exploited. In effect, in the context of alluvial deposits, only cobbles, which are normalized blocks of the same morphology, are available. Due to this regularity in the morphology of the unworked cobbles, the residual blocks remaining after debitage are morphologically very similar, resulting very often in significant interpretive confusion.[52] This regularization should therefore be considered *a priori* as artificial. Only techno-productional and techno-functional analyses can successfully identify the real intentions: whether an object served as a block for knapping flakes or as a tool.

In the case where the raw materials are of a variable morphology, exploited blocks with an identical useful volume will be morphologically distinct after knapping. This morphological diversity of the residual blocks can be interpreted as evidence of an aleatory behavior underlying production. However, if one focuses only on the useful volume (the core) a highly normalized behavior becomes evident.

As a result, knowledge of the qualitative and quantitative characteristics of blocks of raw material in the environment is a precondition for any technical interpretation. This attention to raw material is also necessary in the case of debitage of successive useful volumes on the same block. As the second useful volume is chosen in a secondary temporality and as its presence is aleatory, the residual knapped blocks present a large morphological variability.[53] The utilization of a second useful volume, if present, results in a very large morphological variability of knapped blocks. In most cases, regardless of the initial morphology of the block, the aleatory character of the availability of a second or third useful volume means that the global morphology of the block changes. This is a non-homothetic series of blocks. The refits of High Lodge (Ashton et al., 1992) or of Monte Poggiolo (Peretto et al., 1998) show that the successive useful volumes knapped on a cobble alternate on the same pole (Forestier, 1993), giving the residual impression of a chopping tool and evoking an early[54] industry of cobbles/tools, which is clearly not the case.

Therefore, the use of the morphology of the residual block as the lone basis for classification of such industries is deceptive. For a single conception of debitage, an exclusive focus on morphology leads to contradictory and false conclusions. Depending on the type of block and the number of successive series, the outcome of technical coherence becomes morphological incoherence, which is taken as a primitive trait, while in the case of the exploitation of cobbles, the same process serves as the basis for the identification of a veritable "cultural facies." Only analysis of the production, which dissociates the useful and non-useful volumes, can make sense of the type of conception of debitage and thus of the type of removals sought.

The removals The characteristics of the removals produced depend on the selection of technical criteria naturally present on the useful volume. In cases where these naturally present criteria result in removals that are sufficient to fill functional needs and the removals do not need a further stage of confection, the tool is left unretouched. Alternatively, the removal may be the object of a significant phase of confection, which in this case is usually applied to the transformative part of the tool and only rarely to the prehensile part.

The absence of a phase of confection is often observed in the exploitation of Type C2- blade removals predating the Saalien, whether in Europe at Tourville-la-Riviere (Guilbaud and Carpentier, 1995) and at Saint-Valery-sur Somme (Heinzelin and Haesaerts, 1983) or in the Middle East at the site of Kaféine in Syria (Figure 2.55) or even in Africa in the Kapthurin Formation in Kenya (Johnson and McBrearty, 2010). This absence of a phase of confection does not mean that the blades do not possess precise techno-functional criteria. In effect, the choice to

Figure 2.55 Unretouched blades derived from knapping of Type C2, Kaféine, Syria. Photo copyright E. Boëda.

produce removals that are twice as long as they are wide indicates the desire for a particular prehensile part, like the tang of a modern blade. To this, there is added the desire for a natural back opposite to a cutting edge or two cutting edges that are parallel and only rarely convergent.

The presence of a phase of confection is often associated with exploitation of Type C1, as can be observed in the collections of High Lodge (Figure 2.56). This retouch is generally restricted to the transformative part, adjusting the contact with

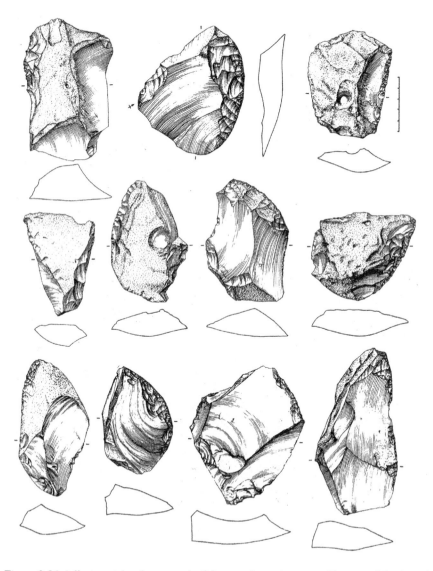

Figure 2.56 Adjustment (*aménagement*) of the transformative part without modification of the prehensile part (Ashton et al., 1992).

the worked material. The retouch only rarely modifies the general morphology of the flake and even more rarely the prehensile part.

In other cases, a more precise selection of the useful volume allows for production of removals that are very close to the eventual tools. This type of production is found in sites such as Guanyindong, province of Guizhou, China (Li, 2014). Depending on the type of useful surface selected, the exploitation of Type C1 permits the production of removals/tools with convergent edges that a simple supplementary confection finalizes (Figures 2.56–2.59).

To conclude, exploitation of Type C appears to be the first volumetric conception capable of exercising a forward-looking control (anticipation) of the eventual removals that will be used as they are or will be object of a confection stage. This volumetric conception is applied to a part of the block, designated as the useful volume. It is the result of selection in relation to the type of removal desired. During the early periods,[55] one finds this type of exploitation on all the continents.[56]

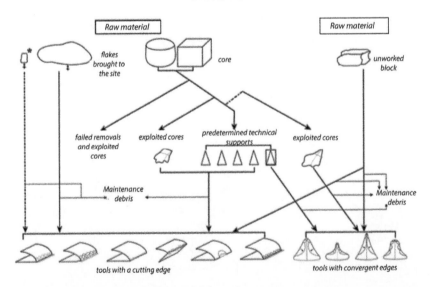

Figure 2.57 The technical system of lithic production for the site of Guanyindong, Guizhou, China. Operational schemas of Type C. These schemas allow for a wide range of flakes, of which some with convergent edges are sought after to be transformed into specific tools.

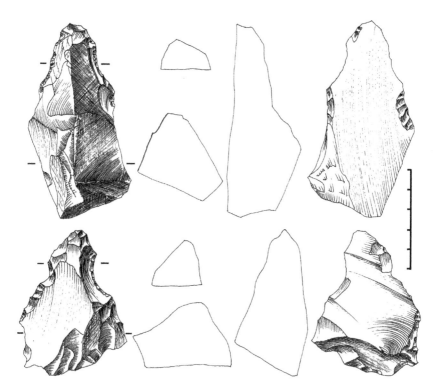

Figure 2.58 Guanyindong, China. Tools with convergent edges made on flakes with a triangular transversal section. The stage of shaping reinforces the convergent form resulting in chamfered or pointed end.

USEFUL VOLUME OF TYPE D

The useful volume of Type D is the result of preparation, as opposed to the useful volume of Type C, which was selected for its natural characteristics. In other words, for a useful volume of Type D to be ready for knapping it must first be prepared. This preparation is applied to the debitage surface and eventually to the surface of the striking platform (Figure 2.60). This preparation is only applied to the useful volume, leaving the rest of the block in its natural state.

Thus, the block held in knapper's hand is composed of two components: a prepared useful volume corresponding to a core (*sensu stricto*) and a non-useful volume. Depending on the objectives of the knapper, the non-useful volume may or may not be exploited, partially or in totality, for a second series of removals on the condition that this subsequent volume is first prepared to be operational.

Identifying exploitation of Type D is not a simple matter. A morphological and/or partially technological analysis leads most often to efforts to name categories of objects or debitage that deviate from nominal forms,[57] as is evident in the frequent use of terms using suffixes such as pseudo, pre, proto, or para. It is thus that one

86 *The techno-logic of evolution*

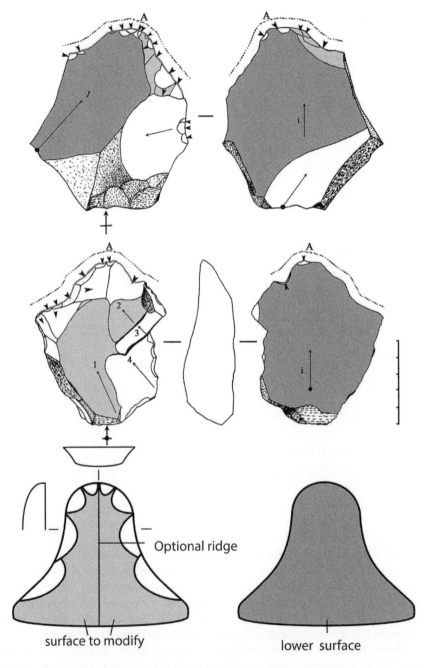

Figure 2.59 Guanyindong, China. Tools with a chamfered end (after Li, 2014).

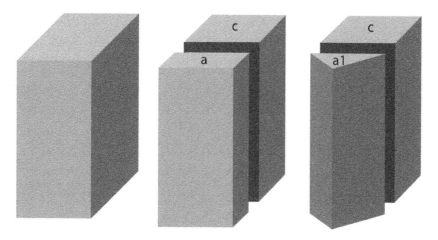

Figure 2.60 Conception of Type D. Left: the selected block. Center: the block is conceived as two subunits, the future useful volume (a) and a future non-useful volume (c). Right: the useful volume a1, designated as the core prepared for knapping (a1), and the non-useful volume (c).

speaks of para-Levallois debitage and proto-Levallois[58] (Bordes, 1961b). There even exist Levallois cores for proto-Levallois flakes, which signify that one is "on the way" but that "it is not yet completely there" (Bordes, 1961b)! The names of the sites where certain cores are found are also used in creating a taxonomy for these objects such as *Victoria West* or proto-Levallois cores (Van Riet Lowe, 1945, Lycett, 2009), the *Tabelbala-Technghit* technique/*Levalloissienne* technique (Tixier, 1957), the *Kombewa* method (Owen, 1938, 1939; Tixier et al., 1980), or the debitage of type *Roucourt* (Otte et al., 1990). Another solution is to equate the identified types of cores to cultural facies: Mousterian, Abbevillean, or Acheulean cores (Bordes, 1961b). In other cases, it is the mode of production that defines the type of core: orthogonal core (Heinzelin de Brancourt, 1962), unidirectional core, semi-rotational (*semi-tournant*), bidirectional, and so on.[59]

Another classic confusion arises because the knapper selects a block on the basis of natural surfaces that possess the required technical criteria, although these are insufficient making a phase of preparation necessary. This can result in the misperception that a partially prepared block is of Type D—see the discussion of Types E and F. Another possible source of confusion that might confound Types E and F with Type D is when the phase of initialization is abandoned early on because of issues related to the quality of the block. The knapper can anticipate failure and rapidly abandons the block.

To avoid all these errors, one must work on a complete collection. Only envisioning the totality of the technical intentions makes the conceptual reality of Type D, which allows for the production of removals with a certain number of predetermined criteria, apparent. This conception is far more common than it might seem.

					Type D			
				D1 flake	D2 elongated		D3 triangular	
					blade	bladelet	Levallois typo-point	Levallois pseudo-typo point
method	initialization		selection	x	x	x		x
		maintenance	Kombewa	X		X		X
			unidirectional parallel	X	X			
			unidirectional convergent		X	X	X	x
			diverse crests		X	X		
			bidirectional					
			peripheral	X				
	production		preferential	X			X	X
		recurrence	unidirectional parallel	X	X	X		
			unidirectional convergent		X	X		X
			bidirectional		x	x		
			peripheral	X				

Figure 2.61 Table of the potential variability in the methods of initialization and production of a useful volume of Type D.

Variability of the modes of initialization and production   The potential variability of production of useful volume of Type D is utilized to produce a wide range of removals, including flakes, blades, and triangular flakes (Figure 2.61).

The useful volumes that serve to produce flakes are designated as Type D1, those that are used to produce blades are designated as Type D2, and volumes exploited for triangular flakes are designated as Type D3. As we will see later with the archaeological examples, some of the removals possess technical criteria similar to so-called Discoidal or Levallois removals. However, keep in mind that one must distinguish between types and techno-types, in particular in the case of Levallois points. In effect, a Levallois point might well be produced by a debitage that is of a non-Levallois conception. The point is thus of type Levallois but is not Levallois in terms of techno-type. For a point to be techno-typologically Levallois, it must be produced by the Levallois conception of debitage.

Just as for debitage of useful volume of Type C, but in a far clearer fashion for categories D1, D2, and D3, there is variability in methods of initialization and production. For the methods of initialization, a phase of preparation compensates for the reduced role of selection. This phase of preparation can be expressed in various ways, by one or several modes of initialization. It is the traces of initialization, evident on the residual volume, that lead to classificatory confusion.

The methods of production are, in and of themselves, generally not very diverse. One can observe a first distinction between the production of a preferential removal—in general flakes or typological points, and more rarely blades—and a recurrent production of flakes or blades. The methods of production by recurrent series are very generally unidirectional, more rarely bidirectional, orthogonal, chordal, or even centripetal.

Type D1   The variability of exploitation of Type D1 is evident primarily in the phase of initialization, which involves the preparation of the useful volume. Many variants are possible.

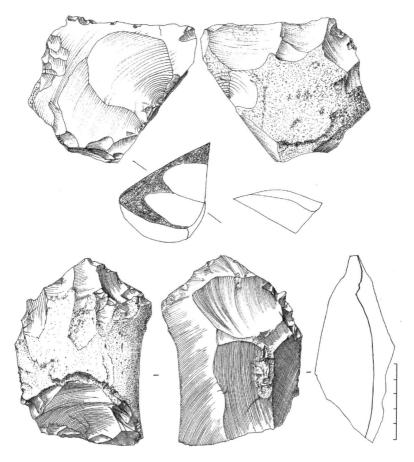

Figure 2.62 Level C'3, Barbas, Dordogne, France. Cores of type D1, Kombewa-type initialization.

Initialization of Kombewa type   The utilization of the ventral surface of a flake as a useful volume is one of the possible solutions. The number of flakes removed from this surface, designated as Kombewa or semi-Kombewa, is variable but does not exceed two or three removals (Figure 2.62; Boëda et al., 1996; Boëda, 1997). The removals are produced off the ventral face of a flake in the convex area that corresponds to the bulb of percussion. Once this convex volume has been utilized, the flaking ends. Depending on the particular variant, Kombewa or semi-Kombewa, flakes can be transformed into bifacial pieces, as at Barbas (France) level C'3 (Figure 2.63),[60] or into backed pieces as at Korolevo (Ukraine) level CII (Figures 2.64 and 2.65).[61] This mode of production is also present in the early African phases dating back to more than one million years, such as at the site of Fejej in Ethiopia (Figure 2.66; de Lumley et al., 2004).

90 *The techno-logic of evolution*

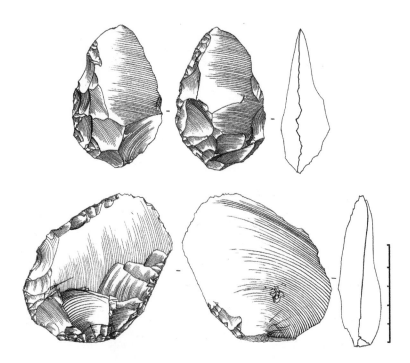

Figure 2.63 Level C'3, Barbas, Dordogne, France. Kombewa flakes that have served as the support for the fabrication of different tools.

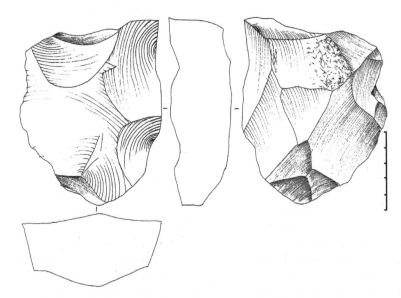

Figure 2.64 Korolevo, Level C.II, Ukraine (Micoquian). Useful volume of Type D1 with Kombewa initialization.

The techno-logic of evolution 91

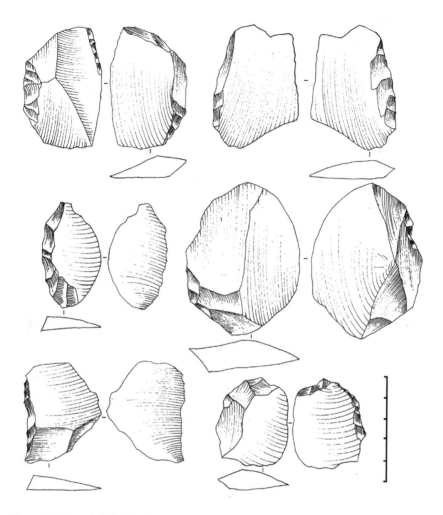

Figure 2.65 Level C.II, Korolevo, Ukraine (Micoquian). Modified Kombewa flakes.

Initialization that can resemble Levallois without being Levallois The useful volume is in this case prepared by removals. This type of core has frequently been classified under the Levallois category, although chronologically it appears earlier than Levallois debitage. As a result, in certain contexts, such as at Cagny-La-Garenne, France (Figure 2.67), these cores are considered as the precursor of Levallois debitage (Tuffreau, 2004). However, this type of exploitation has no relation to a Levallois conception because the useful volume is not prepared in order to reinitialize the block. This absence of a possibility of continuity in knapping can be observed on the part of the block opposed to the useful volume, designated in the case of Levallois debitage as the striking platform surface, which in the current

92 The techno-logic of evolution

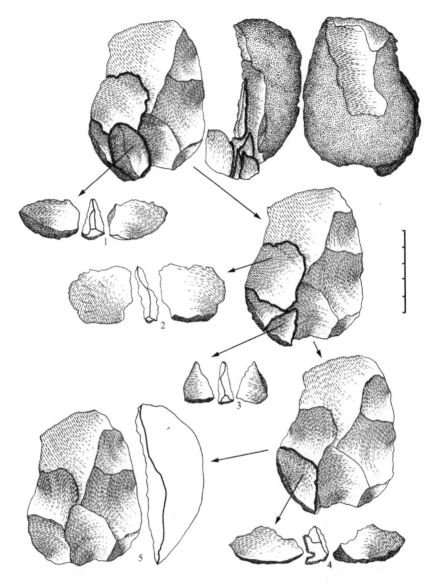

Figure 2.66 Fejej, Ethiopia, Type D3. A recurrent series of removals to produce flakes with an adjacent or opposed back (de Lumley et al., 2004).

case completely lacks preparation except for the removal of a single desired or multiple desired flakes. In some cases, the method of production of removals from the debitage surface leads to the production of flakes somewhat similar to those that result from Levallois debitage.[62] Even if these flakes are technically identical to Levallois flakes resulting from a Levallois production, we should establish

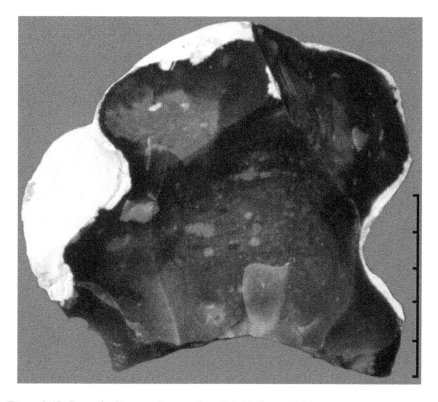

Figure 2.67 Cagny-la-Garenne, France, Type D1 (Tuffreau, 2004).

a distinction and name them differently. It is thus that we designate these flakes resulting from a non-Levallois production as "Levallois typo-flakes" because typologically they are identical. We reserve the term "Levallois techno-type flake" for the removals from a Levallois production.[63]

Initialization: Victoria West Cores Victoria West cores have been the object of several designations. The most familiar are *proto-Levallois core* (Van Riet Lowe, 1945) or *para-Levallois* (Bordes, 1961b). These designations indicate that these cores are considered as the precursors of Levallois debitage. Nonetheless, as in the preceding case, the type of general preparation distinguishes Victoria West cores from Levallois cores. The problem is not related to the debitage surface that is prepared with a small number of removals, giving some of these cores an "archaic" character, but rather the global conception of the core (Figure 2.68). The non-Levallois character is due to a preparation of the useful volume that is limited to a part of the block. Once this volume is exploited, the rest of the block does not present the technical preparation that is necessary for a repreparation of the volume.

94 *The techno-logic of evolution*

In contrast to the Levallois core, the Victoria West Core does not show any anticipation of a possible continuity integrated into the global volume of the core. The angle formed by the surface of the striking platform with the surface of debitage is too close to 90° to allow for a successful resumption of knapping. To eventually continue knapping, it is necessary to reestablish the totality of the construction of the useful volume as well as the surface of the striking platform. In a Levallois conception, for example, in the Ault Onival dans le Somme type of debitage, or at the sites of Champ Bruquette and Tio Marche in the Pas-de-Calais (Valin et al., 2006), the core is conceived in such a fashion that once a desired removal is knapped, one can without difficulty restore the technical criteria lacking from the useful volume to the same debitage surface and surface of striking platforms.

Type D2 Type D2 consists of the exclusive production of removals twice as long as they are wide. We should distinguish between two different objectives possible within this type of exploitation: the one producing blades and the other producing bladelets.

Figure 2.68 Victoria West Cores, South Africa. Photo copyright Kathleen Kuman.

In both cases, the production presents variability in the modes of the initialization of the useful volume. This variability allows for the adjustment of the type and the number of blades or bladelets produced per prepared surface. The modes of initialization are classic and consist of the preparation of an arch (lateral convexity) and of the carination (distal convexity) through laminar cortical removals. The use of anterior and/or posterior crests as well as a striking platform surface varies depending on the modality of percussion—internal or marginal—which leads to the production of blade/bladelet removals with distinctive technical traits (Figure 2.69). Once the useful volume is exploited, usually through a series of very short removals, the production is ended. Because the configuration of the core does not incorporate the possibility of a partial reinitialization, the cores are either abandoned or reinitialized using another part of the block or by taking the old debitage surface as a point of departure and integrating the remaining criteria.

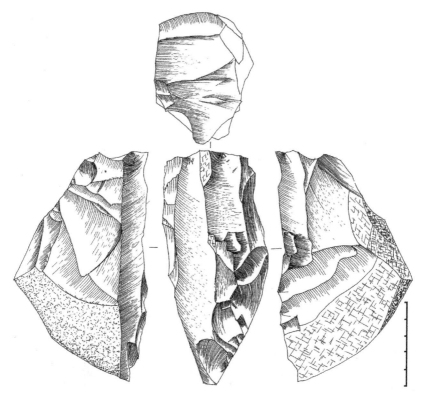

Figure 2.69 Kaféine, Syria, Type D2. Preparation of a useful volume by an anterior crest and a posterior crest. The useful volume, which is extremely small, only allows for the controlled production of two or three blades. Internal percussion with a hard hammer.

96 The techno-logic of evolution

IN THE ARCHAEOLOGICAL CONTEXT, THE EXPLOITATION OF TYPE D2 IS VERY COMMON

Debitage of blades of Type D2   From the earliest blade industries in Europe, Africa, and the Middle East—that date to Oxygen Isotope Stages 8–4—we find the exploitation of Type D2 used either exclusively or in association with other blade production systems: C2, E2, or F2 (see discussion of E2 and F2 below)[64]. In general, the removals are produced with the use of either hard or soft percussion, internal or marginal. It seems that internal percussion dominates during the earliest periods; however, the current technical studies are too limited to confirm the exclusive use of this technique of knapping. This impression rests only on our own studies in the Near East and Europe. On the other hand, beginning in Oxygen Isotope 3 in the circum-Mediterranean, marginal percussion becomes the dominant, even exclusive, technique of knapping, without this leading to the abandonment of exploitation of Type D2. On the contrary, we find this system once again during the initial phases of the Upper Paleolithic in the Near East[65] in the so-called transitional or intermediate Paleolithic of Syria (Boëda and Bonilauri, 2006, Figure 2.70). In the European Upper Paleolithic, the exploitation of Type D2 is also present, particularly in the earliest phases (Figures 2.71–2.73).

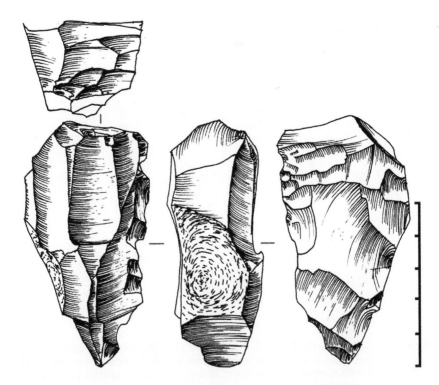

Figure 2.70   Umm el Tlel, Syria, Type D2. Preparation of a useful volume by one or two postero-lateral crests and through the integration of a natural surface on one of the sides of the arch. Internal percussion with a hard hammer.

The techno-logic of evolution 97

Figure 2.71 Barbas III, Dordogne, France. Aurignacian core of Type D2. Partial preparation of the carination. Photo copyright S. Oboukhoff, CNRS photographic service, MAE-Nanterre Médiathèque.

Figure 2.72 Barbas III, Dordogne, France. Aurignacian core of Type D2. Partial preparation of the carination. Photo copyright S. Oboukhoff, CNRS photographic service, MAE-Nanterre Médiathèque.

Debitage of bladelets of Type D2 Bladelet production using this type of exploitation is only documented anecdotally, but it is nonetheless present, well before the Upper Paleolithic, in both Europe and the Near East. However, it is in the transitional industries of the Near East that this production represents a techno-functional objective. As is the case for the debitage of blades, the first evidence of bladelet production is of Type D2. One can distinguish multiple categories of useful volumes depending on whether the desired form of bladelet is straight in profile or torqued (Figure 2.74). The initialization is varied as is the mode of percussion.

98 *The techno-logic of evolution*

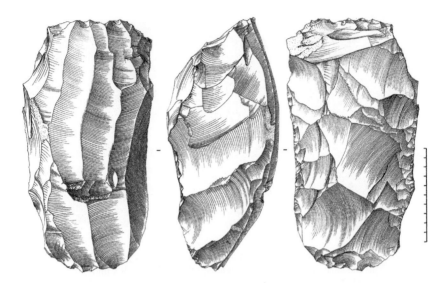

Figure 2.73 Barbas II, Dordogne, France. The preparation covers the entirety of the core, although the useful volume is limited to only a part of the block. This volume is organized to obtain large blades. Once these blades have been produced, the useful volume is exhausted. The further pursuit of knapping is impossible except for work aimed at the recreation of a new useful volume regardless of the type of laminar objectives sought.

There exists a particular case where the debitage of bladelets is intercalated with the production of blades or Levallois points[66] that we have observed in the Transitional levels of Umm el Tlel, Syria (Figure 2.75). In this case, the debitage of one or two bladelets takes place along the axis of the ridge of a flake scar.

In Europe and in the Middle East, this type of bladelet knapping, intercalated in a blade sequence, is known notably in the Magdalenian (Karlin and Ploux, 1994), Gravettian (Nespoulet, 1999), Proto-Aurignacian (Schmider, 2002; Bon, 2002; Bordes, 2006) and early Baradostian of the Zagros (Bordes and Shidrang, 2009).

Type D3 Type D3 consists of an exclusive production of triangular points. We must distinguish two distinct objectives: one producing what can be designated as Levallois typo-points and the other as Levallois pseudo-typo-points.

Debitage of Levallois typo-points The Levallois typo-point can be the result of different conceptions of knapping (Boëda, 1991). When we put forward this idea in 1991 following extensive experimentation, we did not have the entirety of modes of operation capable of providing this typo-point. Type F1, otherwise designated as Levallois, and Type E2, designated as pyramidal, were the only relevant modes of operation clearly characterized at that time.

The discovery of the site of Villiers-Adam, Val d'Oise (Locht et al., 2003), has confirmed the experimental intuition. This site includes, along with other

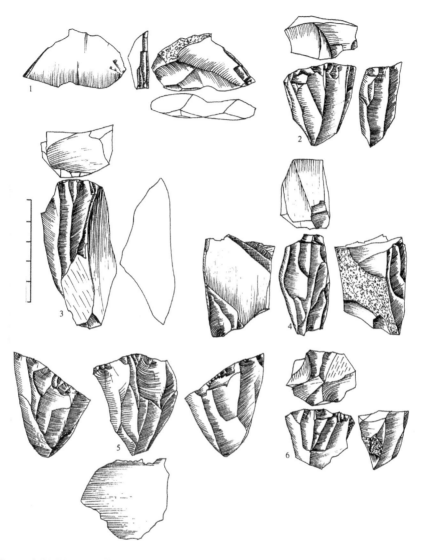

Figure 2.74 Umm el Tlel, Level II base, Syria. Different categories of bladelet cores. The preparation of the useful volume in the case of Piece 1 is through an oblique truncation. In the case of Pieces 2, 5, and 6, the preparation is through overpassing cortical flake removals. In the case of Pieces 3 and 4, one observes several orthogonal flake scars that are difficult to interpret. The percussion is mixed, internal, and marginal.

objectives, the exhaustive production of Levallois typo-points (Figure 2.76) without any evidence whatsoever of Levallois point cores (Figure 2.77).

The general organization of the cores shows that only a single part of the core is prepared. This construction is confirmed by a very large number of refits

100 *The techno-logic of evolution*

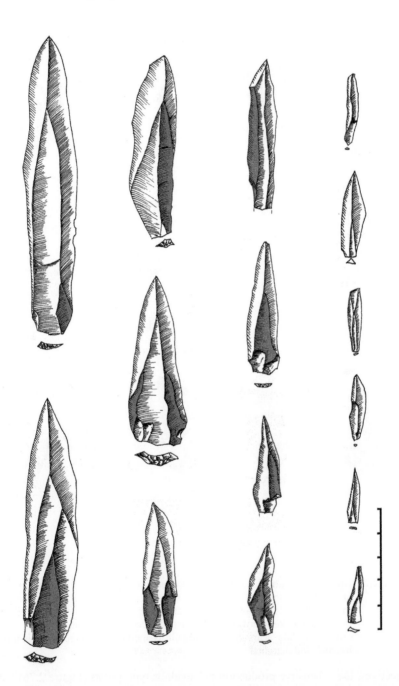

Figure 2.75 Umm el Tlel, Level II base and III 2a, Syria. The gray zones represent the scars of bladelets intercalated within the knapping of laminar products.

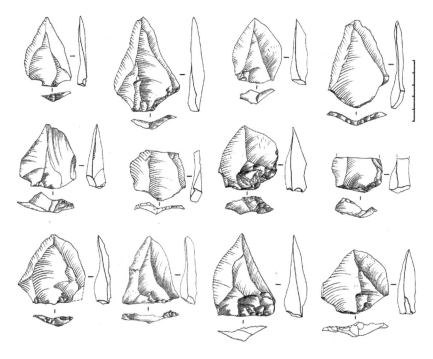

Figure 2.76 Villiers-Adam, Val d'Oise, France. Production of Levallois typo-points (after Locht, 2003).

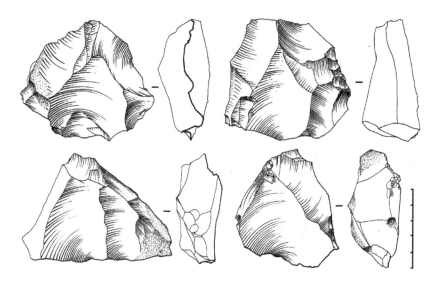

Figure 2.77 Villiers-Adam, Val d'Oise, France. Non-Levallois cores despite their morphological appearance of Type D3 with the production of Levallois typo-points (after Locht, 2003).

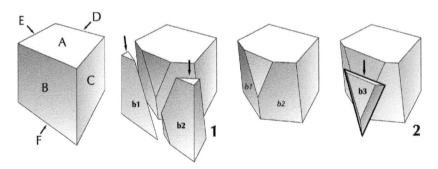

Figure 2.78 Villiers-Adam, Val d'Oise, France. A schematic representation of refit number 11. Type D3 with a Levallois typo-point with a unidirectional convergent initialization.

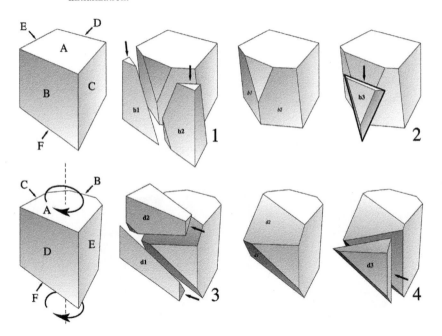

Figure 2.79 Villiers-Adam, Val d'Oise, France. A schematic representation of refit number 34 with two debitage surfaces (independent useful volumes). Type D2 with two Levallois typo-points obtained through the same method of initialization (Locht, 2003).

(Figure 2.78). After the initialization of a useful volume, a triangular flake is obtained. There are multiple modes of initialization that are adapted to the morphology of the initial block.

Some refits show the multiple productions of Levallois typo-points in succession. However, each time, this production takes place on a new useful volume, independent of the first, that is selected depending on the technical criteria of the block (Figures 2.79 and 2.80).

The techno-logic of evolution 103

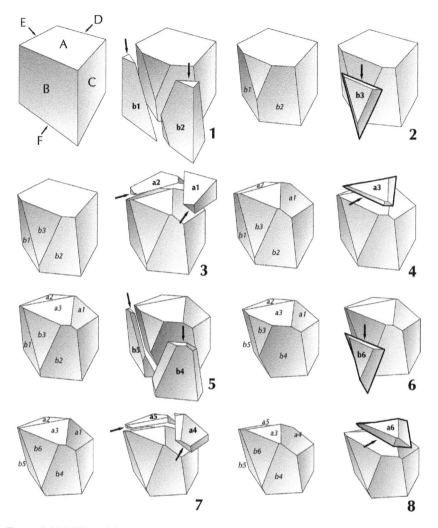

Figure 2.80 Villiers-Adam, Val d'Oise, France. A schematic representation of refit number 5 with four independent debitage surfaces (useful volumes). Type D3 with four Levallois typo-points obtained utilizing the same mode initialization.

The excellent archaeological example of Villiers-Adam in the Val d'Oise confirms the existence of this type of production, which is more common than it would seem. Obtaining a unique production—a Levallois typo-point—is dependent on the possibility of forming a new useful volume on the block. Each volumetric exploitation is independent. There is clear evidence of the partial modification of the block at every stage of production.

On the other hand, this fashion of obtaining Levallois typo-points is *a priori*[67] rarely observed in the Near East[68] where exploitation of Types E2 and F1 is more frequent (Figure 2.81).

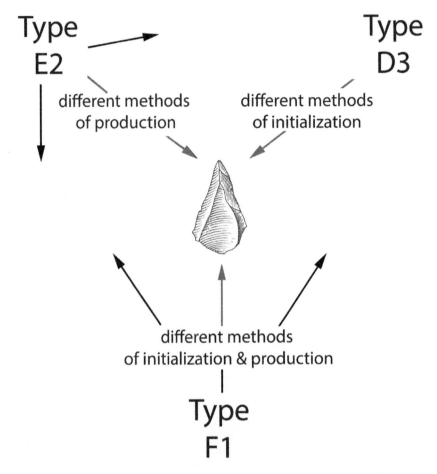

Figure 2.81 A Levallois typo-point can be produced by three distinct types of volumetric structures: F2, E2, and D3.

Debitage of pseudo-Levallois typo-points   This type of debitage is found under numerous designations: centripetal debitage (Texier, 1995), convergent debitage, or discoidal debitage.[69] The term "discoidal" is employed when the production is clearly oriented toward the production of a pseudo-Levallois typo-point. In some cases, despite the presence of this type of objective, there is a tendency to refer to centripetal debitage. In essence, this involves the production of a small series of two or three removals, of which the last has convergent edges. This notion of convergence is, in our opinion, important because this mode of exploitation allows for the production of this particular trait (convergence) without taking into account the global morphology of the flake.

The useful volume obviously represents a part of the block. The volume that is knapped can be a block of any form, a cobble, or a flake. In the case of a block or a cobble, the preparation is limited to one or two removals and the production of the convergent piece is immediate. Generally, after this series, it is impossible to continue the knapping, for technical constraints such as the presence of a step fracture or obtuse angles. This fact is one of the clearest indications that the preparation applies exclusively to a single useful volume on each block. When the block to be worked is a flake, the ventral face is preferentially selected, due to the existing natural convexity. This type of exploitation is found notably in the sites of Champ-Bossuet in Gironde, France (Figure 2.82; Bourguignon and Turq, 2003), and Asprochaliko, Greece (Papaconstantinou, 1987). Nonetheless, the ridge between flake scars on the dorsal surface of a flake can also form the basis for preparation and exploitation.

In conclusion The volumetric conception of Type D covers a far more significant archaeological reality than we might have imagined, and this is found in all variants of production: blades, flakes, triangular flakes, Levallois typo-points, and pseudo-Levallois typo-points. The variability is largely a consequence of the phase of initialization, as we have seen through a number of archaeological examples.

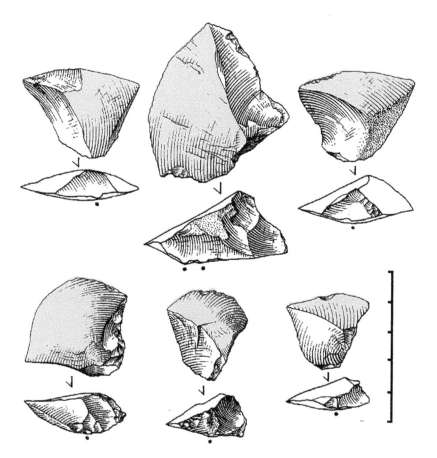

Figure 2.82 Champ-Bossuet, Gironde, France. Pseudo-Levallois typo-point with Kombewa initialization (Bourguignon and Turq, 2003).

106 *The techno-logic of evolution*

The utilization of this type of exploitation can be contextualized in more than one way. The first is chronological, such as in the case of Type D1 that precedes the Levallois, or the case of debitage of Type D1 that develops after Type C2 and is always antecedent to Type F2, while Type D2 is often contemporary with Type E2. The exploitation of Type D can also be an economic response to types of raw material. Exploitations of Type D3 are a solution *au minima* to produce Levallois typo-points and pseudo-Levallois typo-points on difficult raw materials. Types D2 and D3 can be the expression of an economy of debitage and correspond to specific moments that only require a small number of removals and one thus finds this type of exploitation associated with Type F1 and more rarely to Type E2.

It is thus, thanks to a recognition of exploitation of Type D and of its different variations that we can avoid an arbitrary reductionism, facile groupings, and rough designations to allow a much greater complexity, that is closer to reality, to emerge.

Concrete volumetric structures

A second ensemble groups together the technical systems of production that require the entirety of the block to achieve their objectives. In this ensemble, the useful volume corresponds to the integrality of the volume of the block, which can therefore be called a core. The block consists of only a single entity, integrated into the same synergy of production.

The techno-functional criteria of the tools are largely achieved through the process of production. As a result, the supports produced are very close in form to the tools that will be used. One can distinguish two distinct volumetric structures: Type E and Type F.

TYPE E

The exploitation of Type E involves the adoption of an organized recurrence of the removals such that they allow for the establishment on the core of the convexities necessary to arrive at the desired objectives. The block must continuously be exploited by the same range of removals at the risk of losing the predetermining character of these removals and altering the operational volumetric structure. In other words, it is the consistent objectives that maintain a volumetric structure, allowing for continued production. In this group of volumetric structures, we make a subdivision between what we have defined as discoidal, here designated as Type E1 (Boëda, 1993), and pyramidal debitage, here named Type E2.

TYPE F

The exploitation of Type F involves the preliminary preparation of the integrality of the core to create the particular technical characteristics that allow for a control over the technical and morphological criteria of the removal to be produced. Multiple conceptions of debitage belong to this ensemble. The most familiar is the Levallois conception. We also include certain blade production methods that one finds in the Upper Paleolithic and the Neolithic. The lack of a detailed terminology to designate these various production methods, in contrast to the situation for flake production (Levallois, Discoid, Clactonian, etc.) or for blade production of the Lower and Middle

The techno-logic of evolution 107

Paleolithic, can be explained by the fact that within the blade production of Type F there is only a single, or perhaps two, distinct volumetric conceptions. Until now, the observed variability has been at the level of the precise pattern of exploitation, as is the case of Levallois debitage. But the recognition of the precise pattern of exploitation, which we will call here methods, has taken place without truly exploring the underlying volumetric conception or at the very least making an effort to dissociate the method—the precise pattern of exploitation—from the volumetric concept. In general, there is a degree of confusion between what we refer to here as methods and concepts. It is interesting to consider that in the history of the discipline, most researchers amalgamated concept and method for the Lower and Middle Paleolithic, referring to the manner of debitage by its method.[70] In Type F volumetric conception, we have also made a division between what we have previously defined as Levallois, now designated as Type F1 (Boëda, 1994), and certain types of blade production of the final Late Pleistocene and Holocene, here designated as Type F2.

Useful volume of Type E

The different structures of Type E form a very distinct group consisting of conceptions of Type E1 (discoidal) and Type E2 (pyramidal) (Figure 2.83). Before providing a detailed description of these conceptions of debitage, we have attempted to map out their respective objectives. As discussed in the introduction, the evolution of objects is generally the cause of the evolution of structures. In the framework of these evolutions toward increasing techno-cultural constraints, the discoidal (E1) conception makes it possible to normalize a range of possible forms, while the pyramidal (E2) allows for the creation of particular technical criteria. In a way one can say that these two conceptions are complimentary.

TYPE E1

Discoidal exploitation of Type E1 allows for a continuous heterogeneous production of four well-characterized types of flakes as the result of knapping in two

				Type E	
				E1	E2
method	initialization		selection	X	X
		maintenance	Kombewa	X	
			unidirectional parallel		X
			unidirectional convergent		X
			peripheral	X	
	production		preferential	X	
		recurrence	unidirectional parallel		X
			unidirectional convergent		X
			centripetal & cordal	X	

Figure 2.83 Table of the potential variability of the methods of initialization and production of a useful volume of Type E.

108 *The techno-logic of evolution*

Figure 2.84 Queyssac, Dordogne, France. Core of Type E1. Photo copyright S. Oboukhoff, CNRS photographic service, MAE Médiathèque, Nanterre.

directions: cordal and centripetal (Figure 2.84; Boëda, 1993, 1995a and b). The flakes from a centripetal direction are either longer than they are wide or quadrangular (Figure 2.85).

TYPE E2

The pyramidal exploitation of Type E2 tends toward the production of systematic removals that are twice as long as they are wide (blades), except for accidents (Figures 2.86–2.89). The production is either (1) homogeneous consisting of blades, as in Amudian case (Figure 2.90; Meignen, 1994) of Tabun Cave (Garrod and Bate, 1937; Garrod, 1956; Jelinek, 1975, 1981, 1982, 1990) or the Abri Zumoffen (Garrod and Kirkbride, 1961), or (2) heterogeneous consisting of blades and elongated triangular flakes similar to the Levallois typo-points, such as the Leiliras of Australia (Figure 2.91; Mulvaney, 1975; Bordes, 1976–1977; McCarty, 1976; Spencer and Gillens, 1912) or the assemblage of Level 4 of Boker Tachtit in the Negev (Marks and Volkman, 1983).[71]

CONCEPTUAL SPECIFICITY

The specificity of exploitation of Type E is based on a paradox: products that to a significant degree are predetermined are obtained without an extensive phase of initializing the core as is found in exploitation of Types D and F. For exploitation

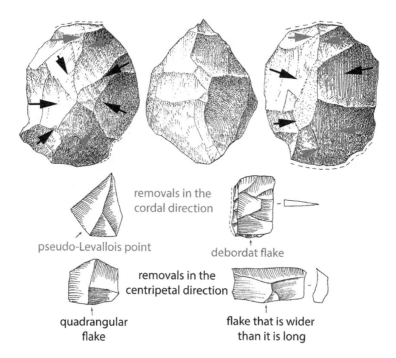

Figure 2.85 Külna, Czech Republic, Micoquian Level. Discoidal core with bifacial exploitation, with the production of four categories of flakes.

Figure 2.86 Kaféine, Syria, Anté-Mousterian industry. Core of Type E2. Photo copyright S. Oboukhoff, CNRS photographic service, MAE Médiathèque, Nanterre.

of Type E, the phase of initialization involves the selection of the block to knap and a very short phase of production consisting of two or three flake removals, for which the objective is to rapidly produce the one or two first flakes specific to each conception. As soon as the production is underway, a process of the auto-configuration of the core unfolds. This is to say that each removal is predetermined

110   *The techno-logic of evolution*

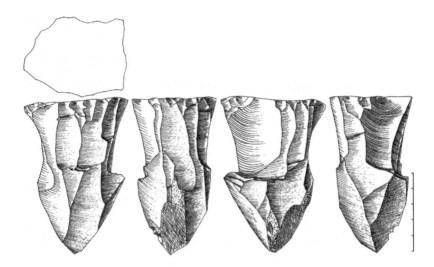

Figure 2.87 Kaféine, Syria, Anté-Mousterian industry. Core of Type E2. Photo copyright S. Oboukhoff, CNRS photographic service, MAE Médiathèque, Nanterre.

and predetermining, thus permitting for the maintenance of a controlled production. Of course, this production does not allow for the realization of other types of removals, which would risk breaking the recurrence and thus the production of normalized removals. These are closed conceptions, which in order to function must always produce the same type or the same series of objects with the same rhythm.

At the point of departure, the useful volume is only a part of the block. In order to be operational, the core requires only a partial useful volume, localized in one area of the block. But in clear and significant contrast to what we have described in the precedent types of exploitation—Types A, B, C, and D—where following the exploitation of the useful volume the subsequent algorithm has no obligatory relationship with its precedent, in the current case of exploitation of Type E, there exists a functional interdependence between removals of one sequence and the subsequent series. The first "algorithm," realized off the initial useful volume, puts in place the technical criteria necessary for a second algorithm, and this continues through the exploitation. In this way the exploitation of the initial useful volume engenders the creation of a second useful volume and so forth. Thus, the part of the block that is not operational constitutes a reservoir, in the proper sense of the term. This reservoir immediately becomes a useful volume as soon as, following the exploitation of the first series of removals, the pursuit of qualitatively and quantitatively defined objectives makes this necessary.

The pyramidal or discoidal cores are a sequence of useful volumes, one volume generating the next, such that the exploitation of the initial block can be almost total. This interdependence means that the production does not ever involve the addition of a new useful volume. This is an integrated structure but one which at the beginning only exists virtually. For this reason, one cannot use the term "*mise en forme*," which roughly translates as configuration (Soriano, 2000). In effect this is

The techno-logic of evolution 111

Figure 2.88 Saint-Firmin-des Prés, Loir-et-Cher, France, Excavations of V. Lhomme. Core of Type E2 (Lhomme et al., 1999).

not an integrated structure that first takes the finished form of a configured core, as we see in Type F, but rather an integrated structure that is in perpetual construction.

Exploitation of Type E becomes very interesting to analyze because it is the subject of many difficulties in recognition and interpretation. The perpetual state of becoming has as a consequence a shift in the morphology of the core depending on the quantity of desired removals. This is in the case of pyramidal cores where one can pass through anterior stages that are quarter or semi-pyramidal[72] (Figure 2.92). This morphological variability is also found, to even a greater extent, in the case of discoidal cores. In effect, in the case of discoidal debitage, nothing requires the knapper to maintain two surfaces at once, as the work can focus on a single face, or

112 *The techno-logic of evolution*

Figure 2.89 Saint-Firmin-des Prés, Loir-et-Cher, France, Excavations of V. Lhomme. Core of Type E2 (Lhomme et al., 1999).

even a single portion of one surface[73] (Figure 2.93). It all depends on the quantity of desired objectives and the unfolding of operations. As a result, there are as many different morphologies of cores as there are removals produced!

The E1 and E2 conceptions are controlled by the rule that "whoever does the least, does the most." The incessant shift in morphology makes these volumes non-homothetic structures (Boëda, 1997). Therefore, although they result from the same structure, these cores present, regardless of the method utilized, variable morphologies depending on the number of desired removals. The essence of this genre of debitage rests on a necessary morphological transformation. Thus, what could appear to be evidence of the use of different methods is in reality simply a measure of the intensity in the utilization of the initial block depending on the quantity of desired objectives.

If there is a perception of different methods, it is situated at the level of the quantitative representation of the possible objectives. It is in the choice of one assemblage of removals or another that the difference in method is expressed. These methods thus involve the problems of how to combine interrelated sequences of

The techno-logic of evolution 113

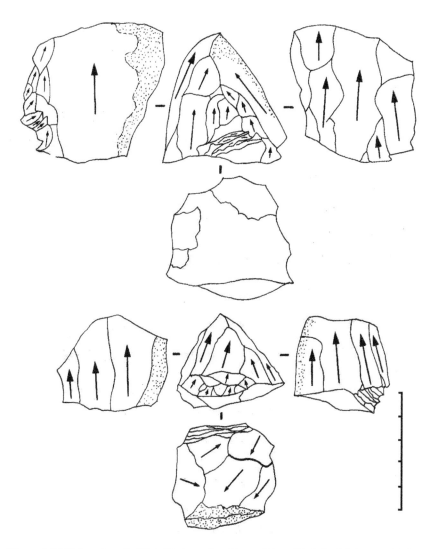

Figure 2.90 Tabun, Israel—Unit XI, Amudian. Core of Type E2 (after Meignen, 1994).

removals. In the case of the Discoid—Type E1—we could have thus defined multiple methods[74] and objectives:

1 A method of preferential removals, such as the pseudo-Levallois point (Bourguignon and Turq, 2003).
2 A method with a mixture of dominant elements: *Débordant* (edge of core) flakes and pseudo-Levallois points. (Depaepe et al., 1994; Locht, 2003).

114 The techno-logic of evolution

Figure 2.91 Australian Leiliras (after McCarty, 1976).

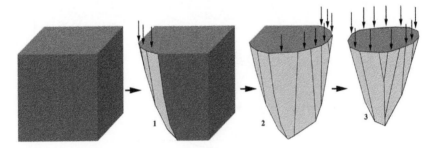

Figure 2.92 Pyramidal core with its potential variants. (1) Quarter pyramidal. (2) Semi-pyramidal. (3) Pyramidal at the end of its potential.

3 One or more methods of diversified removals (Boëda, 1995a and b; Brenet and Folgado, 2003).

Similarly, in the case of the pyramidal Type E2, multiple methods allow for the production either exclusively of blades or, alternatively, a mixed production consisting of blades and triangular removals, thus points that appear Levallois.

On the other hand, in both pyramidal and discoidal, the direction of removals does not form the basis for the differentiation between methods. In effect, in order for the

The techno-logic of evolution 115

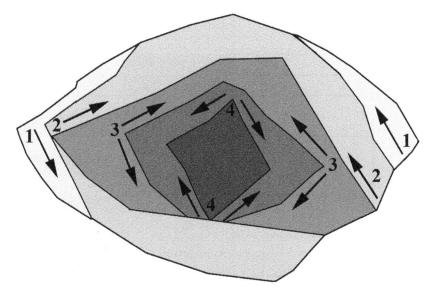

Figure 2.93 Non-homothetic debitage of Type E1. The exploitation can take place through removals of one or two faces in succession or alternation. Regardless, the range of removals does not change. In Case 4, one can even see a change in axis as is observed archaeologically at the site of Beauvais (Locht, 2003).

exploitation of an initial useful volume to lead to a second useful volume, it is necessary, in the case of the discoidal, to produce removals from multiple directions, and in the case of the pyramidal to produce removals from a single direction. The changing or stable direction of production is clearly the result of a structural necessity rather than the expression of a cultural characteristic, in opposition to what will be seen with the Levallois cores and certain blade cores of the Upper Paleolithic.

In fact, Types E1 and E2 are not really subject to the full potential range of variability found in Type F1. To an extent, this is explained by the essential characteristics of this production. Is it not necessary, to remain operational, to always produce the same range of products? The variability is therefore limited to the frequency of one type or another of removal.

In light of our new proposition of types, we can return to the distinction between the exploitation of the surface of a core as opposed to the exploitation of the volume of a core that we formulated beginning in 1988 (Boëda, 1988a and b, 1997). Almost all of the types of abstract structure correspond to a volumetric exploitation of a surface, which corresponds to a limited useful volume. The types of concrete structure bring together debitage based on volumetric exploitation. In this sense we have shifted from what we were able to say in the 1990s because at that time we conceived of the Levallois as the exploitation of a surface rather than a volume. In practice, the categories of abstract type and concrete type do not correspond

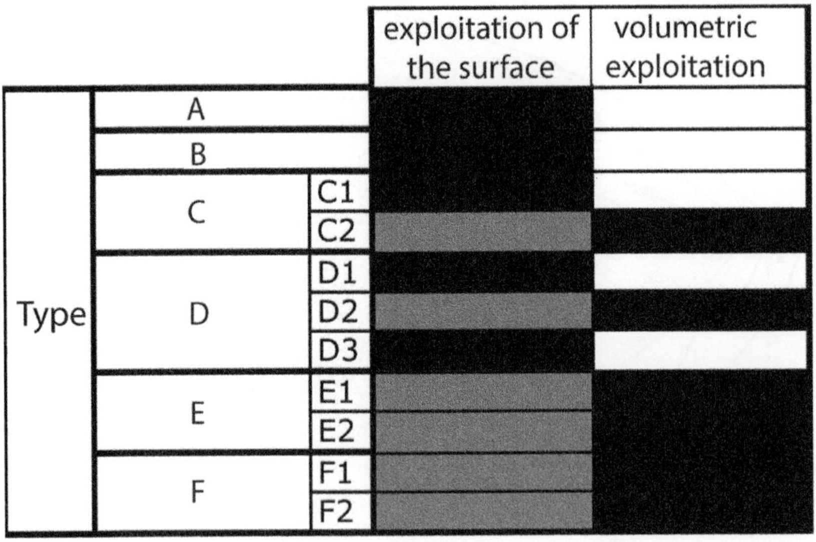

			exploitation of the surface	volumetric exploitation
Type	A		■	□
	B		■	□
	C	C1	■	□
		C2	▦	■
	D	D1	■	□
		D2	▦	■
		D3	■	□
	E	E1	▦	■
		E2	▦	■
	F	F1	▦	■
		F2	▦	■

Figure 2.94 Correlation between different types of useful volumes and the exploitation of volume versus surface. Black: Essential to the volumetric structure. Gray: Possible but not structurally essential, "whoever does the least, does the most."

directly to the notions of surface and volume, as we have just suggested, to the extent that these types do not represent the same phenomenon. Each type, and thus each useful volume, possesses its particular potential for the production of predetermined removals. Depending on the extent of the useful volume, it might be limited to a single surface, and thus be an "exploitation of a surface," as in the case of Types A, B, C1, D1, and D3, or might encompass multiple surfaces, "exploitation of a volume," as in Type C2 and D2 (Figure 2.94). In the case of Levallois, which is discussed in the next section, each phase of production is the exploitation of a surface. However, since the volumetric conception includes the reinitialization of the core and the continuation of a similar or different production, the Levallois is a volumetric exploitation. In fact, it is the potential of this particular type of structure that allows for a total volumetric exploitation. Generally, the tendency is to move from an exploitation of surface, which is the domain of the abstract structures, toward a volumetric exploitation that groups together the concrete structures and, in some cases, the abstract blade structures.

Useful volume of Type F

The useful volume of Type F corresponds to the volume of the configured block ready for exploitation. The configured block in its totality is the core. This configuration takes place following a stage of initialization, which is essential for obtaining the desired technical criteria for each of the objectives as well as for the overall exploitation of the core.

Thus, we distinguish two clearly distinct technical stages of equal importance: the stage of initialization that creates the core and the time of actual exploitation for production of the desired objectives. This temporal division in the process is different from Type E where the phases of configuration and initialization are integrated into the same synergy such that the configuration is renewed through the process of exploitation.

THE PHASE INITIALIZATION

The capacity of the core to become useful in its quasi-integrality while also being able to provide at any moment the desired artifact or artifacts depends on this phase. One usually thinks of this stage as a significant and complex process of preparation. However, there exists a second option that is not often recognized, which involves a draconian choice of the block to be exploited. Such a strategy might or might not be combined with a stage of preparation.

The use of overall preparation is by far the more frequently used strategy, regardless of the degree to which there is selectivity in the choice of the block of raw material (Figures 2.95 and 2.96). The method of preparation will vary depending on the qualitative and quantitative objectives without necessarily implying a strict fit between the method of preparation and a particular objective or objectives. On the other hand, the configuration of the core is specific to each major class, particularly for blades and bladelets. As mentioned earlier, a phase of selection can be included, which reduces the extent of preparation. However, this supplementary phase does not follow any fixed or rigid rules, as one might expect, by arguing, for

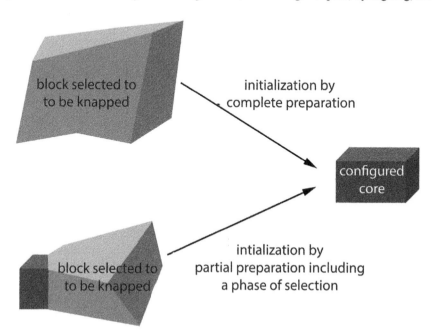

Figure 2.95 Configured core of Type F obtained following a stage of initialization through alteration with or without a preliminary selection.

118 *The techno-logic of evolution*

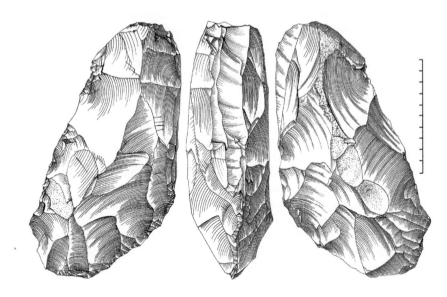

Figure 2.96 Villazette, Dordogne, France, Magdalenian. Configuration modifying the totality of the block with the goal of blade production.

example, that there is regularly a high degree of fit between the raw material and the desired type of configuration. In reality, the full range of variability is present and deserves in-depth analysis.

The option where "the selection is everything" is rare but nevertheless present on several continents—Europe, Asia, and South America.[75] This full selection is generally limited to focusing on the exploitation of cobbles, but there is no selectivity in terms of what type of cobble. The objective is to split the cobble into two identical hemispheres or *splits* (Figure 2.97, Crabtree, 1972). Each *split* is a twin flake with a regular dorsal face and a flat dorsal face, like a Levallois flake. The choice of the cobble is thus of fundamental importance because it must possess all of the characteristics of the eventual support, as well as all the technical criteria needed to enhance the likelihood of success in the production stage. This requires two punctiform surfaces for simultaneous impact with a hammer and anvil.

The production phase for *splits* is carried out through bipolar percussion on an anvil with a hard hammer. Only a single blow is possible. Bipolar percussion is the only mode of fracture capable of splitting a cobble into two hemispheres. Without a draconian selection, there is no chance of success. Thus, it is not the mode of percussion that accounts for the *splits* but rather the selection of the cobble. In effect, in Africa, we know of numerous Mousterian and Neolithic industries that use bipolar fracture with the objective of producing variable flakes, from "orange slices" to flat fragments and debris of every type, and, from time to time a fortuitous *split*. In reality, other than the production of *splits* on carefully selected cobbles, bipolar production on other cobble morphologies is difficult to control.

The techno-logic of evolution 119

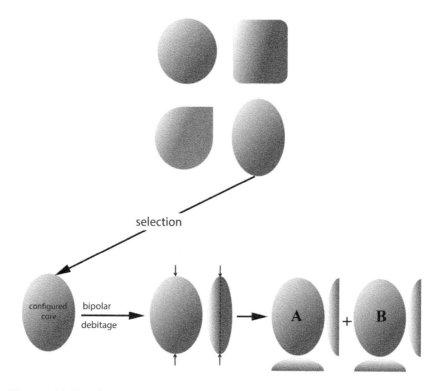

Figure 2.97 The phase of initialization consists of finding the future core in a form that is already ready to be flaked.

In summary, the production of *splits* imposes a very strict configuration of the core that results from a phase of initialization based exclusively on the selection of the block of raw material, in this case a cobble with a very particular morphology. It is interesting to note that this solution is in a sense the acme of efficiency and of the yield of objectives from raw material. The configured core is replaced by the objectives. This substitution is the successful outcome of the technical operation.[76]

OBJECTIVES OF CONFIGURED CORES OF TYPE F

When the phase of initialization is based on the preparation of the core, one can distinguish between two categories of configured volumes that are dependent on the objectives of production. They are designated as Types F1 and F2.

A configuration of Type F1, or Levallois debitage, has as its objective the production of a diverse range of artifacts. While in the case of configuration of Type F2, the objective is more restrictively focused on the production of blades and bladelets.[77]

120   *The techno-logic of evolution*

When the initialization is limited to selection, the objectives are essentially flakes, where only the relationship between length, breadth, and thickness can vary depending on the desired functional objectives. This mode of production is designated as F3.

THE SPECIFIC CHARACTERISTICS OF TYPES F1 AND F2

The techno-types produced from configured cores of Types F1 and F2 are in no way novel, as these can be obtained with the exploitation of Types C, D, and E. Blades can be produced from Types C2, D2, and E2; the Levallois typo-points can be produced with Types D3 and E2; and the Levallois typo-flakes from Type D1. Therefore, there does not appear to be a one-to-one fit between a type of product and the structure of the useful volume from which it is obtained (Figure 2.98).

One can therefore question the utility of the specific structural characteristics of exploitation of Types F1 and F2. Why configure the entirety of the block to be knapped? There is not a single direct answer to this question. There seem to be several concurrent factors involved that are difficult to rank. We distinguish three factors underlying the configuration of the entirety of the block found in the exploitation of Types F1 and F2.

FIRST FACTOR: NORMALIZATION OF THE PREHENSILE PART

The first reason to configure the entirety of the block is related to a significant regularization of the technical characteristics of the desired products that relate to their prehensile part. In the case of Types F1 (Levallois) and F2 (blade), it is clear that the prehensile part is a major objective, to the same degree as the transformative part. The typological focus on the transformative part[78] of tools has obscured the notion of support—the product of debitage in its integrality. The notion of the support—as we have developed at length, is essential because it provides the link between the means (the useful volume) and the tool. If one shifts the analytical perspective to ask what the supports produced by exploitation of Types F1 and F2

			flake	blade bladelet	point pseudo-point
Concrete structure	Type F	evolutionary gradient			
	Type E				
Abstract structure	Type D				
	Type C				
	Type B				
	Type A				

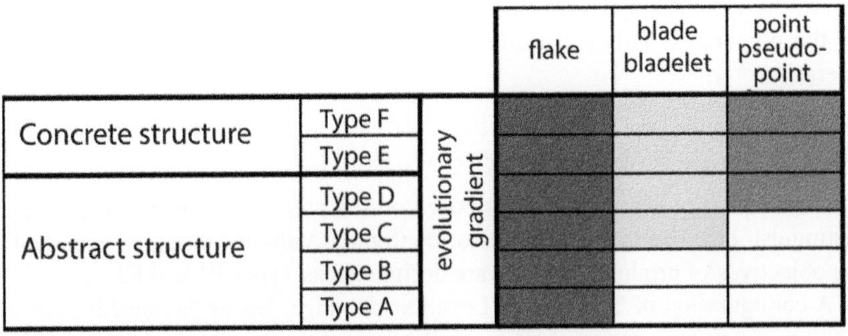

Figure 2.98 Following this table, there is not a fit between the type of product and the volumetric structure of the core.

have in common, instead of focusing on the distinctions between these types, it becomes evident that from the stage of the configuration of the core, the prehensile part is the object of unexpected investment. This normalization is certainly linked to the notion of hafting. This rationalization of the prehensile part has already been evoked for blade production but rarely for the Levallois debitage where emphasis is always placed on the silhouette.

SECOND FACTOR: PRODUCTION IN SERIES, DIVERSITY/UNITY

This aspect of the exploitation of Types F1 and F2 is distinctive for each type.

F1 PRODUCTION OR THE NECESSARY DIVERSITY OF ARTIFACTS: A STRUCTURAL ADVANTAGE

In the case of exploitation of Type F1, there is the production of potentially differentiated supports, except when what is involved is the production of a preferential removal (Figures 2.99 and 2.100). Even when, as in the case of preferential exploitation, there is only a single removal per surface, this does not prevent a variability in products resulting from differences in initialization. This variability allows for the production of supports of the same silhouette but with edges that are structurally different (Figures 2.101–2.103).

On the other hand, structural variability is almost obligatory in the case of recurrent methods of debitage (Figure 2.104). In effect, it is practically impossible to succeed in producing a single type of removal within a single recurrent series (removals off a single prepared volume). This diversity applies to the silhouette of the removal and a large number of technical criteria, including those of the dorsal face. When one considers the support from a functional perspective, by distinguishing

Figure 2.99 Core with a preferential flake removal of Type F1. The method of initialization is centripetal and the method of production is preferential. Syria, Palmyra Basin. Photo copyright S. Oboukhoff, CNRS photographic service, MAE Médiathèque, Nanterre.

122 *The techno-logic of evolution*

Figure 2.100 Point core of Type F1. The method of initialization is bidirectional and the method of production is preferential. Photo copyright S. Oboukhoff, CNRS photographic service, MAE Médiathèque, Nanterre.

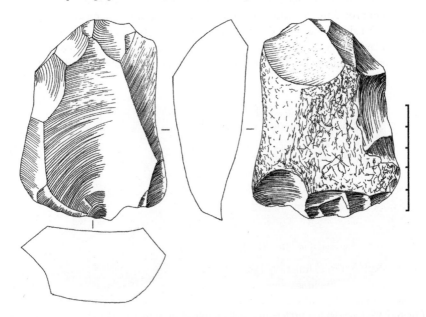

Figure 2.101 Core for production of a preferential triangular flake of Type F1. The method of initialization is centripetal at the distal end and unidirectional at the proximal end. The method of production is preferential. Syria, Palmyra Basin.

The techno-logic of evolution 123

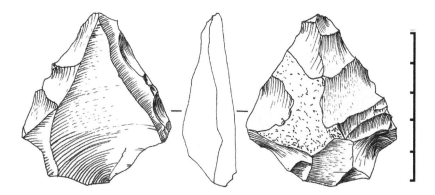

Figure 2.102 Preferential core for production of a Levallois point of Type F1. The method of initialization is centripetal and the method of production is preferential. Umm el Tlel, Level VI 3a', Syria.

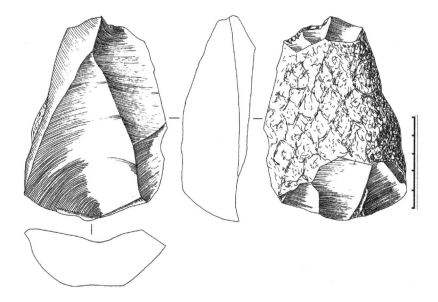

Figure 2.103 Point Core of Type F1. The method of initialization is bidirectional and the method of production is preferential. Palmyra Basin, Syria.

between the prehensile and transformative parts, one realizes that the typo-technological variability is largely restricted to the future transformative part rather than the prehensile part. The shape of the transformative part may be long or short, and/or convergent, bi-angular, ogival, arced, and so on. The transformative part may or may not be associated with an additional technical characteristic such as a natural back, the edge of a flake, parallel flake scar ridges, or convergent flake scar ridges.

124 *The techno-logic of evolution*

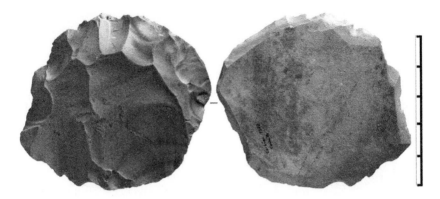

Figure 2.104 Corbiac cavaille, Dordogne, France. Recurrent core of Type F1. The method of initialization is centripetal and the method of production is recurrent unidirectional parallel. Photo copyright S. Oboukhoff, CNRS photographic service, MAE Médiathèque, Nanterre.

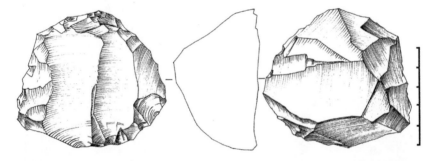

Figure 2.105 Level C'4 Lower, Barbas I, Dordogne, France. Core with recurrent removals of Type F1. The method of initialization is centripetal and the method of production is recurrent unidirectional parallel.

This diversity is made possible by the large number of methods of initialization and recurrent production—unidirectional parallel, convergent, bidirectional, and centripetal—within exploitation of Type F1 (Figures 2.104–2.110).

Most of the recurrent methods allow for production of characteristic removals that are clearly distinctive and easily recognizable. However, the recurrent centripetal exploitation of Type F1, whether the analysis is based on cores or products, is often confused with debitage of Type E1. This situation is partially the result of carelessness in the designation of modes of debitage based on a lack of semantic clarity that can allow for a single term to have multiple meanings. The term "centripetal," like the term "unidirectional," is a red herring that results in the grouping of different things within the same category. For the differentiation of cores, compare Boëda (1993) and the discussion that has been developed in the current work (Figure 2.111).

The techno-logic of evolution 125

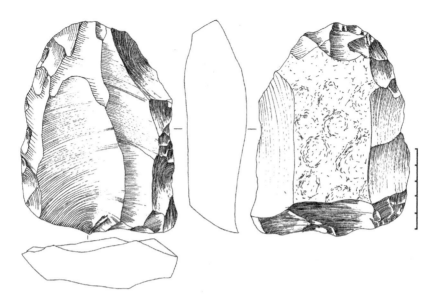

Figure 2.106 Bicheri, Syria. Recurrent core of Type F1. The method of initialization is centripetal and the method of production is recurrent unidirectional parallel.

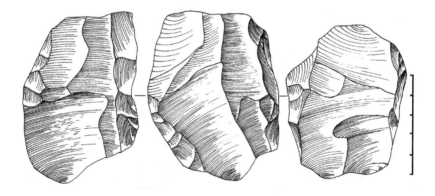

Figure 2.107 Biache-Saint-Vaast, Pas de Calais, France. Core with recurrent removals of Type F1. The method of initialization is centripetal and the method of production is recurrent bidirectional parallel.

If one focuses on the objectives of production and avoids privileging one type of removal at the expense of others, one realizes that the centripetal recurrent production of Type F1 is clearly distinct from exploitation of Type E1. In the case of debitage of Type F1, the production can easily be diversified, which is not the case for Type E1. As a result of the different modalities of debitage relative to the plane of intersection of the two surfaces, parallel for Type F1 and secant for Type E1, the

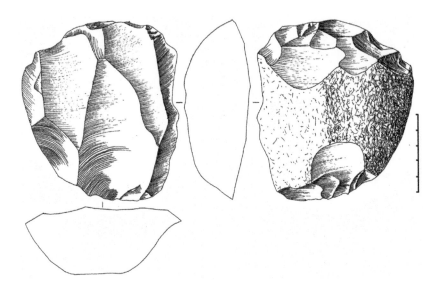

Figure 2.108 Palmyra Basin, Syria. Recurrent core for point and convergent flake production of Type F1. The method of initialization is mixed unidirectional parallel and centripetal. The method of production is recurrent bidirectional.

Figure 2.109 Palmyra Basin, Syria. Recurrent Levallois point core of Type F1. The method of initialization is unidirectional parallel and the method of production is recurrent bidirectional. Photo copyright S. Oboukhoff, CNRS photographic service, MAE Médiathèque, Nanterre.

section of the cores along their longitudinal axis will be different (Boëda, 1993). However, as in all debitage with a majority of centripetal and cordal removals, the production of off-axis convergent edges is a significant component and likely a desired characteristic. This overlap in objectives, even if only partial, results in a degree of confusion (Figures 2.112 and 2.113). So, why dissociate modes of production that have objectives that are at times identical?

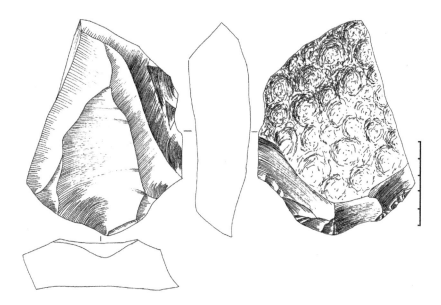

Figure 2.110 Palmyra Basin, Syria. Core for recurrent point and laminar flake production of Type F1. The method of initialization is unidirectional convergent, and the method of production is recurrent unidirectional convergent.

These examples confirm that the same products may result from different methods and that a single method can produce different products. This signifies that one cannot make an absolute correlation between a type of product and a mode of production. Remember that an object only exists and can only be defined within the technical assemblage to which it belongs.

This observation can be extended by studying the modes of initialization. The method of initialization cannot be a factor in the identification of one type of debitage or another. We have already raised this problem in the case of knapping of Type D. We must emphasize this point because the debitage of Type F represents a significant progress in the role of initialization. One often reads in the analysis of production of Type F that there are cases of partial initialization leaving the implication that the configuration applies to part of the block. This possibility must be considered, but it is also logical to consider the modalities of initialization: is this a phase consisting exclusively of a phase of preparation or is there also an aspect of selection that precedes this phase? Technical criteria that are naturally present on the block can be integrated as criteria of initialization (Figure 2.114). This brings us back, yet again, to the point that only a structural perception of the ensemble of products allows for an understanding of the technical stakes at play in relation to precise objectives.

The potential for variability in exploitation of Type F1, regardless of the particular method employed, makes it almost impossible to produce a recurrent series with

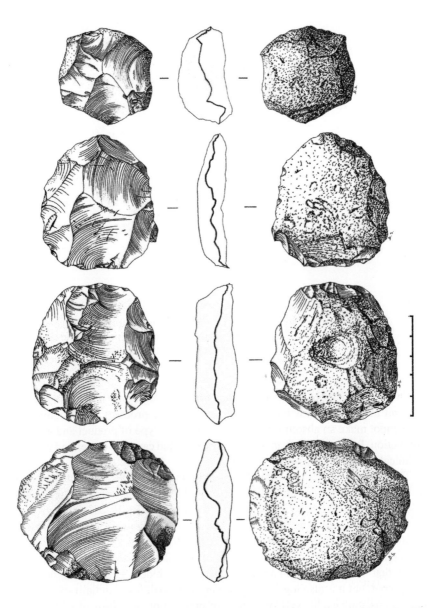

Figure 2.111 La Bouloie, Crenay, Haute-Marne, France. Recurrent cores of Type F1. The method of initialization is centripetal and the method of production is preferential (Boëda, 1993; Amiot and Etienne, 1977).

the goal of a single objective. Based on numerous refit cores and extensive experimentation, one realizes very quickly that the recurrence, in order to be maintained, requires an essential diversity in the production of artifacts, whether it involves the production of flakes, points, or elongated flakes. The case of blades provides

The techno-logic of evolution 129

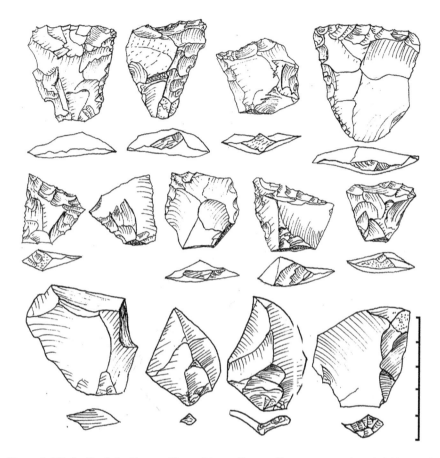

Figure 2.112 La Bouloie, Crenay, Haute-Marne, France. Recurrent centripetal debitage of Type F1. Production includes unretouched and retouched flakes with convergent edges (after Amiot and Etienne, 1977).

the clearest example. The goal of utilizing an exclusive predetermined support/product, such as blades, is one of the technical reasons for the abandonment of F1 debitage (Levallois) in preference for specific methods of blade production of Type D2 and E2, and then very soon afterward of Type F2.

DEBITAGE OF TYPE F2 OR THE OPTION OF NORMALIZATION
OF A SINGLE TYPE OF ARTIFACT

The goal of debitage of Type F2, on the other hand, is the normalization of a silhouette: the blade. Of course, technical and metric variability in the removals is inevitable as in all recurrent production, but it is impossible to introduce other shapes, such as rectangles or triangles, using this type of debitage at the risk of interrupting the recurrent blade production and being forced to reconfigure the core.

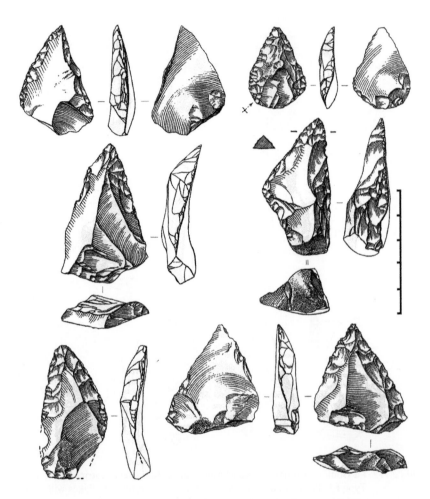

Figure 2.113 Des Forêts, Dordogne, France. Recurrent centripetal debitage of Type F1. Production includes unretouched and retouched flakes with convergent edges (after Brenet and Folgado, 2003).

The variability of the blade silhouettes will gradually attenuate to the point of disappearance as a function of the structures of debitage, ultimately reaching a production that is quasi-normalized at each stage of production. This propensity toward normalization is the result of changes in the modality of the detachment of removals without any structural modification of the core. This particularity is specific to debitage of Type F2: it is inherent in the structure. Among all the other structural configurations that we have been able to study, the structure of Type F2 is the only case where we see an evolution in the modes of detachment, with a succession of direct and indirect marginal percussion, followed by pressure flaking, and subsequently the interaction of indirect percussion and pressure flaking

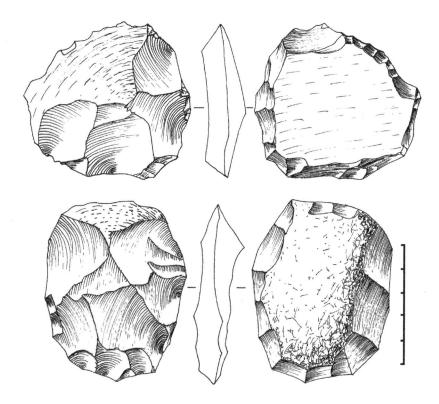

Figure 2.114 La Bouloie, Crenay, Haute-Marne, France. Centripetal Levallois debitage of Type F1. The selection is based on the selection of a naturally convex surface (the result of fracture from freeze-thaw) that is partially altered. Depending on how the debitage evolves the appearance could lead one to think that there are different types of debitage, but a technological analysis of the totality of the assemblage immediately eliminates this possibility.

(Pelegrin, 2006).[79] These new modes of percussion applied to the debitage of blades are preceded by a long period of the exclusive use of internal percussion (Figure 2.115).

The introduction of marginal percussion, at first direct and then indirect, followed by the adoption of pressure flaking, is the result of the pursuit of normalization,[80] which is only made possible by the volumetric structure of Type F2. More than the invention of indirect percussion or pressure flaking[81] in and of itself, what seems critical to us is the capacity of the structure to respond to new objectives. There is a kind of structural and functional coevolution. This evolution of the process of detachment is absolutely not present in the case of debitage of type F1,[82] which, throughout its evolution, requires an internal percussion from specific striking platforms, that makes it possible to obtain a degree of homogeneity of the prehensile part[83] but not of the totality of the support.

132 *The techno-logic of evolution*

evolutionary gradient	F2	pressure	evolution of the modalities of detachment
		indirect percussion	
		marginal direct percussion	
	E2	internal percussion	structural evolution of the useful volume
	D2		
	C2		

Figure 2.115 Evolution of the modes of detachment by laminar types of useful volume.

These two first factors: normalization and recurrence in series, whether in the case of Type F1 or F2, thus both trend toward a normalization towards the future tool or of a component of a new tool. This is certainly associated with a functional complexity, without doubt rendered in a larger range of gestures. This functional complexity does not signify that a greater number of elements intervene in the tool, but that the synergy between the different parts of the tool is augmented toward a greater concretization of the tool.

THIRD FACTOR: A LINKAGE BETWEEN THE VOLUME OF THE CORE
AND THE VOLUME OF THE ARTIFACT

The third factor involves one of the particularities of Structure F, the relationship between the volume of the core and the volume of the artifact produced. From this perspective, the modalities F1 and F2 are a response to an increased productivity.[84] This structural response does not take place through the structural evolution of the core because with this type of exploitation we approach "a sort of auto-regulation or auto-adaptation and in a fashion also of auto-correlation" (Simondon, 1958). The configuration of the core allows a response to a large number of problems that arise during the debitage, and also that result from changes in objectives. This involves a sort of internal adaptation to external circumstances. We define the autocorrelation, the overall internal coherence, as a core that integrates through its structure a systematic organization of different technical components, which makes it possible to compensate for missing criteria of predetermination from one pole of the core—the striking platform surface for cores of Type F1 and a crest or the striking platform surface for cores of Type F2.

In the case of Debitage of Type F1, it is possible at any moment to correct the debitage surface from the surface of the striking platform. It is for this reason that in 1986, we defined the Levallois concept (Boëda, 1994) in terms of hierarchically related surfaces. This hierarchy must exist in order to maintain the operational character of each of the surfaces at every moment. This characteristic is apparent in the silhouette of the core viewed in cross-section. The ratio between the perimeter of the surface and the thickness is high. The cores are therefore always flat, thus allowing for the permanent availability of a good striking angle between the two surfaces. This capacity of "autocorrelation" is expressed by the maintenance of the original silhouette of the core through the entire sequence of knapping. In effect,

The techno-logic of evolution 133

the morphology of the core remains as it is through the entire operational process, regardless of the method of production used and the phase of the operational process. As long as the structure of the core is respected, that is, the synergy of technical criteria is set in motion, the "form" of the core is invariant. This is a homothetic process: the debitage of Type F1 is a homothetic structure[85] (Figure 2.116).

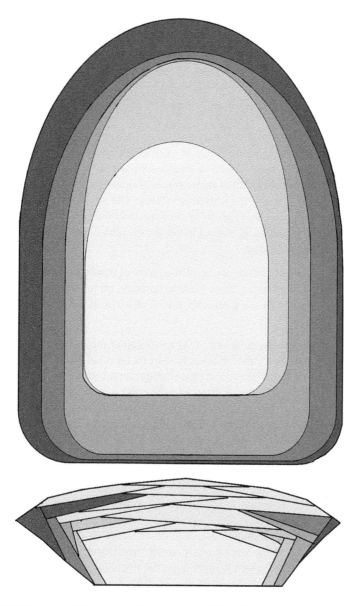

Figure 2.116 Schema of the exploitation of a core of Type F1, presenting the characteristic of "auto-correlation."

134 *The techno-logic of evolution*

AN ADDITION TO THE DEFINITION OF DEBITAGE OF TYPE F1: AUTOCORRELATION

The volumetric configuration of a core of type F1/Levallois is controlled by five criteria, which we defined in 1986 and published in 1994. These include:

Criteria 1 and 2: A plan of intersection (criterion 1) delimiting two distinct surfaces that each play a specific and non-interchangeable role (criterion 2), and this applies equally to both the phase of initialization and the phase of production.

Criterion 3: The removals from the phases of initialization and production are detached exclusively by internal percussion with a hard hammer.

Criterion 4: The function of the phase of initialization is to put into place the criteria of predetermination—convexity and/or flake scar ridges—on the debitage surface in order to respond to the objectives and to configure the striking platform surface.

Criterion 5: The predetermining removals from both the debitage surface and the striking surface platform are secant to the plain of intersection, while the predetermined removals have a plain of detachment that is parallel or sub-parallel to the plain of intersection of the two surfaces (Figure 2.117).

Criteria 6: Finally, there is an additional criteria that we have not previously introduced and that seems to us to be fundamental: the placement in synergy of the ensemble of technical criteria listed above, which introduces a capacity of "autocorrelation" able to:

- Correct accidents in the course of the phase of production.
- Reestablish the characters of predetermination on the debitage surface from the surface of striking platforms, which as a result can itself be constantly maintained.

This sixth criterion is the evidence of the evolution of the lineage, whether from a historical or evolutionary perspective, toward its terminal phase. The debitage of Type F1/Levallois is the last volumetric configuration capable of a mixed production of artifacts. The position of Type F1 as the end of a lineage is the result of its inability to respond to normalized blade production. The termination of a lineage signifies that the exterior milieu, which in the current case includes, at least to an extent, the motivation for a new production, has changed and the structure in place can no longer respond. One can therefore qualify the hyper-specialization of the Levallois core as hypertelic (this term refers to excessive growth in an organ or body part in the evolution of an organism, i.e., the antlers of an Irish Elk) as it is unable to adapt to a change in the associated milieu. However, this hypertely is not fatal (Simondon, 1958). The longevity of debitage of Type F1/Levallois and its wide geographic distribution are clear evidence of this. The progress, in both the technological and the evolutionary sense, that blade production of Type F2 might be thought to represent is more apparent than real. Rather, what one sees is a change, a rupture in the lineage of objects, where each lineage requires its own structures which become the object of their own evolutionary cycle as do all the other structures. The cause of the change that takes place is to be found in the new

The techno-logic of evolution 135

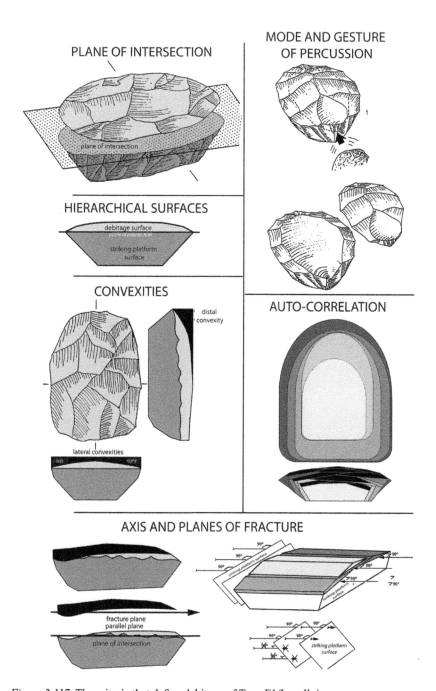

Figure 2.117 The criteria that define debitage of Type F1/Levallois.

136 *The techno-logic of evolution*

associated milieu. The chronology of specialized blade production can provide several elements of an explanation. As we have already said, the option of specialized blade production dates back more than 200,000 years, whether in Western Europe, Africa, or the Middle East. However, the analysis of the evolutionary stage of the volumetric structures utilized in these periods demonstrates that they did not give rise to an evolutionary cycle. One observes a rupture in the lineage with the appearance of debitage of Type F1/Levallois. This non-evolution of the early cycle of blade production can once again be attributed to the associated milieu. One could say that the debitage of Type F1/Levallois interrupted the evolutionary cycle of blade production by changing the associated milieu. However, this type of production itself would eventually be "dethroned" by the reappearance of blade production of Type F2 with its new associated milieu. Was this in fact the same external milieu associated with the initial episode of blade production? The logical response is no, unless one imagines a stasis in societies, independent of period and geography. This indicates that the changes are to be understood from a historical perspective rather than from the perspective of a techno-logic.

THE "AUTOCORRELATION" OF TYPES F2

In the case of blade and bladelet production of Type F2, the phenomenon of "autocorrelation" is possible and augments as a function of changes in the modalities of detachment. Both indirect percussion and pressure flaking allow the knapper to get the most out of a core by intensifying production and achieving an extreme normalization of the product (Figures 2.118–2.123). The homothetic character of

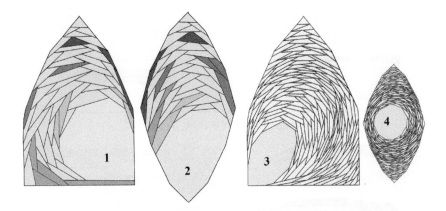

Figure 2.118 Schemas of the initialization and exploitation of a core of Type F2, which present that characteristic of "autocorrelation." Initialization 1: An anterior crest and two lateral posterior crests. Initialization 2: Two anterior and posterior crests. The percussion is direct marginal and requires phases of a partial reinitialization of the debitage surface and striking platform surface. This is made possible as a result of the integrated structure of the core. Initialization 3: Marginal indirect percussion initialization 4: As the yield and productivity increase, the initialization reaches its peak with pressure flaking.

The techno-logic of evolution 137

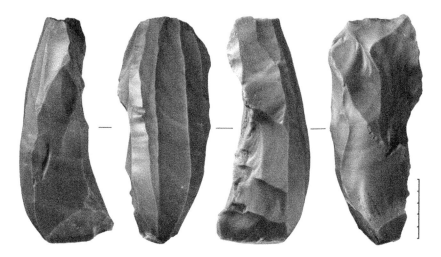

Figure 2.119 Villazette III, Dordogne, France. Magdalenian laminar core of Type F2. Photo copyright S. Oboukhoff, CNRS photographic service, MAE Médiathèque, Nanterre.

Type F2 cores is just as remarkable as for the debitage of Type F2 and becomes all the more so as the modes of detachment develop (Figures 2.121–2.123).

SPECIFICITIES OF PRODUCTION OF TYPE F3

Type F3 applies exclusively to the use of cobbles and as such belongs to a specific lineage, of which it certainly is the terminal phase. Geographically, this lineage is present in Asia and South America with a few cases in Europe, in particular in Italy during the Pontinian. This lineage does not first appear in the form of what one designates classically and abusively as *Choppers* and *Chopping Tools*. Type F3 is significantly more complex and represents an alternative technical approach to the block to be knapped, which one finds in the circum-Mediterranean. An alternative, not something ersatz, as has been claimed at times. As opposed to a block, a cobble naturally offers functional technical criteria proper to the prehensile part. We therefore find the opposite of what we have previously said is the case for the fracture of blocks, where it is the transformative part alone that is invested with a constant techno-functional characteristic: the cutting edge. This contrast characterizes technical options that lead to two different technological worlds that do not overlap: the world of debitage and/or shaping of blocks and the world of cobbles. In the world of blocks, along the course of the evolution of tools we see an integration of the prehensile part and the transformative part in a synergy of effect, while in the world of cobbles the integration is the inverse, the transformative part is constructed while taking the prehensile part into account. Nonetheless, in both cases, one can say that existence precedes essence. The existence of the cutting potential

138 *The techno-logic of evolution*

Figure 2.120 Queyssac, Dordogne, France. Perigordian laminar core of Type F2. Photo copyright S. Oboukhoff, CNRS photographic service, MAE Médiathèque, Nanterre.

of a natural flake or the natural prehensile part of a cobble demonstrates that the debut of the notion of the tool is the encounter of a functional idea and an individual. Remember, however, that this individual might also be a nonhuman primate. Can one not therefore say that the difference between a nonhuman primate and a human primate is nothing other than what they do (Sartre, 1996)?

Type F3 is the most fully realized structure. In the best circumstances, it produces two similar half cobbles whose combined volume is equal to the cobble/core.

The techno-logic of evolution 139

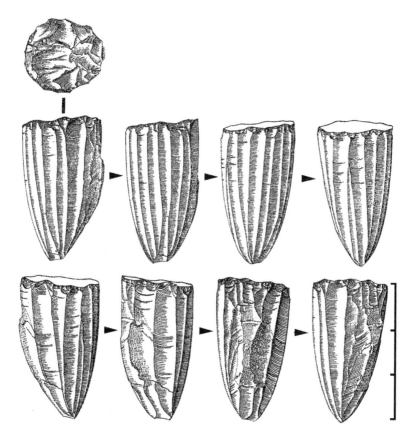

Figure 2.121 Chalcolithic, Susa, Iran. Core of Type F2, pressure flaking. Collection of Macquenem (after Dauvois, 1976).

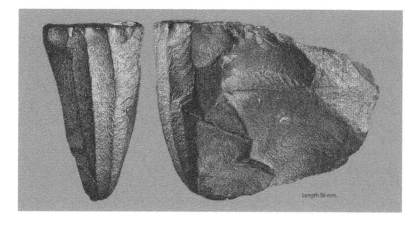

Figure 2.122 Suyaggye, Chungcheongbuk Province, Korea. Upper Paleolithic Yubetsu core. (Yonsei University Press, 2001).

140 *The techno-logic of evolution*

Figure 2.123 Bladelet cores of Type F2, pressure flaking. Northern China. Photo copyright S. Oboukhoff, CNRS photographic service, MAE Médiathèque, Nanterre.

This mode of production is the apex of predetermination. Nonetheless, contrary to what we would have expected, this mode of production remains geographically selective and limited. On the other hand, its chronological position whether in Europe or in Asia within the Upper Pleistocene fits with the expectations of techno-logic. In Europe, the Pontinian (Pannochia, 1950) is considered to be an industry of Charentian time, localized in Latium. The adoption of this mode of debitage in the Pontinian does not seem to fit within a "tradition" of industries on cobbles. This clearly appears to be a local invention where the objective is the development of maximum control over the production of predetermined flakes with a particular volume. The choice of cobbles is possibly the result of the availability of the raw

The techno-logic of evolution 141

material, and the use of the bipolar technique can be attributed to the goal of producing predetermined volumes with dimensions that are greater than what can be achieved through unipolar debitage of the same cobbles. There thus exists a technical synergy of multiple objectives culminating in a "standardized" production. This standardization of flakes/supports is of the same essential nature (*essence*) as the Levallois debitage of the circum-Mediterranean. In Asia, by contrast, it seems that we are situated in a different evolutionary trajectory. In southwest China, we find a final Pleistocene industry[86] that is based on the almost exclusive production of *splits* and tools on *splits* (Figure 2.97). The features of the tools are what we would expect in the Mousterian phase in Europe. However, this similarity is deceptive. Once one takes an evolutionary perspective, in order to understand the relationship between the technical objects, one realizes that this technical option is situated in a lineage for which the technical principle is based on the utilization of a partially standardized volume: the cobble. The idea of recognizing a distinctive "phenomenon" of cobble-based industries and placing it within a circumscribed geographic region was proposed by Hallam Movius in 1944 (Movius, 1944, 1948). But for Movius this regional distribution was temporally limited to Paleolithic periods contemporary with the African Acheulean, representing the eastern range of the second migration of hominins out of Africa, between 0.7 and 0.5 million years ago (Bar Yosef and Belfer-Cohen, 2000). It is not our intention to revive this model that has become over the years a veritable paradigm, and at best is based on a historical rather than a technological point of view.[87] We are interested in the technological aspect. The Southeast Asian technological world presents an undeniable reality: an originality, independent of chronological period, dominated by the exploitation of cobbles and by the integration of the volumetric criteria of the cobble into the schema for the configuration of cores and tools. Three Asiatic industries provide perfect examples: the industries of Longgupo and of Bose in China, and the Hoabinian in Southeast Asia. In the case of the Plio/Pleistocene site of Longgupo (Boëda and Hou, 2011) the cobble serves as the basic matrix that is exploited using bipolar debitage followed by modification and shaping resulting in a wide range of single- or double-edge tools. At Bose (Hou et al., 2000) the industry dates to the Middle Pleistocene and more than 95% of the tools are unifaces[88] on cobbles, with one or two retouched edges. Instead of being on a flake, the future support is developed directly on a cobble which is selected to have a volume that allows for one part—with a flat surface in cross-section—to serve as the future transformative part and another as the prehensile part. This aspect of the selection of the volume to be worked seems to be particularly important because all of the utilized cobbles were capable of producing large flakes that could serve as tools; however, at this stage in the development of production, the form of the resulting prehensile part would have been a matter of chance. The Hoabinian (Colani, 1927, 1929) appears during the final phase of the Upper Pleistocene. Here again the tools are dominated by products made on carefully selected cobbles. The selected cobbles have an oblong form and a trapezoidal or rectangular section that is naturally close to a plano-convex structure which accommodates the manufacture of tools (Zeitoun et al., 2008). The general morphology of the pieces is standardized: a flat cortical surface on one face and a shaped surface on the other. This morphology is obtained by directly shaping a selected cobble or indirectly on a *split* produced using bipolar debitage, which is then shaped.

Type F3 industries that we have documented at the sites of Maomaodong (Figures 2.124 and 2.125) and Chuandong, China, province of Guizhou, provide evidence of a more developed stage because they involve an operation of debitage that results, in a single blow, in the production of two hemi-cobbles for which only the transformative part is shaped further. In the case of these two sites, it is interesting to note that another raw material is available in the form of cobbles and blocks.

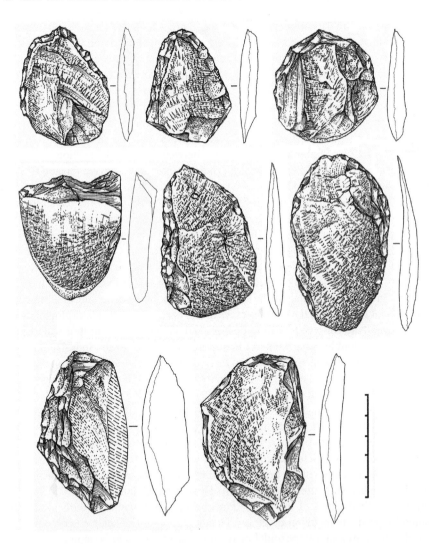

Figure 2.124 Maomaodong, Guizhou Province, China. *Splits* transformed into tools. Drawing copyright H. Forestier.

The techno-logic of evolution 143

Figure 2.125 Splits transformed into tools. Only debitage of Type C will be used to produce flakes with only slightly regularized shapes, as at the site of Maomaodong, Guizhou Province, China. Photo copyright E. Boëda.

144 *The techno-logic of evolution*

This is high-quality flint that could have been used effectively to produce the same volumes. We can add that despite the availability of flint there is no debitage of Type D, E, or F.[89] Technical developments in these contexts are thus based only on the use of cobbles and no other type of support. Although the flint is of excellent quality, when it is used, it only presents an initial stage of evolution, which is not the case for the cobbles. We are clearly in a different realm of technique. This phenomenon is clearly indicative of a cultural alterity (otherness) between the East and West that is often overlooked and certainly richer than we suspect.[130]

Notes

1 In a generic fashion, we prefer to use the term "incise," which simply signifies "making a gash (entaille) with a cutting tool" rather than the verbs cut, carve, and slit, which refer to specific gestures.
2 The possibility in prehistory to observe a temporal duration of over two million years allows us to identify an evolution in the modalities of using manual energy: direct or indirect prehension. This evolution can principally be observed in the prehensile part of tools. But as the classic typological traits apply only to the retouched parts, which are usually the transformative part, the prehensile part plays only a minor role in typological identification, except when they are retouched, as in the case of the Aterian artifacts with a tang.
3 Except in the publications from the nineteenth century, where they make allusion to the grip in the hand and the energy capable of being transmitted, tools have been considered the antique equivalents of contemporary artisanal objects (Chouquet, 1883).
4 Recent ethological data have shown that it is necessary to distinguish between the capacity to make a gesture and the manner of handling the tool (Foucart, 2006).
5 de Condorcet [1793–1794], 1970.
6 This notion of grasp has always been correlated with the anatomy of human ancestors. It is thus "that a comparative analysis of the bones of the hands of Neanderthals and those of modern humans has concluded that the hand of the Neanderthals is capable of a more powerful flexing which leads to the possibility that of a better grasp of the object in the palm" (translated from Villemeur, 1991).
7 This is not the case for other periods for which many studies exist such as the recent work by Rots (2002, 2010).
8 Epiphylogenetic memory (a term created by B. Stiegler: Technical memory; "it records the collective memory, it is the trace inscribed by the collective unconscious, that is deposited in the world of objects. Through this, it makes the collective unconscious possible" (translated from www.philosophie.ulg.ac.be/documents/PhiloCite2008/Stiegler.pdf).
9 But, in fact, can there really exist a non-anthropomorphized space, other than those that one does not think exists? Except in rare cases where populations are suddenly forced to leave their own territory to go to an unknown space, the space in which a group lives, and also the spaces where one does not live, already have an anthropological aspect. They can thus be seen as a reservoir, not culturally invested, but known.
10 Very often we confound territory and space. Territory is a space that is traveled, or not, that we have interiorized. Territory is a constitutive element of our culture. In prehistory this interiorization makes it impossible to truly grasp this aspect of experience, but hints are unmistakable, which are "possibilities" that can never be proven. The best example of the confusion caused by not recognizing the distinction between space and territory is found in studies of the economy of raw materials. Here, one regularly sees the systematic equation of the geographic distribution of a raw material

The techno-logic of evolution   145

with the zone of acquisition of a group. It is as though the geological space has become an anthropoc geographic space. The geological space may be known but is it an element of, in its integrality, a territory from which materials are collected? Do I know all the bakers in my village? No, but I know several, which does not stop me from only frequenting one!

11 Once again it is necessary to acknowledge the cultural and cognitive potential of those making the tools, particularly for the ancient periods. In effect, when the level of technicity of these populations is only perceived through a simple morphological analysis, the behavioral conclusions that follow are rarely to the advantage of the tool maker, described as opportunistic, uninvested, and so on.

12 The schema of selection presents different degrees of complexity depending on the desired technical characteristic for the support of the eventual tool. In effect, on the evolutionary scale of supports, selected supports can represent either one of the initial stages or a concrete stage, as we see later in the case of the Asian industries on cobbles.

13 In this study we only consider incising artifacts. Incision can be accomplished with an edge of a trihedron. The cutting edge serves for actions such as cutting, scraping, slicing (Leroi-Gourhan's *percussion posée linéare*), and chopping (Leroi-Gourhan's *percussion lancée*). The trihedron allows for actions of piercing and grooving.

14 Depending on the type of detached piece used, blade or flake, the mode of proximal (along the morphological axis) or lateral (perpendicular to the morphological axis) grip, the extent and type of hafting, the gesture and the energy transmitted on the part that transmits energy will or will not have a role in determining the success of the objective.

15 In several cases the part for the transmission of energy is the prehensile part. This is the case for tools use with static percussion (*percussion possée*) with a hammer (Leroi-Gourhan, 1943).

16 This is a point of fundamental importance in the framework of human evolution in relation to technique. As is found in the mass of a simple rock, a cutting edge may exist naturally in numerous situations. One can go as far as to say that the act of the invention of a cutting edge did not exist; if there was an invention it was of the gesture of percussion, which thus forms the connection with the objective.

17 From the moment when it is selected by a person.

18 From what we are capable of detecting.

19 In East Africa, this dates back to at least 2.7 million years.

20 This division is artificial. It represents only a tendency that appears to be observable on the periphery of the Mediterranean Basin.

21 Although these differences could be interpreted as the distinctive characteristics associated with different technical and cultural traditions, a strictly behavioral explanation based on differences in activity or raw material is preferred (Isaac, 1976).

22 This reaches the point where we can ask whether these industries would have been recognized as "human" and ancient if it was not for the discovery of human remains (unassociated) in the same periods and in the same localities. In fact, the recognition of the anthropogenic character of very early industries is only valid due to the association of industries and human remains. It is as though the proof of the anthropic character of an artifact is external to the object itself. Imagine a doctor awaiting the death of their patient to have certainty that the illness was in fact fatal!

23 The consequences are perfectly illustrated by the debates concerning some of these tools. For example, one increasingly sees the use of the term "chopper/core." Thus, two things are combined into one, either as an object with a dual functionality or with its individuality denied. In using this terminology, we remove the object from its associated milieu and thus commit a methodological error. However, this error is above all a reflection of the way in which we perceive the technical world: as an element exterior to us, exterior to our culture.

146 *The techno-logic of evolution*

24 Even though this does not directly concern our central point, this failure to take into consideration the entirety of the constitutive elements of an industry, and the act of emphasizing a particular type of piece to the detriment of others has the consequence of creating veritable global "civilizations," which develop as the result of the appearance of a new "hominid." This is the case for the Acheulean and *Homo erectus*. The most interesting example is provided by the recent discoveries in China and Korea, where one sees the extension of the Africa Acheulean "civilization," which is seen as moving out of Africa. However, if we just compare the percentage of bifacial "Acheulean" pieces between sites in West Asia (the Middle East) and East Asia, we find a frequency of bifacial pieces ranging between 70% and 95% for the West Asian ensemble and less than 5% for East Asia (both China and Korea). This can signify only one thing: that the role of bifacial pieces within the ensemble of tools is different in these two regions. If we pursue the consideration of the 5% of bifacial pieces found on the East Asian sites, the differences between assemblages become apparent. These are not the same tools. They only have in common the fact that they are knapped on two faces. If we take into consideration the 95% of non-bifacial objects one observes the same dissimilarity between sites and between regions within China. In the Guangxi Autonomous Region (Bose Basin), more than 60% of the bifacial tools are unifaces supporting a diversity of cutting edges, while in Shaanxi Province (Lantian, Liangshan) and Shanxi Province (Ditsun) the tools are produced on flakes or cobbles (E. Bodin, pers. comm.), which is different from the Bose industries. In Korea there is also considerable variability in the composition of industries with bifacial pieces. In the context of considering this continental-scale comparison between West and East Asia, we could also evoke India where cleaver-based industries are an exception within Asia. We could also consider the dating, the technical stages present, the evolutionary lineages, and more, which are factors that also make it impossible to support the concept of a global "Acheulean." But nonetheless the idea persists! It is essential to dissociate the notion of the Acheulean from the concept of the biface: there is not an Acheulean without bifaces, but on the other hand there are bifaces in cultures other than the Acheulean. Take as an extreme example the sites of Telarmachay in Peru (Lavallée et al., 1985) and Catalan-Chico: Paso Mendionda in Uruguay (Taddei, 1987) where veritable bifaces are described that in other contexts and circumstances would have been identified in one case as developed Acheulean and in the other as an archaic Acheulean. But the rest of the material, made of tools whose epiphylogenetic memory is known to us, prevents us from making this attribution. In fact, two problems coexist. The first, which is well known, consists of only taking into consideration the facts that conform to the dominant paradigm. The second is the result of our strictly morphological approach, which can only recognize elements that repeat, without as a corollary a real technological reflection.

25 In the case of the bifacial, depending on the region—West Asia, Africa, or Western Europe—the frequency of shaped pieces varies between 20% and 95% of the tools. In the case of industries with choppers and chopping tools the frequency is around 40%, as at Longgupo (China).

26 In the current case, we prefer using the term "form" with a simple- or double-beveled edge, because the words *chopper, chopping tool*, or worked cobble (*galet aménagé*) do not consider the techno-functional intention. In the case of Longgupo (China) the technological analysis shows that the hominins sought two forms: a simple beveled edge (chopper) or a double-beveled edge (chopping tool), which were produced as a result of the specificity of the available material (cobbles, split cobbles, or flakes), which have in common the ensemble of the desired technical volumetric characteristics. If we used the terms "chopper" or "chopping tool" only for tools made on cobbles, we would have missed more than half of the forms that are identical to those made on cobbles. In the same fashion, if we had used the term "worked cobble" (*galet aménagé*), we would have eliminated more than a third of the forms of identical volume but made on different supports.

The techno-logic of evolution 147

27 The presence, in each of these large regions, of the totality of the bifacial cycle appears to be the result of convergence rather than successive migrations from Africa imposing and importing their technical culture on the local inhabitants, whoever they might have been. It is difficult to imagine a succession of catastrophic events of this type. On the other hand, in East Asia there was a radically different technical evolution throughout the Pleistocene.

28 This is the case of the so-called Upper Acheulean industries in Europe—some authors have even advocated the term Epi-Acheulean for this type of industry (Tuffreau, 1979) or Mousterian of Acheulean tradition.

29 We could also include India, China, and Korea.

30 The frequent use of the term "Abbevillian" to designate a piece judged to be technically archaic is derived from the bifaces found in the Carpentier quarry at Abbeville.

31 This "vision" is accepted without reservation and without any consideration of the exceptional scale of a technical diffusion of a technique without modification across such a vast period of time and geographical range.

32 Surely much shorter by tens of thousands of years, but this remains difficult to demonstrate due to the paucity of evidence and the uncertainty in many age determinations.

33 This observation is only really possible in northwestern Europe and in Italy where the evidence is best preserved.

34 Levallois debitage, associated with bifacial pieces, had already appeared in the Middle East before this new phase. The sites that attest to this phenomenon are rare and often undated, so that we must be cautious about their chronological position. Nonetheless, the objectives of this initial Levallois flaking have nothing in common with what is found subsequent to the Hummalian. In the initial phase, production is focused on flakes and elongated flakes, the post-Hummalian Levallois flaking produces mostly triangular flakes and blades. These two Levallois phenomena are independent of one another and are separated by the Yabrudian and Hummalian cultures. When the Levallois flaking makes its reappearance, one observes that this new industry reproduces the same tools as the Hummalian, and it is only that the phase of retouch is far less significant because the unretouched flakes more closely approach the form of the eventual tool. There exists in some cases a sort of functional rather than technical continuity, a phenomenon that is particularly apparent at the site of Umm el Tlel, Syria. Subsequently the Levallois flaking continues to be dominant, but the range of tools changes, and becomes essentially convergent and triangular.

35 The techno-functional and use wear analysis carried out by S. Bonilauri on a sample of hundreds of pieces from Umm el Tlel has shown that more than three-quarters of the predetermined products were hafted with bitumen (Bonilauri, 2010).

36 As we see later, although Levallois debitage produces Levallois tools, the latter as individuals, but not as a diversified ensemble, can be produced by other concepts of debitage. In effect what gives the Levallois concept its specificity is its ability to produce, through either a unique or successive useful volume, a qualitative and quantitative range of Levallois tools.

37 The notion of "blade" applies not only to the morphology of the support but also more broadly to the intention of production. We designate as a blade any product that is longer than it is wide and that is the outcome of production oriented exclusively toward this type of support. In the case of mixed production, as in the case of Levallois production, we use the term "laminar product" rather than blade.

38 Some of the technical criteria of configuration can, of course, be naturally present in the chosen block.

39 This is the source of the stability and the ease of recognition of certain cores such as Levallois cores, at least those exploited to produce preferential flakes. This ease of recognition is expressed by a globally used typological designation.

40 This is a provisional terminology.

41 This is the case, for example, in the Upper Paleolithic with regard to blade cores for which the state of configuration is composed of three crests: two posterior and one

148 *The techno-logic of evolution*

anterior. It is evident that the morphology of the core changes along with the advancement of work. Through the rotation of blade removals, the crests disappear as the process proceeds. This transformation is a necessary consequence of the process of debitage and the state of configuration of the core makes this transformation possible and allows for the integration of technological states with varying morphological consequences. Nonetheless, in the Upper Paleolithic, all of the volumetric configurations do not function in the same way, for example, the cores with two crests (one anterior and one posterior) function much like Levallois cores and are thus homothetic.

42 Until now the various "evolutionary" thinkers, such as Leroi-Gourhan and Simondon, have not dealt with the concept of cycle. For Leroi-Gourhan, tools adapt to the act to be accomplished through changes in form and size, which he defined as "tendance." He never wrote about the structure of the object. For him, there is not a cycle but only lineages. Evolution takes place at the level of the acts to be accomplished. Leroi-Gourhan created lineages of objects having the same use function, in relation to the three major principles of percussion. Simondon also did not write about cycles, but rather of a technical evolution controlled by laws (in the metaphorical sense). The temporality of his analysis is essentially modern, contemporary. For him, the notion of concretization applies only to contemporary objects, not even to the artisanal world, whether historic, or even more so the products of prehistoric artisans!

43 We return to this point later with concrete examples.

44 In addition to temporality, the spatial dimension must also be taken into account. In effect when we attempt to reconstruct the geographic distribution of the different lineages and their process of development, what emerges is in direct contradiction with the dominant paradigms, particularly those that emphasize the role of migration.

45 And not the functions, because these remain the same regardless of the time periods as we continue to cut, slice, cleave, pierce, grate, scrape, and so on.

46 Such as the transition in the Middle East, around 300,000 years ago, from the Acheulean to the Yabrudian, with the production of tools that are 99% on bifacial pieces being replaced by the production of tools 99% of which are on a new type of support derived from debitage. Only a few Yabrudian sites continue to include a minuscule quantity of bifaces or bifacial pieces—in general less than 2%–5% of the assemblage. On the other hand, in Central Europe, up to the shores of the Black Sea, following the Mousterian "Levallois" industries, one sees the reappearance of an industry for which the bifacial support becomes once again the matrix/support for the creation of a range of different types of tools. We can furthermore cite the bifacial industries found in Normandy—dated approximately to the period following Oxygen Isotope 5—between 75,000 and 40,000 years ago (Cliquet et al., 2001a and b), which are intercalated with the Mousterian lineage where debitage is dominant.

47 Experimentation provides the only way of gaining an understanding of the importance of the gesture in obtaining the desired products. With a different gesture, the same flaking surface and striking platform is capable of producing an elongated product, a flake wider than it is long, or a convergent product.

48 To reduce this ambiguity, we combine data based on stratigraphic and taphonomic analysis, such as the presence of post-depositional processes capable of producing eoliths, with reference collections from experimentation and parallel sedimentary contexts where hominins could not have been present. In parallel, a techno-functional analysis is carried out on the archaeological material.

It is important to emphasize that the technical or techno-functional analysis must demonstrate fundamental differences between the objects produced by nature and those produced by humans! This distinction may seem trivial but is nonetheless critical. Humans produce tools for a use function and/or as a sign, while nature creates objects without a use function.

As a result, every technological analysis must respect two axes that guide research:

The techno-logic of evolution 149

- The significance of the artifact without being limited to the mode(s) of support production on which the tool will be made. Analysis is also not restricted to the establishment of diacritical schemas that only take into account the number and order of negative scars visible on the artifacts.
- The coherence of the ensemble of artifacts among themselves, because every artifact is a part of the system to which it belongs.

We must thus reverse our approach by interrogating the artifact as a tool and not as an undifferentiated support. We must discover the functional intentions by way of the technical options employed because it is there that the difference between humans and nature is situated. This is even more emphatically the case at the very beginning of a lineage when only the transformative part of a tool is predetermined: the support, on which the tool is realized, possesses few constraints, except for those that allow for the proper execution of a gesture. It is only later on that one sees the support becoming invested with increasing degrees of techno/cultural constraint, which requires increasingly distinctive modes of production. As a result, when one is interested in the earliest cutting tools, it is essential to focus on the transformative part and the relationship of this part with the prehensile part. In this fashion it is possible to perceive the structuration of the tool, while at the same time working within a diachronic framework, able to establish the evolutionary stage in which this tool is situated. Based on this developmental context of the tool, we can compare it with other objects in other times and places to understand whether we are dealing with a case of invention, innovation, and/or diffusion; in other words, whether the full suite of evolutionary stages is present or if the stages are fragmentary.

49 Consider how in the scientific literature the earliest stone tools are regularly attributed to genus *Homo* rather than Australopithecines, even though we lack proof for this assertion.

50 By blade production we clearly are referring to the exclusive production of products that are longer than they are wide, with a relatively homogeneous morphology.

51 All too often the term "initialization" is reserved exclusively for actions affecting the useful volume. However, from our point of view this term, "initialization" as we have defined it also includes the act of selecting the block of raw material. Thus, in every step of initialization aimed at obtaining a configured useful volume, there are two steps: selection and preparation. The respective roles of these two stages in the process of initialization are variable. In the case of the exploitation of a useful volume of Type C, the selection of the volume to be knapped plays a predominant role, and the preparation is limited to establishing what will become the striking platform surface. As we see later, in the other types of exploitation the balance between selection and preparation can be at equilibrium, can tip toward an emphasis on preparation, or completely disappear, in favor of a complete dependence on configuration.

52 We have already pointed to the problem on multiple occasions. The confusion is manifest in the erroneous use of terms such as chopper, chopping tool, modified cobble, and tool/core.

53 A polyhedral morphology can result from the knapping of multiple volumes of Type C1 pushed to the extreme limit of production. The polyhedral form is due to the aleatory migration of successive series of flake removals.

54 Some of these cores have been identified as either chopper or chopping tools, from which the presence of an "Oldowan" industry has been inferred. The refits clearly demonstrate that these are just simple cores.

55 This does not imply that we cannot find this conception in more recent periods.

56 Because of a lack of information, we cannot confirm this statement for Australia.

57 This eccentric terminology is rooted in the history of research. It is the residue of the development of the methodological evolution of a typological approach that was constructed, from its debut, based on the bias of a "naturalist" approach focused on

150 *The techno-logic of evolution*

morphological essence, in parallel to a more technical approach. It must not be forgotten that this determination to create types is oriented toward comparison. This is the true essence of typology. On the other hand, our work also leads to the creation of types, but the types are created by trying to come as close as possible to the structural characteristics of each object.

58 For F. Bordes, proto-Levallois flaking "is differentiated from true Levallois flaking in the sense that, if one can detect the principal characteristics of this debitage, they are often still realized unskillfully" (translated from Bordes, 1961b).

59 These latter designations are currently so widely used that it is difficult to link them to a particular reference. This rapid propagation is evidence of a craze for the technical approach, which is in our opinion insufficient. In effect, 90% of the removals from a recurrent series are knapped along a single axis from a single end of the core (unidirectional) and following a semi-rotational modality. How can it be done otherwise? We know of very few examples where the knapping is not semi-rotational. This is notably the case for Rubané in Belgium where the blades, with a quadrangular section, are known under the designation of "*frites*" (Cahen, 1988).

Returning for a moment to the case of the bidirectional. This terminology can often lead to confusion between:

—First, flaking for which the detachment of flakes is the result of two opposed shock waves, the shock and counter shock, which has been designated as crushed direct percussion (Bordes, 1947) but more generally is designated as bipolar percussion (Breuil, 1954).
—Secondly, the flaking of two successive recurrent series obtained from opposed ends of the core. This is ultimately two successive series of unidirectional knapping off opposing ends of the core.
—Thirdly, flaking of a recurrent series knapped from two ends of the core from the same flaking surface.

If we desire to establish distinctions and be precise, we must, therefore, ensure care with this terminology. This is equally important for orthogonal and centripetal flaking. If used carelessly, these designations treat the technological reality superficially.

60 In the initial publication of Barbas, we have described these pieces as Levallois cores with a Kombewa method of initialization (Boëda et al., 1996). At that time, we had not yet made the distinction between the different types of production, but we had simply classed this as a variant of Levallois debitage.

61 Would also cite the assemblage from Tares à Sourzac, Dordogne, France: "The inferior face of the large primary supports of scrapers with retouch (Quina) are exploited to produce a Kombewa removal" (translated from Geneste, 1991: 19 or Villiers-Ada, Val d'Oise, France, Locht, 2003).

62 There is nonetheless a significant difference in the type of platforms that rarely have a Levallois character.

63 We have previously introduced this distinction in relation to points (Boëda, 1991), and we extend this to flakes.

64 As we have defined previously, the term "blade" is reserved for removals that result from the exclusive production of blades.

65 We think that this so-called transitional phase can be incorporated, based on the ensemble of its technical strategies, into the debut of the Middle Eastern Upper Paleolithic, in which we are in agreement with S. Kuhn, who was the first to introduce this idea (Kuhn et al., 2004).

66 This observation has been made in the Transition II base and III 2a at the site of Umm el Tlel, Syria. On the majority of the Levallois products—both blades and points— one observes bladelet scars on the dorsal face. Use wear analysis has shown that the

The techno-logic of evolution   151

bladelets had a specific function related to their pointed morphology (Boëda and Bonilauri, 2006).

67 We must remain cautious in our statements as very few technological analyses with this type of approach have been carried out. Nonetheless, as opposed to Europe where the Levallois typo-point is not dominant within the Levallois typo-products, in the Near East the Levallois typo-points are produced using Levallois debitage.

68 Except in their miniaturized form: in the Mousterian levels at the site of Umm el Tlel there is a production of triangular Levallois typo-points that are between 2 and 3 cm. long. These flakes are obtained either off the ridge of the dorsal face of a flake or after minimal preparation, from the dorsal face of a flake. The production consists of a single flake or at most two.

69 This multiplicity of names obviously reflects different realities, in part as a result of problems related to raw material, as numerous authors have mentioned (Mourre, 2003).

70 The definition of the conception of debitage based on cores centripetal, semi-rotational, or unidirectional raises an interesting question. On this basis how would one differentiate between a unidirectional Levallois debitage, a unidirectional "Clactonian" debitage, or even a unidirectional laminar debitage? If each of these is unidirectional, one could think that there is no difference. Nonetheless, we know that these differences exist!

71 There certainly exist a large number of sites with pyramidal cores but because their description in most cases is above all morphological, we prefer to only refer to the best-described cases.

72 If one remains on a strictly morphological level, cores of type C2, D3, and even F1, can, at the end of knapping, have a quarter-pyramidal or semi-pyramidal form. The distinction with flaking of type E2 is essentially due to the orientation of the striking platform in relation to the flaking surface. In effect, this orientation is one of the very first steps of the phase of initialization as it conditions the success of the maximum potential exploitation of the block. A proper orientation allows for the global exploitation of the periphery. If this is not the case one ends up in the categories of cores of abstract type with a useful volume limited to only a part of the block.

73 In this case, as opposed to exploitation of Type D2, the process of flaking can be realized without difficulty. There is no technical impediment to continuing. The potential sequence is only interrupted. And it is not impossible to see associated, in the same archaeological context, exploitation of Types D3 and E2. It is thus interesting to explore the underlying factors: raw material, learning, behavior? To reach a conclusion it is necessary to place the core in its context and compare it to others.

74 Nonetheless, we remain unconvinced that this really suggests distinct methods such as what we find within Levallois flaking, but rather a "procedure of optimization" for augmenting the frequency of a particular type of removal or an entire range of removals. As we can observe in the case of the unidirectional parallel Levallois method, a small difference in the sequence of removals within a single series can change the form of each removal.

75 In Terra del Fuego multiple Holocene sites provide evidence for the existence of Levallois *chaînes opératoires* and at the site of Cabo San Vincente I, Chile, there is evidence of two other associated *chaînes opératoires* (Nami, 1992). One of these might involve the production of *splits* (Morello, 2005). The comparison of *splits* with preferential Levallois flakes shows only a minor volumetric difference. The same is true for tools made on these two types of supports. Does this suggest two different routes for the manufacture of functionally identical objects? The third *chaînes opératoires* is bifacial and consists of the manufacture of very flat pieces with the same volume as the products discussed earlier!

76 We will return to consider this mode of production in greater detail and provide several archaeological examples.

77 Debitage for which the objective must be exclusive, in this case of blades.

152 *The techno-logic of evolution*

78 Except in cases where the prehensile part is the object of very evident alteration as in the case with numerous tools from the European Upper Paleolithic such as the *pointes à cran* and the multiple variations of backed pieces.

79 This hypothesis could be considered to be false if one only considers the knapping of Grand-Pressigny. However, following experimental work it appears that what is involved is a mixed mode of detachment that involves both indirect percussion and pressure flaking.

80 This hyper standardization is also found in bladelet production. The evolution of blade and bladelet production follows the exact same path.

81 The use of pressure flaking has been suggested by several technological and experimental studies to have already been used for the retouch of certain Mousterian tools. The tests that we have undertaken ourselves support this early usage of pressure flaking. Nonetheless, it is important to distinguish between the use of pressure for retouch and the use of pressure for the detachment of supports. In the case of retouch, it is the modification of the technical characteristics of the edge off of which the flake is removed that is sought after rather than the technical characteristics of the removal itself, as is the case in flaking. This simple distinction results in differences in the way the compressor (the tool applying pressure) is utilized. This difference is perhaps the most important!

82 Even if in several rare and anecdotal cases, one observes evidence of marginal percussion.

83 In this context, it is worth noting that some researchers had tried to define Levallois debitage based on the type of platform. This idea was dismissed by F. Bordes. In fact, it is not the *chapeau de gendarme* (a distinctive striking platform found in some Levallois industries) that makes an industry Levallois, but rather it is the idea of the regularization of the prehensile part that leads to the Levallois debitage, and which is in turn expressed in the development of platforms such as the *chapeau de gendarme*. In Levallois debitage there exist another way to create the prehensile part: a faceted convex platform. In terms of frequency, this type of platform is just as common as the *chapeau de gendarme*.

84 This augmentation of productivity is the result of a meticulous and often protracted preparation that, in some cases is described as wasteful in terms of material compared to more direct debitage such as Types D2 (Yubetsu as compared to Setouchi technique, Aita et al., 1991). If in fact, debitage of Types F1 and F2 are generally wasteful of raw material in the phase of initialization the opposite is the case during the stage of production. In the framework of a comparative study of the different types of debitage, it would be interesting to cross-reference this observation with consideration of transport.

85 This particular characteristic made it possible for Levallois cores with preferential flake removals to be recognized very early. This recognition had the consequence of making other modes of debitage that are not homothetic less apparent, resulting in terminological errors for certain categories of debitage.

86 The sites of Maomaodong and Chuadong, Guizhou province, China.

87 In reality, given the sparse available data the prevalence of this paradigm is surprising.

88 Less than 5% of the pieces can be classified as bifaces with a reserved base. The industries from Bose are also used as evidence for a Chinese "Acheulean" in contradiction to the Movius Line. But is it the biface that defines the Acheulean? This question is not of great interest other than to support the paradigm of the diffusion of *Homo erectus* out of Africa. It is more interesting to consider the totality of the industry rather than a single type of object.

89 Note that as in East Asia we are on an East/West axis of diffusion, from a perspective that adheres to the paradigm of the spread of *Homo sapiens* out of Africa one can only be surprised not to find any trace of the technical cultures of Levallois followed by blade production that one finds in the circum-Mediterranean and Central Asia, even though these technical systems are seen as enabling human migration and as evidence of cognitive development and ascendancy over the environment.

3   The anthropological sense

A paleo-history of the lineages
of blade production and blade
products in the Middle East
during the Pleistocene[1]

In considering the technological phenomena of prehistory, we can take either a historical or an evolutionary perspective. The historical perspective, as was suggested by Leroi-Gourhan, treats the phenomena in their temporal context (a dated object) and in space (a situated object). The evolutionary perspective is approached through the notion of tendency (*tendance*) by treating the phenomena in their morphological context[2] (Leroi-Gourhan, 1945/1973). The concept of *tendance* is both overly synthetic and too limiting[3] because it aims to develop *a priori* rules. It is presented as a potential substitute for the impossibility of a complete knowledge of the historical succession (Guchet, 2005). In effect, in trying to give a historical direction to this evolution, history is subsumed by a rationalized conceptual framework. To avoid this limitation, it is necessary to replace the *tendance* with a *techno-logic*. One thus reorients toward a structural comprehension of objects by investigating the interconnections among objects despite the fact that these objects are not static but rather undergo change. It is by exposing and understanding the specific functional synergies, specific to each object of a lineage,[4] that we can discern the evolutionary logic. At a more basic level, regardless of the lineage of objects there is no evidence of "reversed invention" that goes from a concrete object toward the more abstract. Even today, in our modern world, a Prius does not come out before a Model T Ford because a techno-logic exists. Nonetheless, not every structure necessarily follows a linear path. For Simondon (1958), technological evolution does not take place in opposition to history,[5] but on the contrary, in relation to history (Guchet, 2005). It is not the goal to create a separate world, but rather to establish the basis of a structural explication to understand the evolution of objects within the same lineage by taking into account the rules that regulate change. This is the point of analysis that aims to identify the lineage to which an object belongs and the place that it occupies. This is in no sense a case of determinism because the process of development is not inescapable. Nonetheless, the potential for the development of structures gives a sense to evolution. This involves a potential reflexivity that is distinctive to each stage, which must be considered before one attempts to address the historical aspect. In fact, the effect of an event, of an invention, can be perceived at a distance. In this regard, Merleau-Ponty (1960) writes of a history of depths. The history of depths can be detected particularly well in the long temporal scale of prehistory where the invention, such as the "biface"

DOI: 10.4324/9781003359081-4

154   *The anthropological sense*

or Levallois, through their longevity, provides a trace of a way of thinking, a norm that is projected in time and space. There is another superimposed history, a history of the explanation of changes, bifurcations, halts, or repetitions within a single lineage or from one lineage to another. This level of analysis is of a historical rather than evolutionary order because the changes are related to social or environmental (and biological) contingencies. In other words, historical temporality describes the fashion in which the evolutionary stages unfold. This is also the time within which the genealogical discourse of the mythico-evolutionist narrative of actors and consumers is constructed.[6]

The blade phenomena

To illustrate the relationship between a historical and evolutionary approach to technology, we examine the lineage of blade production through the Pleistocene and the lineage of blade products inherent to these modes of production.

Evolutionary preamble

We have defined the elements of a lineage as every object having the same use function and implementation of the same principle (Deforge, 1985). The case of the blade lineage thus includes all volumes that have as a technical finality the exclusive production of objects longer than they are wide, which are designated as blades and that employ the fracture of hard rock as the means to production.

As discussed earlier, the lineage of blade production is found beyond the Middle East: In Africa by 240,000 years ago in the Kapthurin formation, Kenya[7] (McBrearty et al., 1996); in Western Europe where numerous sites existed during the Isotopic Stages 6–4 (Heinzelin and Haesaerts, 1983; Delagnes, 2000; Koehler, 2009); and in Central Asia at the site of Khonako III in Tajikistan (Shäfer and Ranov, 1998).

The lineage of blade products is, in the framework of this book, deliberately limited to exclusively blade production. In effect, our goal is to understand why these productions are oriented exclusively toward obtaining such a standardized type of product. This is, furthermore, the first knapped product to be so standardized and that coincides with the emergence of a specific technical lineage. As a result, it is the exclusive production of blades that is the phenomenon (such as it appears to us[8]) that first needs to be investigated rather than the "blade"[9] phenomenon that existed far earlier. In our opinion, the phenomenon of "blade" takes on a completely new meaning from the moment when it becomes the object of a specific production. In other words, one moves from a lineage of a few blade products to a lineage of blades.

The ontological approach that we propose avoids the purely technical apory, which leads one to endlessly debate the primacy of either the blade or its mode of production. It is neither the necessity to produce a blade that leads to an exclusive mode of production nor the desire for an exclusive production that results in the exclusive production of blades. Rather, it is particular or multiple exterior societal,[10]

The anthropological sense 155

thus historical, necessities that led to a change in the mode of production in order to create a unique tool and/or support. Keep in mind that the blade product is not an end in and of itself, it is only a means. But this can only become material if the necessary technicity is available. So, do we have the technical means needed? This question leads back to the structural capacity of the means of production to respond to this goal. The response may be positive if a small step toward the concretization of the structures of production is all that is needed, or negative, requiring the invention of a new structure of production in its initial abstract form.

Consider Levallois debitage. Levallois precedes the exclusive production of blades and allows for production of blade supports. This method could have persisted. But it did not persist. Why? Perhaps it presented the inconvenience, from a perspective that is not obvious to us, of not being able to contract to the production of a single uniform techno-type of standardized objects. From an evolutionary point of view, it is probable that as a result of new objectives/needs, Levallois debitage became hypertelic, displaying a degree of elaboration that cannot be explained based on function. This hypertely is related to an excessive specialization of the object. In the current case, Levallois debitage had become overly specialized for the production of a heterogeneity of techno-types.

One can conclude that the phenomenon of the "blade" is the appropriate response to new "technical" options for which the only response is the structural adaptation of the modes of debitage through the creation of a new lineage. But, as we will see, the technical potential of the blade only emerges gradually. The lineage of modes of production is thus only the response to the evolutionary potential[11] of the blade as a support for tools.

Historical preamble

A global perspective reveals that the phenomena of blade production and of exclusive production of blades do not have the same history in terms of both geography and chronology. In terms of geographic distribution, the phenomenon of Pleistocene blade production is absent from the West African and East Asian subcontinents. The moment when blade production appears varies from one continent to another, and the duration of this type of production is highly variable. The position of blade production with respect to other modes of production is similarly diverse, particularly in relation to Levallois debitage. If Levallois knapping always precedes the phenomenon of blade production, it does not imply that these are always two sequential developments. In most regions where these two technical phenomena exist, they can be associated and/or blade production can alternate with Levallois debitage, sometimes for more than 200,000 years. However, in the long term, only exclusive production of blades persists.

The history of the phenomenon of tools on blades is just as surprising. At first, the blade, whether in West Europe or the Middle East, appears to lack any adjustment through retouch. This does not mean that all these blades are the same tools. In the case of the Middle East, during the Amudian blades with a natural back are desired and obtained through a specific organization of debitage. We will return in

156 *The anthropological sense*

greater depth to this particular situation. In Europe, the situation is more complex. The first blades are also lacking retouch and do not appear to be associated with any particular technical characteristics—except the two cutting edges, as found at Saint-Valery-Sur-Somme (Heinzelin and Haesaerts, 1983). Subsequently, the situation is more varied. The blades may remain unretouched, as found at Saint-Germain des Vaux (Cliquet, 1992), or they can be retouched, as found at Seclin (Revillon and Tuffreau, 1994) and Riencourt-les Bapaumes (Tuffreau et al., 1991; Ameloot-Van Der Heijden, 1994). In South Africa, the case of the Howieson's Poort is just as surprising, with blade production essentially oriented toward the production of a single type of retouched object (Lombard, 2005; Soriano et al., 2007; Porraz et al. 2008; Villa et al., 2010). The history of blade production across the modes of production and of the resulting products is thus far from being as linear as one might expect.

Techno-logical temporality

The modes of production

The historical discourse can only be established based on the concept of evolution. One must examine the blade production lineage on a structural level before engaging in its history.

According to the "law of evolution," which we have developed in the course of this work, we can group together four structures that we have already defined: C2, D2, E2, and F2. These structures are ordered in time, in the sense that each one of these technical solutions corresponds to a stage of structural integration that is superior to its predecessor. Nonetheless, as we will see, this does not signify that these different evolutionary stages appear in a linear and continuous sequence at every time and in every place. This aspect of the material becoming of the lineages is within the scope of their history. Remember that every structure is the signifier of a group, of a society, as is every other human production. The evolution, fluctuation, and disappearance of lineages are contingent. Keep in mind that every element of a lineage is a "being in itself" within a system of objects (Deforge, 1985).

The products

The changes in the mode of production are responses to new cultural demands. The structural evolution of tools applies to the integration of the three parts of the tool: prehensile, transmissive of energy, and transformative. Changes in the elements of the tool are regulated by the same "law of evolution" that was described for the modes of production. In general, one observes a change toward increased integration of the prehensile part with the rest of the tool. Nonetheless, the reason that a tool exists as a material object is to provide the ability to transform a worked material. It is therefore first and foremost necessary that a tool possess a transformative part. The prehensile part is nevertheless structurally present and necessary because the gesture and the energy required for the realization of the objective depend on

The anthropological sense 157

it. On the one hand, the success of the transformation depends on the cutting edge in contact with the worked material, and on the other hand, it depends on the prehensile part that is in contact with the necessary energy produced by the person carrying out the act. Are we not once again confronted by an impasse (aporia) that requires us to place the constitutive parts of the tool within a functional logic? The concept of evolution allows us to resolve this rational difficulty by demonstrating that these two functional elements will be transformed both by their ongoing integration over time and by the effect of external constraints.

The modes of production and the products

The lineage of blade production does not appear out of nowhere. In the Middle East, it is found approximately 200,000 years ago. Developing out of non-exclusive blade modes of production, the support designated as a "blade removal" is anterior to the exclusive blade mode of production. The "blade removal" is clearly a product that already has significant technical constraints on the prehensile part regardless of how the transformative part is shaped. Subsequently, the normalization of the blade removal into the blade is such that we observe structural modifications of the debitage, trending toward an increased complexity of the interactions between the different technical parameters of the knapped volume and the technical means of production.

If our observations lead us to talk of normalization, it is difficult to determine what exactly the norm is. Is it a new relationship between the length and width of the tool supports and future tools? If this is the case what is the reason: a way or ways of holding the tool, the gesture/s of tool use, or the transmission/s of energy? Part of an indirect response is provided by the fact that the specific structures of debitage will prove to be necessary and will follow one another creating an evolutionary cycle of variable tempo. The direction of the evolution of these successive blade production structures, which produce only blades, are qualitative, and trend toward an increasing number of blades per knapped volume.

At the scale of a particular industry, the choice of exclusive blade production does not signify that this is the only mode of production. We must dissociate the industries that only incorporate blade production from those where blade production is associated with other structures of debitage, and thus other predetermined supports. These conceptions go back to different options. In industries with only blade debitage, a single type of predetermined support is chosen for the ensemble of tools with or without the same maintenance, use gesture, and energy. In such a case, there might be another associated production but the supports produced will be minimally constrained, with the constraint applying to a minimum of technical criteria and never to the prehensile part.

In the case of blade industries associated with other structures of debitage, the availability of multiple predetermined supports derived from distinct modes of production corresponds to different gestures, which implies differences in energy.

Thus, in the case that interests here, a support that is already standardized and exclusive is elaborated by a process of evolution, which results in the regularization

158 *The anthropological sense*

of the prehensile part and the capacity to produce a wide range of transformative parts. The reliance on a stage of modification is thus required if one desires particular cutting edges, silhouettes, and technical characteristics that cannot be obtained through the process of debitage.

The archaeological application must therefore take into account the ensemble of the points discussed above. But to have any sense, these must be placed in an archaeological context, that is to say, by confronting the ensemble of technical elements.

Beyond a connection based on a logical interaction between the technical facts, there exists a connection based on chronological succession (Bergson, 2009). This temporality of analysis is the time of the creation of facts (*genèse des faits*).

Chronological temporality

The production of blades

For the purposes of our discussion, we distinguish five phases in the development of blade production, which divide into two major cycles.

The first cycle (Phases 1 and 2) begins with the initial blade production, named depending on their characteristics as Amudian, Pre-Aurignacian, or Hummalian. These industries precede the period dominated by Levallois-Mousterian production. The second cycle (Phases 3–5) begins with the so-called Intermediate or Transitional Industries, also designated as the Initial Upper Paleolithic, and ends with the last blade industries of the Holocene.

FIRST PHASE

This phase, which developed between 300,000 and 200,000 years ago, includes the earliest Levantine blade industries, in Israel and Lebanon, known as the Amudian.

The stratigraphic relationship between the Amudian and the Yabrudian is variable. It is either interstratified with the Yabrudian as is the case at Tabun Cave in Israel, Unit XI, where it is dated to 264+/-28 kyr (Garrod and Bate, 1937; Garrod, 1956; Jelinek, 1975, 1981, 1982, 1990; Mercier and Valladas, 2003), or it post-dates the Yabrudian, as is the case at Abri Zumoffen in Lebanon where the Yabrudian is dated to Oxygen Isotope Stage 7 (Garrod and Kirkbride, 1961; Roe, 1983; Sanlaville, 1998). The recent discoveries at the site of Qesem, Israel, dated between 400,000 and 200,000 years ago, are contemporary with, and thus apparently an activity variant, of the Yabrudian[12] (Barkai et al., 2003, 2005, 2009, 2010; Gopher et al., 2005).

SECOND PHASE

During this phase, which developed between 200,000 and 150,000 years ago, blade industries are found in the Levant and the Syrian interior (Figure 3.1).

The anthropological sense   159

Typological phase	Locality	Age	Reference
Amudian	Tabun, Unit XI	306+/-33,000 (TL)	Mercier et al. 1995
	Qesem	Between 330,000-245,000	Barkai et al. 2003, 2005, 2009
	Abri Zummoffen	Oxygen Isotope Stage 7	Sanlaville 1998
Pre-Aurignacian	Yabrud, C. 13 & 15	Younger than 195.000 +/- 15,000 (C18, TL)	Farrand 1994
Indeterminate	Hayonim, E base	150/200,000 (TL, ESR)	Valladas et al. 1998, Schwarcz et al. 1998, Mercier et al. 2007
Hummalian	Hummal Ia, alph h	Possibly younder than 243,000+/- 40,000 and 422,000+/-55,000 (TL for an underlying Yabrudian assemblage	Richter 2006
	Umm el Tlel	Older than Oxygen Isotope Stage 6	Boëda 2009
Indeterminate	Hummal VI, C6b	220,000-150,000 (TL)	Richter 2006
	Kaféine 1	Older than Levaloiso-Mousterian of Oxygen Isotope Stages 5 and 4	Boëda 2000
Djuruchulian	Djuruchule C. 1 & 2	150,000/200,000 (TL, ESR)	Mercier et al. 2010

Figure 3.1 Chronological table of the industries of Phases 1 and 2.

In the Levantine region:

- *The Pre-Aurignacian*: Known at Yabrud (Syria) interstratified with the Yabrudian levels, Yabrud levels 13 and 15 (Rust, 1950; Bordes, 1955, 1958, 1997). This industry does not appear to be older than 195,000+/-15 kyr (TL), the date obtained for level 18, an underlying Yabrudian level (Farrand, 1994; Garrod, 1956).
- *Hayonim blade production*[13]: Known in Israel underlying the Levalloiso-Mousterian sequence of the site of Hayonim—Level F and the base of Level E, which is dated to 160,000–230,000 years ago (TL, ESR) (Meignen, 1998a and b, 2000, 2007, 2011; Valladas et al., 1998; Schwarcz and Rink 1998; Mercier et al., 2007).

In the regions of Palmyra and El Kom in Syria:

- *The Hummalian*: Currently known in stratigraphic context at two sites: Hummal and Umm el Tlel.

At Hummal, the context is somewhat unclear. The Hummalian assemblage was first discovered in 1980. At the time, it was designated as Level Ia (Besançon et al., 1981, 1982; Hours, 1982; Boëda, 1995a, 1997). An initial series of thermoluminescence dates produced an age of 160 +/- 22 kyr for the underlying Level Ib, a travertine conglomerate that contained Yaburdian elements (Henning and Hours, 1982). But this age was questioned based on the contamination of the sediments

160   *The anthropological sense*

by radioactive elements (Mercier and Valladas, 1994). With the reopening of the excavations by J.-M. Le Tensorer in the 2000s, two Hummalian assemblages were exposed. The first, designated as Level h (or alpha h), corresponds to Level Ia from the earlier excavation. The second assemblage is derived from Levels 6 and 7 and designated as Level 6b (or VIb). This assemblage, which has no directly observable stratigraphic relationship with Level h, is dated by thermoluminescence between 250,000 and 160,000 kyr (Le Tensorer, 2005, 2007; Le Tonsorer and Hours 1989; Richter et al., 2011).[14] In 1982 and 1983, the RCP 438 team[15] directly sampled Level 6b and in 1991 we did the same. The analysis we conducted in 1991 on this material, along with a study of the material from Level Ia, clearly indicates these are distinct industries, even if they are both expressions of blade production. As a result, it seems appropriate to us to retain the designation of Hummalian for the industry of Level Ia but not for the Level 6b industry.

At Umm el Tel, the Hummalian level overlies a Yaburdian assemblage situated in a travertine conglomerate dated to 140,000 years ago (Boëda and Al Sakhel, 2006, 2007, 2008, 2009; Copeland and Hours, 1981, 1983). However, this needs verification. It must be used with caution because based on the chronostratigraphy the recent excavations indicate an age for this assemblage that is earlier than Oxygen Isotope Stage 6/7 (Henning and Hours, 1982; Copeland and Hours, 1981).

The Industry of Hummal 6b   (stratigraphy following Besançon et al., 1982; Le Tensorer, 2007; Wotjtczak, 2011).

This industry is distinct from the one found in Level Ia. It involves a specific mode of blade production, resulting in characteristic thick blades with a trapezoidal section. It is difficult to distinguish retouch from substantial post-depositional damage observable on this assemblage. The material is found in a matrix of fine gravel that is indicative of intensive erosion. The stratigraphic relationship of this assemblage to the Hummalian of Leval Ia (alpha h) is difficult to determine despite the renewed excavations. This remains a problem that the new excavations have not resolved. In effect, since the discovery of the locality, in a different sector of the deposits a series of levels—II, III, and IV—that incorporate Levallois products including blades—are clearly described as having a connection with Level Ia (Besançon et al., 1981).[16] Although it is impossible to create a stratigraphic connection between the earlier excavations and the more recent investigations, this information should not be rejected. The observations regarding Levels II–IV provided evidence of a Levallois blade industry of type Tabun D (Blady Early MP), which is also found in the Umm el Tlel sequence (Boëda and Al Sakhel, 2008). Nonetheless, in the current state of knowledge one cannot conclude with confidence that cultural elements of type Tabun D are found stratigraphically overlying the Yabrudian of Hummal. The dates obtained for Level 6b (Richter et al., 2011) must be confirmed taking into account the problem of residual radioactive elements in the sediments (Mercier and Valladas, 1994).

The site of Kaféine   This is a new blade production industry recently discovered in stratigraphic position at the localities of Kaféine 1, 2, and 3[17] (Boëda and Al Sakhel, 2005). Kaféine 1 presents more than six archaeological levels that largely consist of the products of knapping, cores, and a large number of unretouched blades. The base of the sequence is not known. A workshop for the production of Levallois points and flakes was found on the surface, corresponding to Oxygen Isotope Stage 5–4 of the El Kom region. The attribution of an age anterior to the Levalloiso-Mousterian, other than Tabun D (Blady Early Middle Paleolithic), for this industry seems possible. In one of the levels, a patinated Levallois core with very large blade removal scars was discovered. This core might relate to an early Levalloiso-Mousterian period that precedes blade production. There is neither typological nor technological similarity with Level 6b at Hummal. Nonetheless, this site, together with Hummal 6b strongly, suggests that there is a non-Levallois blade industry in the El Kom Basin that is distinct from the Hummalian and probably either later or contemporary with the earliest Levallois-Mousterian facies.

The southern Caucasus: The Djruchula-Koudaro complex This group of industries is also known as the Djruchulian (Liubin, 1977, 1989; Meignen and Tushabramishvili, 2006, 2010; Golovanova and Doronichev, 2003). Although located well to the north, along the southern flanks of the Caucasus, these industries and in particular the assemblages from the site of Djruchula in Georgia belong in terms of technique and technology to the blade industries identified in the Middle East at the sites of Hayonim E (base) and F (base), Hummal Ia (Copeland, 1985), and Abu Sif (Neuville, 1951), even though the Caucus assemblage have distinctive elements, such as bifacial retouch (Meignen and Tushabramishvili, 2006, 2010). At the site of Djruchula, two periods of occupation characterized by blade industries are dated respectively, to 260/210,000 years ago and 140,000 years ago using thermoluminescence (Mercier and Valladas, 2011).

TECHNICAL CHARACTERISTICS OF PHASES 1 AND 2

These assemblages have been analyzed using a range of approaches and methodologies. In fact, with rare exceptions, syntheses have proven to be difficult and can lead in different directions depending on the characteristics considered. At a minimum, any synthesis will recognize that a large number of the blade cores indicate a Levallois concept of debitage, that the percussion is direct with a hard or soft mineral hammer, and that the point of impact is internal and not marginal.

Identification of the presence of Levallois debitage must be made with great care. In some cases, the "diagnosis" is made on the basis of a small number of products, particularly points.[18] Researchers with experimental experience are very aware of the danger of such an approach. In other cases, it is the cores that are emphasized. However, as we have shown previously, some cores of a volumetric conception of Type D might mimic the appearance of a Levallois conception. Lastly, some non-Levallois blade products of Type D might, depending on their stage of abandonment, give the impression of being of Levallois conception. In reality, this is actually just similarity in form, while the underlying conceptions are radically different. We have conducted extensive experimentation with the

162 *The anthropological sense*

Hummalian modes of blade production to confirm the process of "morphological succession" that allows for the conservation of blade production that is not continuous but rather follows the knapping of useful volumes. We think it is particularly important to emphasize this point. In effect, the analyses of technique are above all aimed at recognizing the procedures of production—concepts and methods—and the result has been significant progress. However, it nonetheless remains the case that an overemphasis on classification has resulted in an inflexible system. This is particularly true for certain non-homothetic modes of production. There is a major confusion between the concept and the method. This is particularly true for blade production,[19] which gives rise to numerous paradoxes. For example, on the one hand, there is evidence of Levallois blade production, thus a recognized and confirmed volumetric concept, without having clearly and precisely defined the method or methods (with the exception of the unidirectional). On the other hand, there is mention of non-Levallois blade production, with extensive detail on the methods without the least reference to a volumetric concept. As a result, there is a rich vocabulary that is semantically diverse and evocative such as revolving (*tournant*), semi-revolving (*semi-tournant*), unidirectional, and pseudo-pyramidal. But at a conceptual level what are these? Conceptually, what does a non-Levallois production signify? What do these expressions mean at the level of concepts and in terms of finality? It is necessary to go beyond this stage of recognizing the facts to reach an analytical level. This is a supplementary step that must be breached. Because at this stage we are always confronted with problems that result from the effects of classification and the dynamics of the development of taxonomy. Each time one arrives at a new stage of comprehension, one is tempted to reify it by creating an overly rigid classification that is in a way reassuring because it allows for the production of a discourse. Once again, the facts are forced into a single mold!

THIRD PHASE

In this phase, we group together the chronologically more recent industries that still include a specific blade production that can be associated with Levallois debitage. The sites are few, distributed across a vast territory and chronologically scattered. These industries are distinct from the industries of type Tabun D (Early Blade Middle Paleolithic) where the Levallois blade component is clearly dominant along with the production of short supports—flakes and/or points (Copeland, 1975; Meignen, 2007).

For the Levant:

- The site of Rosh Ein Mor dated to approximately 80,000 BP (U/Th) (Marks and Crew, 1972; Marks and Monigal, 1995; Schwarcz et al., 1979).
- The site of Ain Difla dated between 90,000 and 180,000 BP (TL, ESR, U/TH) (Lindly and Clark, 1987; Clark et al., 1988, 1997).

For the regions of Palmyra and El Kom:

- Levels VI2 alpha a and VIII1a at Umm el Tlel dated, respectively, between 60,000 and 70,000 BP (TL) and between 70,000 and 110,000 BP (TL) (Boëda and Al Sakhel, 2008).

The anthropological sense   163

FOURTH PHASE

The fourth phase begins with the industries designated as[20] *Transitional, Levantine Early Upper Paleolithic*, or *Initial Upper Paleolithic* (Garrod, 1951, 1955; Azoury, 1986; Copeland, 1970, 1975; Ohnuma, 1988; Bar Yosef and Belfer-Cohen, 1988; Belfer-Cohen and Bar Yosef, 1999; Gilead, 1991; Marks, 1983a and b, 1993; Kuhn et al., 2004; Brantingham et al., 2004b; Meignen and Tushabramishvili, 2006, 2010) as well as *Intermediate Paleolithic*[21] (Boëda and Muhesen, 1993; Boëda and Bonilauri, 2006). The term "transition" suggests a phylogenetic relationship with the various cultures that come before and after, while the terms "Upper Paleolithic" or "Initial Upper Paleolithic" indicate both a rupture with preceding cultures and the beginning of something new that will go on to flourish.

In reality, the choice of terminology depends on the characteristic that one chooses to emphasize. In certain cases, it is the persistence of an archaic trait, such as the Levallois point, produced by Type F1/Levallois debitage or some other conception, or the presence of Emireh points is emphasized, despite the presence of characteristic Upper Paleolithic tools. In other cases, primacy is given to the tendency toward blade production and/or the presence of Upper Paleolithic tool types—endscrapers and burins—made on blades. One therefore talks of Leptolithic artifacts, particularly for the Western and Central European industries (Breuil, 1912; Kozlowski, 1988; Kozlowski and Kozlowski, 1996), indicating that the existence of these tools signifies an evolution toward the Upper Paleolithic.

However, the principal characteristic of all of these industries is a mixture of "apomorphic"[22] and "plesiomorphic"[23] technical criteria and depending on whether we choose to emphasize one or the other we will view this as either the terminal stage of a process or, to the contrary, as the beginning of a new process of development. But why should we attribute more value to one or the other?

Of the numerous known sites, we will only cite the most well known: Ksar-Akil, Lebanon (Azoury, 1986; Ohnuma, 1988), Boker Tachtit, Israel (Marks, 1983a, b), Tor Sadaf, Jordan (Fox, 2003; Coinman, 2004), Umm el Tlel, Syria (Boëda and Muhesen, 1993; Boëda and Bonilauri, 2006) and Üçagzli, Turkey (Kuhn, 2004; Kuhn et al., 2004).

The geographic distribution of this phenomenon covers the Middle East, from the Mediterranean to the Euphrates, and even well beyond that we find it in Central Asia at Obi Rakhmat and Khudji (Ranov and Amosova, 1984; Vishnyatsky, 2004), in the Altai at Kar-Bom (Goebel, 2004), and very clearly in northern China at Schidongou (Brantingham et al., 2004a).

The duration of this phenomenon in the Middle East is brief, as it is limited between 45,000 and 47,000 BP based on the age of the earliest levels—Boqer Tachtit 1 (Marks, 1983a, b)[24] and 35,000 BP for the most recent levels located in the steppe zone (Boëda et al., 1996). In the regions further to the east, we have earlier ages that are in the process of verification.

This fourth phase extends geographically beyond the Middle East, providing evidence of the circulation and technical adoption of this new idea that transcends geographic and ethnic regions.

164 *The anthropological sense*

FIFTH PHASE

The fifth and last phase groups together all of the industries postdating the so-called Transitional industries until their disappearance.

These blade industries are known from 43,700 BP at Kebara—Unit IV–V (Bar Yosef et al., 1996; Bar Yosef, 2000). After 36–35,000 BP at Kebara—Unit IIf, a new type of industry designated as the Aurignacian or Levantine Aurignacian appears that lasts until 21,000 BP as found at Ksar Aqil (Mellars and Tixier, 1989). This industry occupies the same area in the Middle East[25] as the Ahmarian, without there being a real substitution of one by the other (Goring Morris and Belfer-Cohen, 2003; Mellars, 2004). In effect, the Ahmarian is a complex of industries that one finds during and after the Aurignacian period rather than a homogeneous entity (Bar Yosef and Belfer-Cohen, 1977; Bar Yosef, 2000). The final phase of the Upper Paleolithic in the Middle East is often equated with the final facies of the Ahmarian or the *Late Ahmarian Complex*, particularly in Syria (Ploux and Soriano, 2003) and in Jordan (Coinman, 1993, 1998; Olszewski, 1997; Byrd, 1988; Byrd and Garard, 1990). After this final phase, the Ahmarian is followed by the Geometric Kebaran around 17,500–14,600 cal BP, then by the Natufian between 14,600 and 12,900 BP (Belfer-Cohen and Goring Morris, 2003; Maher et al., 2011; Godfrey-Smith et al., 2003). The beginning of the Neolithic designated as PPNA and PPNB, between 9000 and 7000 years ago, sees the further development of blade production (Abbès, 2003; Calley, 1986; Cauvin, 1968, 1977, 1990, 1994). This tradition reaches its culmination in the Early Bronze Age (Neuville, 1930; Rosen, 1983, 1997) with the so-called Canaanean blades.

The blade products

THE DEBUT OF THE BLADE PHENOMENON

The Amudian and Hummalian blades   For the debut of the blade phenomenon, the empirical data on the tools is not very precise. There are significant differences in analytical approaches from one site to another. In contrast, the data set is rich for the periods after 45,000 BP.

Nonetheless, for the initial industries, we have tried, in tabular format, to synthesize the available data as well as possible. Taking into account what is known about the chronology, it is possible to distinguish two major tendencies.

A first tendency is characterized by blades that are mostly unretouched, which does not signify that these are not tools. Where the use wear on these blades has been studied, these analyses confirm that most of these unretouched blades functioned as tools. The function of unretouched blade tools was initially detected through a technological analysis of the production schemas without the help of use wear analysis, for example, in the case of the Amudian (Meignen, 1994, 1996). The techno-functional characteristics of the blade tools are integrated into the schema of production with the result that they are present once the blades have been struck from the core. Each blade produced is thus an artifact ready to be used. Only the energy of the gesture is missing for them to become tools.

The anthropological sense 165

With regard to such a system, two observations can be made. The first is that the potential to use retouch to transform the blade into a different tool is rarely, if ever, realized. This situation leads to another level of reflection regarding the complementarity of tools in the same assemblage. Two solutions can be considered. The simplest is to imagine that we are considering sites with specialized activities that only require a minimum diversity of tools. In the case of the Amudian this is conceivable because in most sites it is found associated with Yabrudian tools. In theory, this association might be rejected out of hand because the underlying technical conceptions seem different and even opposed. Unless this opposition is what actually connects these different techno-functional conceptions in making them complementary? The alternative hypothesis is to consider the Amudian facies as a technical entity with a diversity of tools that is not apparent to us at first glance. Combining a techno-functional study with use wear analysis, the research undertaken at the site of Umm el Tlel (Bonilauri, 2010), although limited to the Levallois industry of convergent tools, demonstrates that retouch was not required for the realization of objectives as varied as working vegetal material or meat, whether by cutting or scraping. Similarly, the Amudian blades could have been utilized for many different tasks, without requiring any specialization whatsoever.

The second observation is made within an evolutionary framework. Given that we are in the first phase of the emergence of a blade system, one could imagine that the structural potential of the blade has not yet been developed because it is still at its first stage. Only the capacity of the unretouched blade is recognized and is judged to be sufficient. This comment does not in any way contradict what we said earlier. On the contrary, they actually lead in the same direction. Is it not the same in Europe? There also there is a techno-logic.

The second tendency provides evidence of the use of a blade as an ideal support for the fabrication of a variety of artifacts with a single or multiple operational schemes (Figure 3.2). All of the structural potential of the blade is thus exploited, a point to which we return. Put simply, the unretouched blade tool becomes the support for tools. Thus, the blade is utilized as a matrix to be shaped. From a purely descriptive perspective, taking the case of the Hummalian that we know well, it is possible to distinguish there again two tendencies of retouched artifacts. We use the term "artifact" rather than tool, as is done in ergonomics, because in this case, this distinction is particularly important. In effect, if one only considers the type of retouch, it is only possible to identify a first tendency in which we group together the retouched artifacts that belong to the type "sidescraper" [*racloir*] following Bordes' terminology: simple sidescraper, double sidescraper, and retouch of Quina type. The second tendency groups together a wide range of convergent tools that we have previously evoked. Note the absence, except for rare exceptions, of end-scrapers and burins. The recent analysis we conducted demonstrates with certainty that the rare burins are in reality cores for bladelets of 3–4 cm in length.[26]

Let us return to the first tendency and integrate the techno-functional criterion that distinguishes the blade: the prehensile part. The first observation we can make is that one cannot really designate a blade tool as a scraper in the same way that one applies this term to a flake tool. We prefer to use the term "retouched blade" even if the function is the same as a scraper. The structure of a blade forces the tool

Locality	Natural or managed crest	Absence of retouch		Upper Paleolithic types**	Blade retouched on one edge	Blade retouched on two edges	Retouched convergent edges	Blade retouched on dorsal face	Levallois flake, point, blade production	Yabrudian Production	Bladelet production
Non-Levallois laminar production (Typological characterization)									**Macro-characterization of production**		
Tabun, Unit XI	X	X	X	X	X	X				X	
Qesem	X	X		X	X	X					
Abri Zummoffen	X	X		X	X	X					
Yabrud C. 13 & 15	X	X	X	X	X	X					X[0]
Kafiéne	X	X									
Hayonim E base & F		X			X	X	X	X	X[#]		X
Hummal Ia*		X			X	X	X				X
Umm el Tlel		X			X	X	X				X
Djuruchule C.1 & C.2		X			X	X	X	X	X[#]		
Hummal VIb*		***			***	***	***		X(?)		

* Study based on material collected in 1982/83 and 91; **Chatelperronian point, endscraper, burin; *** Taphonomic problem; # Production of luminaire removals probable; X(?) The cores are of Type D3; [0] Based on the technical characteristics of the carinated endscrapers; X Significant frequency

Figure 3.2 The structures of blade production and types of tools (in the classic typological sense in the Near East).

to be held differently, resulting in different energetic potential and gestures. This therefore implies, due to the essential distinctiveness of the operational schemas, that these are different tools. The second observation follows from a comparison with the tools that precede the Hummalian, particularly the Yabrudian. There is a genuine ergonomic rupture between the Yabrudian and Hummalian.

This rupture is largely confirmed by the second tendency, which is represented by the convergent blade tools. In relationship to the preceding artifacts/tools, these suggest truly novel tools. These are not simply objects with convergent edges. The convergence of the edges, in the case of the Hummalian, is used to obtain a variety of tool types. Thus, we distinguish different types of convergence:

- Symmetrical along the morphological long axis of the blade in plan view and also symmetrical along the perpendicular axis.
- Symmetrical along the morphological long axis of the blade in plan view and asymmetrical along the perpendicular axis.
- Offset along the morphological axis of the blade in plan view and along the perpendicular axis.
- Offset along the morphological axis of the blade in plan view and along the perpendicular axis.

The anthropological sense 167

Another element of variability, based on the type of modified cutting edge, can also be taken into consideration, further multiplying the range of tools.

In summary, the phenomenon of the Hummalian, and its homologues in the Levant and the Caucasus, represents a genuine ergonomic revolution, with the integration of new energies and new gestures. On an evolutionary level, we are within the trajectory of the evolutionary potential of blades.

We can also consider the evolution of the Hummalian system of production which is globally the same as for the Amudian.

This observation corroborates what one can observe of the intensity of retouch in the Hummalian. In general, there is not a correlation between the type of support and the shape of the desired tool. The lack of fit is corrected by extensive retouch. Numerous experimental replications of the Hummalian modes of production demonstrate the considerable technical and morphological diversity of supports produced. The principal objective of debitage is a discontinuous production of blades. The resulting variability can be corrected with retouch of the transformative and prehensile parts (see the discussion of the Hummalian in Chapter 2). It is very interesting to note that at the site of Umm el Tlel, the industry overlying the Hummalian is a Levallois industry of type Tabun D, Blady Early Middle Paleolithic (MP), that is characterized by the same type of convergent tools, but with much less substantial retouch. The unretouched Levallois support is in effect a support that possesses, from its production, the shape and the technical characteristics of the future tool. The retouch only has the role of making the cutting edges functional, depending on the desired objectives. As for the prehensile part, these are practically unretouched. One finds the technofunctional characteristics of debitage of Type F1/Levallois, which we have discussed previously, consisting of a highly normalized prehensile part and a transformative part that closely approximates the future silhouette of the tool.

Keep in mind that the Levallois debitage, in the case of industries of type Tabun D (Blady Early MP), also serves to produce other types of supports such as Levallois points. This variability in production explains the abandonment of debitage exclusively focused on blades, even if these elongated flakes, often with convergent edges, continue to be produced.

THE POST-HUMMALIAN

After this period of retouched blades, the industries with a high proportion of blades become rare during Oxygen Isotope States 6 and 5 when the emphasis is on Levallois debitage of Type F1. Only a small number of short-lived episodes of blade production appear during this period. The technical information on these types of tools is rare, but it is clear that in no case are these of Hummalian-type. It appears that most blade products during this time interval are unretouched.

BLADE AND BLADELET PRODUCTS: FROM THE TRANSITION TO THE NEOLITHIC

It is only with the so-called Transitional period (Middle to Upper Paleolithic), 100,000 years later, that there is the reappearance of a lasting emphasis on blade

168 *The anthropological sense*

tools, which then persists this time until the Neolithic. But this is not the repetition of earlier tool types. Rather, there is the appearance of new tools along with the linked appearance of tools on bladelets. This period is marked by the initial development of the debitage of bladelets.[27] Admittedly, one does find in the final periods of the Mousterian several bladelet cores, but these remain very marginal and the production is very limited. Once bladelet production appears in the Transitional contexts, bladelet removals represent a significant component of the predetermined products.[28]

Tools on blades are dominated by backed blades, pointed blades, endscrapers, and burins. It is interesting to note that endscrapers and burins are present during the Mousterian phases, admittedly in low frequency, but nonetheless in sufficient quantities to be recognized consistently. However, during the Mousterian the supports for these tools are for the most part the predetermining flakes rather than the predetermined flakes of Levallois F1 or other types. The characteristic of non-predetermination is significant because it provides evidence of a lack of regularization of the supports and thus of irregular shapes. This does not signify that the supports do not have to possess certain technical characteristics. These characteristics are found among the available flakes, they are not obtained as the result of specific debitage procedures leading to a support with normalized prehensile or transformative parts. The fact that beginning in the Transitional period the same transformative parts (endscrapers and burins) are systematically associated with a new type of support, which moreover is the only type of normalized support, signifies a profound change. Does one not see at the same time the disappearance of debitage of type F1/Levallois as well as every other heavily structured mode of production such as type E1? These are thus new tools that imply changes in ergonomics, gesture, and energy.

The tools on bladelets belong to another category of tools. Where bladelets appear within the technical system it is not to support the same transformative parts as the blades. On the contrary, the transformative parts are always unretouched, and only the prehensile part is subject to partial modification as in the case of Ahmarian and Aurignacian bladelets, or of a more substantial modification to obtain a good silhouette as in the case of the Kebaran. Nonetheless, it is necessary to distinguish the bladelets from the Transitional period because they are in general unretouched and characterized by a specificity related to a mode of prehension. The techno-functional analysis of the transitional levels at Umm el Tlel provides evidence of hafting along the axis of debitage, which is also the morphological axis of the bladelet. In this context, the gesture with which the tool is used is influenced by the unretouched shape as there is a correlation between unretouched shape and particular techno-functional categories (Boëda and Bonilauri, 2006). In the Aurignacian, the prehension of the bladelet becomes essentially lateral for both flat and torqued bladelets.

During the PPNA and PPNB phases, the production of bladelets disappears in favor of the exclusive production of blades and of classic tools on blades: endscrapers, burins of all types, arrowheads designated as Aswad, Byblos, Jericho, Amuq, or other types, and denticulated or non-denticulated sickle blades. At the end of the PPNB, blade production loses its importance and tools are produced on flakes

(Nishiaki, 2000; Ibáñez and Urquijo, 2006). Only the production of obsidian blades by pressure flaking persists.

The anthropological sense: at the crossroads of the chronological and evolutionary data

A technical paleo-history of the modes of production and the tools produced

FIRST PHASE: THE AMUDIAN FROM 300,000 TO 200,000 YEARS AGO

The structures of blade production and the tools produced   The very first structures of blade production appear in their abstract form, evidence that this is the debut of a lineage (Figures 3.3–3.4). We can propose two alternative hypotheses:

- This is the result of a purely local process of invention.
- The invention took place elsewhere and arrived before the evolution of the lineage developed.

In the current state of knowledge, the first hypothesis seems the most likely. If one considers the anterior and/or contemporary industries—the Acheulean whether completely bifacial or the Yabrudian—the evolutionary rupture is

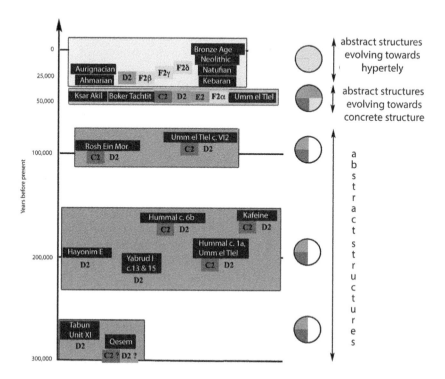

Figure 3.3 The evolution of the structures of production in the Near East.

170 *The anthropological sense*

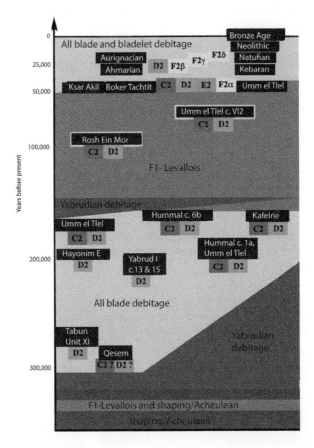

Figure 3.4 The evolution of the ensemble of structures of production in the Near East.

apparent. But this rupture is situated within a deep history of ruptures that begins with the transition from the Acheulean, which is completely bifacial, to the Yabrudian, which is totally flake based.[29] This transition involved the abandonment of shaping that allows for the regularization of supports in favor of an exclusive reliance on debitage, or to be more precise, a reliance on exclusive debitage together with exclusive confection. In the case of the Yabrudian, the normalization is mixed because the stage of confection results in both the volume and the cutting edge of the tool. Given the importance of this stage of confection, we could separate an initial stage of shaping that develops the regularized volume and the second stage of confection in the strict sense of the term that involves only the cutting edge. But this subdivision is not really of importance because what is critical is that the process of the production of normalized supports is already complex if one takes into account the stage of debitage.

The anthropological sense   171

Throughout the subsequent process of evolution that we can follow with blade production: C2, D2, E2, and F2 and the Types D1, D3, E1, and F1, there will be a convergence toward the normalization of supports. The blade production that follows the Yabrudian is a new rupture. Even if the stratigraphic position of the Yabrudian and this initial stage of blade production is not very clear, the emergence of blade production is evidence of a new orientation that leads to the Hummalian and its homologues such as at Hayonim in Israel and Djruchula-Koudaro in the Caucasus.

When looking at the initial blade assemblages, one observes a lack of retouch. This absence has two evolutionary explanations, but for this, we must disassociate the analysis of the tool from the analysis of the support.

The abstract stage of the tool   In the framework of an evolutionary lineage very often the tool is unretouched because it is structurally at an abstract stage. This does not mean that the diversity of tools is limited; on the contrary, use wear analysis has consistently shown that a simple cutting edge can serve a diversity of functions. Expecting the lack of retouch to indicate a lack of tool diversity is not the hypothesis of a technologist. After all, even a basic familiarity with our tools today demonstrates that if we only paid attention to the simple cutting edge, and do not take into consideration the volume on which it is created, we would place burins, scissors, planes, and obviously all of the different types of knives in the same category.

The stage of the concretization of the support   During the stage of concretization, there is a trend toward normalization. The process of debitage is the response to the new demands of exclusive blade production (*tout laminaire*). In the case under consideration, the support becomes normalized, which is to say that it arrives at a stage of concretization, even of hypertely (extreme overdevelopment) as in the case of Chalcolithic blade production. This normalization applies above all to the prehensile part, it is this element that structures the support and as a result the knapped volume. There is, as we see below, an evolution of the modes of production toward the production of supports that come as close as possible to the eventual form of the tool, as will be the case in the debitage of Type F1 and F2. In the case under consideration the ergonomic demands related to the exploitation of new energies and gestures lead to supports with a particular silhouette.

It remains to explain, in terms of the dynamics of society, the rupture with the Yabrudian, as well as the rupture of the Yabrudian with the preceding Acheulean. Even though this is not our principal goal in this work, there are several paths for reflection.

The first is geographic. The Near Eastern phenomena of Acheulean,[30] Yabrudian, and Amudian with their variants, are limited within a geographic space that ranges from the Zagros Mountains in the north, the Euphrates in the East, and the steppe zone to the south. In terms of environment, there is no obvious fit

172   *The anthropological sense*

with the appearance and disappearance of these cultural phenomena. Similarly, explanations based on migration can be excluded, at risk of recreating a new *Out of Africa*.

The aspect worthy of consideration is at an evolutionary level. Contrary to the sense of geographic stability, we are within a dynamic of technological rupture and instability. We are thus not dealing with changes within a particular lineage. We must dissociate the transition from the Acheulean to the Yabrudean and the transition from the Yabrudian to the Amudian blade production. The first transition from Acheulean to Yabrudian takes place at an evolutionary level. In effect, the bifacial structures of the Acheulean have reached their stage of concretization. In other terms there is no longer the possibility of further structural evolution of the "biface" volume that relies on manual energy: it has reached its ultimate evolutionary point, for which reason a rupture is expected. In contrast, the second transition, from the Yabrudian to the Amudian, is unexpected. The Yabrudian appears as a technical solution apparently associated with the societal need to use new modes of prehension and as a result new energies and gestures. Is it because we are in an "energetic revolution" that blade production arrives at almost the same time as the Yabrudian retouched flake? Should one push the reflection further, in assuming that the stratigraphic uncertainty that we have emphasized between the Yabrudian and the Amudian is not in fact a stratigraphic problem but rather a reflection of our technical blindness that leaves us unable to explain this change? In reality, the Yabrudian and the Amudian are evolutionarily similar and thus potentially contemporary, each one being the expression of a different ergonomic solution: exclusively flake/tools as with the Yabrudian and the exclusively normalized blade/tool with the Amudian (Figure 3.5). Are we not faced with a new technical idea that is expressed in different ways with complimentary functional goals, rather than two evolutionarily successive ideas? Is it not because both the Yabrudian and the Amudian disappear that the Hummalian blade production develops? We think that the Yabrudian is a strategy to mediate between the debitage of poorly normalized supports and highly normalized tool volumes. On an evolutionary level, the Yabrudian is thus at the same level of evolution as the Amudian, even if the latter is its techno-functional opposite. The Amudian is another way of normalizing a support that is new and clearly different. Could these two approaches not

	normalization of the support by shaping		mixed normalization of the support flake by debitage/shaping (*façonnage*)/confection			normalization of the blade support	
	shaping (*façonnage*)	confection of transformative part	debitage of minimally normalized support	shaping (*façonnage*)	confection of transformative part	debitage of normalized support	confection of transformative part
Acheulean							
Yabrudian							
Amudian							

Figure 3.5 The modalities for normalizing supports according to the different technical facies. Acheulean: shaping and confection; Yabrudian: debitage and confection; Amudian: debitage.

The anthropological sense 173

be complementary? On the one hand the absence of structural exploitation of the potential of blades in the Amudian would seem logical as a first evolutionary stage, and at the same time could be accounted for by the possibility of realizing certain types of tools on "Yabrudian" flakes.

This association is only a working hypothesis. We need more sites and to find the same sequence in other parts of the Near East. In effect, the Amudian in its Levantine form does not appear to be present further to the east, in Syria, even though there is a blade production without retouch that appears to be associated with bifacially retouched scrapers. In this region of eastern Syria, the Yabrudian is present but is not associated with blades.

SECOND PHASE: THE HUMMALIAN AND THE BLADE LEVALLOIS, 200,000–150,000 BP

Blade production and associated tools During this phase, "all-blade" production continues, while the Yabrudian flake production disappears (Figure 3.4). But the blade industry has changed in terms of the tool assemblage. The blade has become the support for a range of distinct tools. Thus, one can distinguish more than 15 different variants. On the other hand, the structures of debitage have not changed, they are identical to those known from the Amudian.

In the Levant, the Hummalian or its Hayonim variant appears to follow the Amudian, and the situation is similar in the East, in the continental steppe zone— the regions of Palmyra and the El Kom Basin. The Hummalian *sensu stricto* seems to itself be followed by a phenomenon without retouch. As such, we may be dealing with an evolutionary lineage where only the structural potential of the blade is evolving.

Experimentation, combined with techno-functional analysis of these tools, has demonstrated that the retouch has a double objective. The first is to regularize the support of the desired tool. Blade production involves the knapping of an uninterrupted series of blades without intervening repreparation of the debitage surface. The knapper alters the debitage surface in the course of production to create the best configuration. The result of this process is the production of numerous blades per core, with a diminution of size in the order of 5 cm between the first and last blade produced, and products with very diverse morpho-technical criteria. There is not, as is the case in the Amudian, a specific goal of one or two types of products that orients the entire process. Debitage of Hummalian type—essentially of Type D2—is a less normalized production that offers products with a greater diversity of technical criteria, which allows for the selection of a type of support depending on the type of tool desired. As a result of this paradoxical specificity, the retouch becomes crucial for finalizing the desired silhouette. This is the reason for a stage of confection that can be significant and that can be applied to both the prehensile and transformative parts (Figure 3.6).

In summary, with this second phase, we are looking at an evolution of the blade lineage that, rather than refining its methods of production in order to more closely

174 *The anthropological sense*

| | normalization of the blade support by debitage | | |
	debitage of a normalized support	confection of the prehensile part	confection of the transformative part
Amudian			
Hummalian			

Figure 3.6 Modalities of normalizing supports according to the different technical facies. Amudian: debitage. Hummalian: debitage and confection.

approximate the ideal silhouette, is oriented to the exploitation of the laminar potential of blades. For the first time, one sees the development of an entire new range of specific tools connected to a unique method of prehension: the tang. Toward this end, the confection of supports goes beyond a simple functionalizing of the cutting edge because it makes it possible to obtain a new generation of tools that partially disappears with the blade debitage of Type F1/Levallois. This shift in the role of shaping is partly a result of an orientation of production during the Tabun D-Blady Early MP that follows the Hummalian period toward the same types of convergent tools, but in the case of the supports from debitage of Type F1/Levallois the prehensile part is not shaped by retouch. The function of debitage of Type F1/Levallois is to normalize the support, in both the prehensile and the transformative parts, to come as close as possible to the silhouette of the tool.

Debitage of Type F1 and tools of Hummalian type.[31]   The Hummalian-type debitage disappears along with its exclusive blade mode of production in favor of F1/Levallois debitage. If, as we will argue, this mode of debitage is in some ways a return to an aspect of the production of blades and of Hummalian type tools, it is also a rupture, as it includes the introduction of new types of supports such as so-called Levallois points and flakes. The novel products are shaped by lateral retouch that formerly was applied to blades. With the F1/Levallois debitage, one is witness to a breakthrough that does not correspond to an evolution. Everything changes, or at least almost everything!

The F1/Levallois debitage had already made its first appearance during the Acheulean[32] in the north of Syria and the El Kom Basin (unpublished personal observation). But the techno-functional character of this early use of Fl/Levallois debitage is clearly distinct from the industries of the F1/Levallois debitage found in the Tabun D-Blady Early MP that appears in the Levant after the Hummalian. If, as is too often the case, one maintains a simple dualism between non-Levallois/Levallois these critical techno-functional differences will be overlooked, and one will have the impression of a continuum. However, taking into account the techno-functional diversity that F1/Levallois debitage makes possible, it becomes apparent that there is not a phyletic relationship between the Levallois industries of the Acheulean and the Tabun D-Blady Early MP. In the case of the Levallois in the Acheulean, this is the production of large removals, with no control of the shape except for the elongation of the support. This elongation provides a profile that the bifacial forms in this context are not able to provide.

The anthropological sense   175

In the case of the Tabun D-Blady Early MP industries, which are present throughout the Middle East and in particular in the El Kom Basin, the F1/Levallois seems to "reprise" the convergent tools found in the Hummalian. In other terms, there is a shift in the support for the same category of tools. This shift is accompanied by a change in the lineage of the mode of production. One moves from the initial structural expression of blade production—D2—to F1/Levallois, which is the expression of the terminal stage of a lineage for the production of diversified removals. This thus suggests a rupture in terms of the evolutionary structure of production. On the other hand, the partial continuity in convergent tools indicates a structural evolution of the normalization of blade supports. To reiterate, the debitage of type F1/Levallois is an evolutionary step toward the normalization of supports. By introducing a spatial or territorial dimension, it is possible to distinguish two potential technological scenarios. The first scenario is strictly local. It is framed within a territorial continuity. F1/Levallois debitage, which is present at the end of the Acheulean, "survives" in refugia and subsequently redevelops, in a new form due to the impact of a range of Hummalian convergent tools, while also continuing to produce the specific tools that require a diversified production of type F1. The second scenario is initiated by populations exogenous to the Near East that have as technical baggage F1/Levallois debitage. In this case, the impact will be reversed, it will be these "exterior" populations who will adopt the local traditions, without requiring any transformation of their modes of production. This would suggest a simple technical enrichment that would also follow in the evolutionary direction: an increased integration of the different parts of the tool.

THIRD PHASE: SPORADIC BLADE PRODUCTION—LEVALLOIS
AND NON-LEVALLOIS, AFTER 150,000 YEARS AGO

Blade production and the associated tools   Rather than a proper phase, this is more of a case of sporadic occurrences of blade production (Figure 3.4). As we have already indicated, the data is limited. What we do know is that the modes of production are "reprised" in the identical state without any sign of evolution. This suggests multiple reinventions of the "all blade" (*tout luminaire*) and its modes of production without any offshoot. This sporadic and non-evolutionary repetition is likely indicative of a near absence of contact and/or diffusion of people, leading, as a result, to local reinvention and re-innovation and thus of relative autonomy of this Middle Eastern Levalloiso-Mousterian world. It is interesting to note that, once we have a chronostratigraphic sequence, as at the site of Umm el Tlel in Syria where there are 50 individualized archaeological layers, one realizes that this monotony is part of a broader picture. Among the 50 archaeological assemblages present at Umm el Tlel, more than 30 are distinct, although all use the debitage of Type F1. As a result, the sporadic appearance of blade production is only the expression of a supplementary diversity, certainly essentially distinctive, but belonging to the same pattern of change. These changes are clearly indicative of a far greater spatial mobility than is perceived based on the dichotomy F1/Levallois-D2/blade non-Levallois.

176   *The anthropological sense*

This mobility thus fits within the framework of the geographic extension of Levallois knapping. As for the blade industries, they remain at the same evolutionary stage without any change in the tools made on blades.

FOURTH PHASE: THE TRANSITION, 45,000/47,000–36,000

The tools   This fourth phase is usually designated as the phase of transition of the Early Upper Paleolithic (Figures 3.3, 3.4, and 3.7). These two terms signify a phase of change that, depending on the technical arguments for "apomorphy" or "plesiomorphy," is perceived as either an intermediate phase that is "half and half" in terms of change or as an initial phase leading toward something different.

What exactly are the predetermined supports for retouched tools?

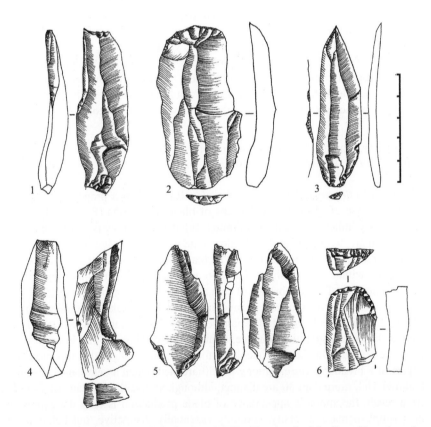

Figure 3.7   Umm el Tlel, central Syria. Level III2b: First level of the Transition phase between 42,000 and 35,000 years.

The anthropological sense 177

Predetermined supports:

- Novelties

  - o Blades
  - o Bladelets
  - o Elongated Levallois techno-points with a narrow base

- No longer produced

  - o Levallois techno-flakes
  - o Large and small Levallois techno-points with a wide base

Retouched tools:

- Novelties

  - o Typo-endscrapers and typo-burins
  - o Retouched blades—backed, pointed, and so on
  - o Retouched flakes

- No longer produced

  - o The various types of typo-scrapers: simple, double, convergent, and so on
  - o Nahr Ibrahim truncations
  - o Retouched Levallois points

Blades become the main predetermined support for retouched tools, with the exception of a few retouched flakes or "typo-sidescrapers." Despite the occasional presence of F1/Levallois debitage, oriented toward the production of elongated Levallois points with a narrow base, and of several blade products, the "typo-sidescrapers" are made on predetermining (preparation) flakes, or even on cores. Is this still the same tool? The structural difference between typo-sidescrapers on predetermined as opposed to those made on predetermining flakes applies *a priori* to the prehensile rather than the transformative part. In effect, because the transformative part is shaped by retouch, it can be similar regardless of the type of support. As a result, the fact that a predetermining flake is chosen as a support implies a less rigid modality of prehension, because the prehensile part is not predetermined. This does not imply that specific technical characters are not sought after in selecting the support.

The abandonment of the production of Levallois techno-flakes[33] imposes an *a posteriori* selection of the future tool supports. The choice of support is made among an assemblage of predetermining flakes that played a role in the realization of diverse predetermined removals. This implies a lack of emphasis on techno-functional criteria and signifies a weak constraint on the prehensile part.

For the endscraper and burin category of tools the situation is different, or even the inverse. They are henceforth almost exclusively made on blade supports. The prehensile part becomes uniform. As for the transformative parts, they remain

178 *The anthropological sense*

unchanged. Here again, this observation indicates very clearly that if there is a change, it applies above all to the prehensile part of the support, with an inevitable suite of functional consequences, which we elaborate on below. These observations converge on the fact that the crux of the change is the prehensile part of the supports. But from a structural perspective, what are these new tools?

In attempting to comprehend the emergence of new tools on a previously known support, we must return to the simultaneous disappearance of predetermined flakes and of the typo-sidescrapers that could lead to a sort of techno-functional "determinism." One might conclude that there cannot be typo-sidescrapers on blades. But this apparent correlation is false. In effect, the history of the typo-sidescrapers shows that all types of supports are possible: Acheulean and Micoquean bifacial pieces, Levallois, Discoid, and other predetermined techno-flakes, predetermining flakes, and blades were all retouched into type-sidescrapers. From a typological point of view the ensemble of these typo-sidescrapers varies in terms of a number of factors:

- The localization of retouch (simple, double, etc.)
- The orientation of convergence (symmetrical, asymmetrical, etc.)
- The different types of retouch, and the presence or absence of Quina retouch

In the *long term* (*temps long*), there thus does not exist an exclusive relationship between the type of support and the class of typo-sidescrapers. During each period, this type of tool is present on a different support. But why when blade production reappears in this fourth stage have the typo-sidescrapers fairly definitively disappeared? We can expand the question by asking if the disappearance of this tool type is accompanied by the termination of the functions associated with these tools, regardless of the type of support. If the response to this latter question is positive, it would mean that an entire suite of functions, that had existed for at least two million years suddenly disappear. This is hard to imagine because this would imply the existence of a deterministic relationship between a class of tools and a function. However, the history of techniques shows that the same function can be filled by different tools and that the same type of tool may be used for different functions.[34] As a result, one can logically conclude that the disappearance of the typo-sidescraper is not the result of the loss of the functional objectives associated with this tool. These same objectives were very surely filled by the new tools made on other mineral materials, osseous or vegetal materials, which implies new types of transformative contacts and new gestures.

On the other hand, the concomitant augmentation of the typo-endscrapers and the typo-burins is not synonymous with an intensive specialization of existing functions. The augmentation of these types might suggest new functions for identical transformative parts that are now on different supports, supports that conceal a still unused structural potential.

In this fashion, we avoid the apory that results from us endlessly asking whether it is the endscraper that led to the blade or vice versa.

The anthropological sense   179

The novelty is the integration of two long-known technical elements that had long been separate: the transformative part of typo-endscrapers and typo-burins with the blade support as a predetermined support. As a result, a new range of tools would develop. It is thus the structural capacity of the blade, until this time underexploited, that will be revealed through the integration of a new spectrum of transformative parts. This utilization of unexplored capacity should not be associated with a cognitive factor. Remember that during the Howieson's Poort of South Africa, although we are already in the presence of *Homo sapiens sapiens*, the blades are limited to the fabrication of a single type of tool or more precisely of one element of a tool, as one finds during the Upper Paleolithic of the Middle East and the Kebaran.

On the level of the evolution of techniques, we must therefore reformulate the reasons for the development of this fourth phase. The blade, as a predetermined support, presents a structural potential that, once it is fully exploited, allows for the appearance of new tools. At the same time, these novelties are accompanied by the definitive disappearance of a large number of diversified tools but certainly not the disappearance of their functions. From a historic perspective, what is the structural significance of such a breakthrough, such a revolution in the tool assemblage? To explain an event of this magnitude, it is necessary to consider the use of a new energy, or at the very least, the progressive exploitation of a new energy: kinetic energy, an energy that over time is generalized and affects all functions.

As a result of their structure, blades allow for the emergence and continuity of a series of technical characteristics. The first group consists of emergent characteristics:

- A specific zone for handling (*maintien*), such as a tang, allows for multiple modes of prehension, which generates new gestures, new modes of operation (*fontionnement*), and as a result new functions.
- New transformative parts create a new function and new modes of operation.
- The increase of potential energy through the elongation of the techno-functional unit designated as the part for the transmission of energy, situated between the prehensile and transformative parts.
- A new energy: kinetic energy, linked to the length of the part that transmits energy and the mode of operation.

The second group consists of characteristics with the potential for continuity:

- The same zones for handling as on flakes, for example, backing.
- The same types of transformative parts as those present on flakes.

The exploitation of an energetic potential: an exteriorized transformative part   The choice of blades, with their functional partitioning that opposes and distances the prehensile and transformative parts along the axis of the support,

180 *The anthropological sense*

as the sole support for tools has the consequence of putting into play the part that connects these elements: the part for the transmission of energy. While this part has the potential to connect the transformative and prehensile parts, it can also distance them. It is in this potential for distancing that the possibility for kinetic energy develops. To paraphrase Leroi-Gourhan, who spoke of the appearance of the tool as a phenomenon of exteriorization in relation to the body, we think that, in the framework of the evolution of techniques, the potential of the blade allows for the exteriorization of the transformative part with respect to the hand, through the intermediary of the part for the transmission of energy which creates the potential for a new energy (Figure 3.8).

A new realm of technical development is now thrown open with all its fantastic and innovative consequences. But this technical revolution at the same time marks the end of the "all-blade" debitage! In effect, the "all-blade" debitage is the last production based on the mineral world. Metallurgy will follow.[35]

The exteriorization of the transformative part of the tool in relation to the prehensile part does not appear suddenly during the fourth phase. Recall that already during the Hummalian, more than half of the tools on blades are convergent tools, evidence of this exteriorization. But these tools, although convergent and hafted along their morphological axis (Figure 3.9) are characterized by transformative parts that are lateral and not axial, thus limiting any potential augmentation of the part that transmits energy. As a consequence, this particularity of Hummalian tools has a functional loss.

In the framework of a continuous evolutionary process of exclusive blade debitage, this fourth phase could have followed the second phase without interruption. In effect, whether in terms of the tools or the modes of production, strictly based on a techno-logic, following the Hummalian, we should have observed the

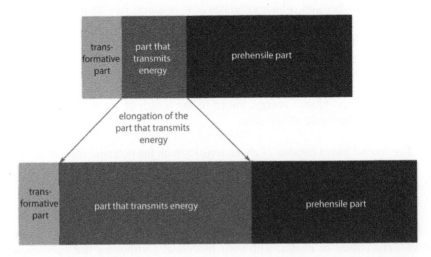

Figure 3.8 The phenomenon of the exteriorization of the transformative part in relation to the prehensile part.

The anthropological sense 181

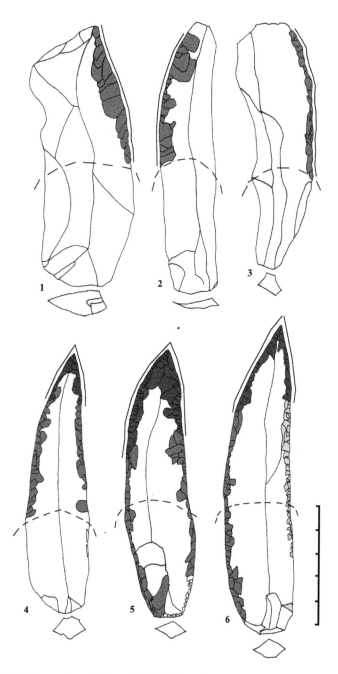

Figure 3.9 The Hummalian of Umm el Tlel: 1–3: tools with lateral retouch; 4–6: convergent tools.

182 *The anthropological sense*

development of new tools that explore the structural potential of blades, but also, in response to this evolution, we should have observed a modification of the modes of production trending toward an increased normalization of the supports. However, these changes did not take place.

The appearance of the F1/Levallois knapping after the Hummalian might be at the root of this halt in the evolution of the blade production lineage over the course of tens of thousands of years, as a result of the capacity of F1/Levallois debitage to produce diversity. Inversely, the eclipse of the F1/Levallois debitage in the fourth phase of the evolution of the blade production lineage is the result of the inability of F1/Levallois debitage to exclusively produce blade supports, and thus to exploit the potential for energetic development offered by these products.

On a structural level, the confrontation of these two systems of knapping is unequal. The blade production is at its abstract phase of development while the F1/Levallois is at the apogee of its lineage[36] (Figure 3.10). The F1/Levallois debitage has the structural capacity, as a result of its normalized products, to come very close to the technical characteristics of the desired tools without further modification, but also to produce a technically diverse range of normalized supports. Normalization and diversity are the characteristics of F1/Levallois debitage. This mode of debitage made possible a better route toward the normalization of blade supports by reducing the phase of modification found on Hummalian blades (Figure 3.11). Moreover, F1/Levallois debitage made it possible to transfer the lateral retouch of blades to a larger range of removals: flakes, points, and their variants.

This structural potential of supports of Type F1 is situated within the framework of the evolution of the supports for tools, independently of their mode of production. The normalization of supports and the potential diversity of the modalities of exploitation (and thus of the resulting supports) within a structure of Type F1 allows the tools to evolve through improved integration of their functional elements. From our perspective, between the Hummalian and the facies of type Blady Early MP, there exists a rupture in terms of production and an evolutionary continuity in the criteria for the normalization of supports. However, with the fourth phase, the rupture applies as much to the tool as to the modes of production. It is also worth emphasizing that the methods of debitage of Type F1/Levallois, utilized during the final phases of the Levalloiso-Mousterian, produce supports that are the opposite of those produced during the Blady Early MP phase, which explains this impression of a rupture.[37]

To summarize, the new tools are, in our opinion, evidence of a choice of a type of energy made possible by blade production. This energy was systematized, thus modifying the panoply of existing tools, resulting in the creation of new tools that conserve the same functions. It is important to emphasize another point regarding the panoply of tools. In effect, if one considers the ensemble of sites belonging to the Transition in the Levant, Negev, and eastern Syria, the quasi-totality of Upper Paleolithic tools is already present. The majority of these tools are invented sporadically across a large territory, adopting a new energetic potential such that each combination of tools is the reflection of local particularity, evidence at once of a single cultural-technical zone and many sociocultural zones.

The anthropological sense 183

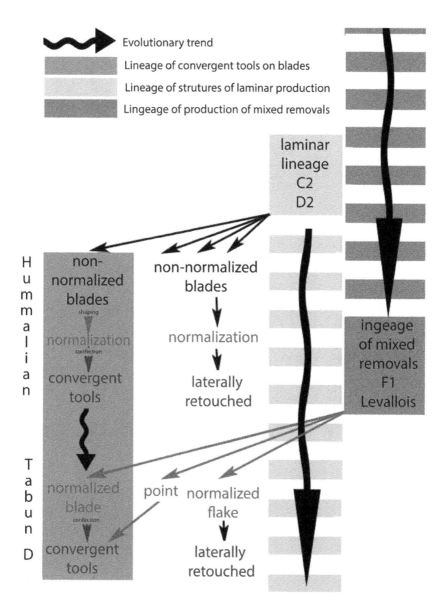

Figure 3.10 The laminar volumetric structures represent the initial evolutionary stages (C2 and D2) in contrast to debitage of type F1/Levallois, which is the last evolutionary stage of the lineage of the production of diverse flakes. There thus exists a discontinuity in the structures of production that is not found in the structures of the tools where one sees a structural evolution of supports.

184 *The anthropological sense*

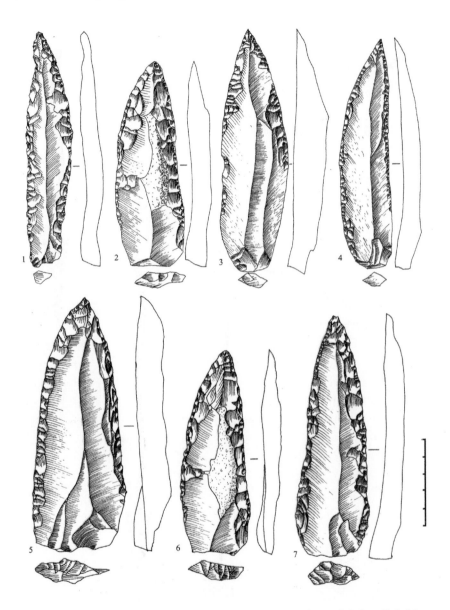

Figure 3.11 Umm el Tlel, Syria. 1–4: Hummalian convergent pieces; 5–7: Levallois-Mousterian pieces of Tabun D facies.

Blade production From an evolutionary perspective, the exclusive blade production initially appears in debitage of Types C2 and D2, identical to the preceding laminar industries. This reinvention is explained by the structural incapacity of the F1/Levallois mode of production to exclusively produce blades. Nonetheless,

The anthropological sense 185

the debitage of Type F1 does not disappear. In a general fashion, it is present when elongated Levallois typo-points with a narrow base are desired. However, in certain cases, these typo-points are produced within the debitage of Type E2,[38] as at Boker Tachtit (Marks and Volkman, 1983). In this context the debitage of Type F1/Levallois is absent.

The historical reality of this process is far from being cut and dry. In effect, one finds multiple technical solutions. In this regard, the Intermediate Paleolithic sequence of Umm el Tlel is very instructive (Boëda and Muhesen, 1993; Boëda and Bonilauri, 2006). From the base of the sequence upward, an initial industry (III2b') follows the final Mousterian level, marked by a clear technical rupture. The debitage of Unit III2b', produced using Type C2 and D2 debitage structures, consists exclusively of blades and a range of classic tool types that do not include Levallois typo-points, which might explain the absence of debitage of Type F1/Levallois. The two subsequent industries—III 2a' and II base'—are characterized by the use of two debitage structures: F1/Levallois and C2/D2. Although the Levallois debitage is associated with typo-points, this is also the source of a large part of the blade and particularly bladelet production[39] (Beoda and Bonilauri, 2006). Another assemblage that is not correlated stratigraphically—of Qualta type—attests to the exclusive use of debitage of type F1/Levallois: the typo-points and the blade removals are produced within the same sequence.

The stratigraphic sequence of Boker Tachtit in the Negev is equally informative. Level 1 at the base of the sequence attests to a double production, F1/Levallois and C2/D2, while the three overlying strata (Levels 2–4) consisting of the same range of tools based on typo-points is made using debitage of Types C2, D2, and E2, while debitage of type F1/Levallois has disappeared.

The situation at Boker Tachtit is thus the opposite of what we observe at Umm el Tlel. The presence of debitage of Type F1/Levallois is often perceived as an archaic trait. We think that it is preferable to view all of these variants, from a historical perspective, as indications of the diffusion and acceptance of new ideas that undergo the cultural filter distinctive to each group, evidence of a past and present technical alterity. These responses cover the range of technical possibility, evidence of both innovation and conservatism, which eventually are reconciled in the fifth phase. If in some regions, such as the Negev, one observes a "history" that follows the course of evolution, tending toward a greater interaction of the structural elements of the core to better achieve the objective, the case of Umm el Tlel demonstrates that populations can choose invention, complementarity, or improvement.

The means of blade production   In general, blades are produced by internal or partially tangential percussion with a soft stone, identical to the means used in the production of Type F1.

The bladelet phenomenon: its tools and production   The existence of bladelet production has only recently been widely recognized for periods prior to the Upper Paleolithic *sensu stricto* in the Middle East. The final phase of the Levallois-Mousterian demonstrates, in a few rare sites, a distinct debitage of bladelets on a limited range

186 *The anthropological sense*

of cores. This is no longer the case during the so-called Transition period where the production of bladelets becomes frequent, with percentages[40] that can exceed some Aurignacian and Ahmarian industries. The recognition of the role of bladelets in industries dating to the Transition period is due in part to the numerous sites in the El Kom Basin in Syria, particularly Umm el Tlel (Figure 3.12; Boëda and Bonilauri, 2006) as well as in Jordan at Tor Sadaf (Fox and Coinman, 2004).[41]

Blade and bladelet production appear with the fourth phase of blade production and not beginning with the fifth phase as is usually claimed. How can this correlation be explained from the techno-logical perspective? Chronologically, each

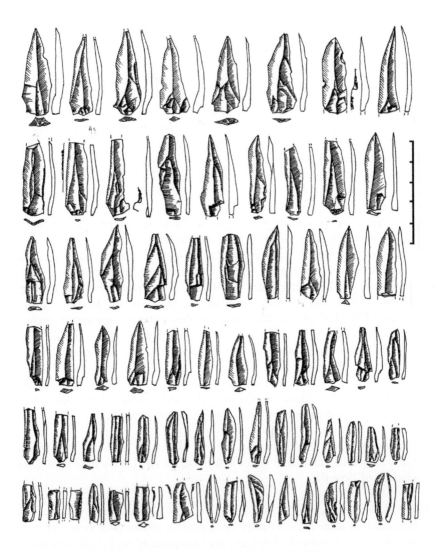

Figure 3.12 Umm el Tlel, central Syria. Bladelets from Level c.II base.

time that the phenomenon of exclusive blade production appears with a diversity of retouched tools on blades, bladelet production is present. There thus exists an undeniable structural correlation between these two modes of production and the diversity of tools.

In the discussion of the Hummalian, we mentioned the presence of bladelets produced by specific modes of debitage without including a description. In the case of the Hummalian of Umm el Tlel, the situation appears considerably more complex than a simple dichotomy between blades and bladelets. In reality, the assemblage includes all the dimensions of blades in the range between 15 and 4 cm in length and 2 and 0.5 cm in width. Within the assemblage, the smallest bladelets are in the minority but these small bladelets are the products of specific cores and are made the object of particular goals. There thus exist true bladelets. In terms of modification, we note a clear distinction. The smallest blades and bladelets (lengths less than 5 cm) are never retouched. The lack of retouch on these pieces is in sharp contrast to the larger blades.

The "unretouched" character of the bladelets is also found in the Transition industries in eastern Syria, but apparently not in Jordan. When we consider the shape of the bladelets from the Hummalian in comparison to those from the Transition industry, a noticeable difference emerges. For the bladelets from the Transition industries, it is clear that the goal is the production of rectilinear bladelets with convergent edges. These technical criteria are not found in the Hummalian bladelets.

In terms of the function of the bladelets, use wear data is rare and applies only to the bladelets from the Transition industries. The small number of studies available indicate a hafting on the axis of the bladelet and the use of the distal part and the adjacent lateral edge; this techno-functional intention has a corollary in the choice of the methods of debitage, as we will see (Figure 3.13; Boëda and Bonilauri, 2006). Several bladelets, in a small percentage, are used laterally in the same way as the Aurignacian and Kebaran bladelets at Umm el Tlel.

The axial attachment[42] of the bladelets during this fourth phase transforms into a mainly lateral attachment beginning with the fifth phase. This observation applies equally to blades. In effect, during the fifth phase, certain blades will be attached

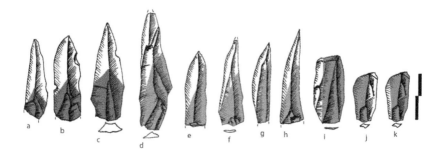

Figure 3.13 Umm el Tlel, central Syria—traces of hafting. a–h: hafting along the morphological axis of the bladelet; i–k: lateral hafting (Boëda and Bonilauri, 2006).

188   The anthropological sense

laterally—in relation to their morphological axis—to achieve a variety of functions. This similar evolution of function confirms the complementarity between the blade and bladelet, within a sort of structural coevolution.

From a different perspective, could one not suggest that the bladelets be considered to be a phase of miniaturization that anticipates the culmination of the lineage of elongated products? This phenomenon of miniaturization involves the support, the bladelet, and not the composite tool made of bladelets. On the other hand, this phenomenon is correlated with composite tools and the utilization of new energy. Of course, the history of bladelet production cannot be reduced to such a linear scheme. The field data indicate that histories vary from one location to another. But, in the long term, one cannot avoid being astonished that an evolutionary history that follows an inverse trajectory is not found. In sum, this signifies that although a coevolution of humans and technology does exist, there is also an evolutionary direction [*sens*] and a historical direction, and that one must distinguish between an "autonomous technological order" that is the source of invention, and the contexts of invention and innovation that are at the scale of the individual (Gille, 1978).

The relatively classic modes of production are abstract structures of Types C2 and D2 (Figure 3.14) and the technique of knapping is a nonexclusive tangential percussion. The debut of bladelet knapping is achieved based on initial structures, which is indicative of a local Middle Eastern invention.

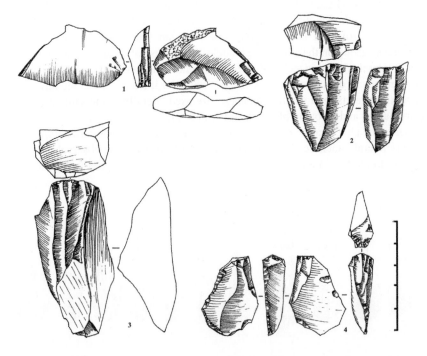

Figure 3.14 Bladelet cores. Umm el Tlel, Syria, level c.II base: 1, 3. Type D2 on a flake, and Type E2. 3. Type C2 on a fragment of block 4. Qualta, Syria: Type D2 on a flake.

The anthropological sense 189

Summary of the fourth phase   When one considers the ensemble of data relevant to blade and bladelet production, we are confronted by a paradox. The duration of the fourth phase is in the order of several millennia across a wide geographic range, stretching from Turkey in the north to the Sinai in the south, while the extension to the east is not known.[43] Whatever the age of the site, whether it is early or late, the structures of knapping are always at the same initial evolutionary stage—C2 and D2. This is consistent with repeated local invention in contrast to the classic diffusionist schema following which one distinguishes between a center of invention—the earliest context—and its subsequent hegemonic extension. The accumulation of evolutionary data—concerning production and techno-functional characteristics—demonstrates that the scenario, if in fact there is only one scenario, does not fit the classic schema. We are thus confronted with the phenomenon of a radical substitution of one assemblage of tools by another that is completely innovative, with all the imaginable ergonomic constraints, and with heterogeneous means of production. This heterogeneity is expressed whether or not a new lineage of production, exclusive blade, is adopted, beginning, in terms of techno-logic, in its abstract forms.

The sequence of Umm el Tel perfectly illustrates this phenomenon. It offers at once the appearance of the radical adoption of new tools, along with the total disappearance of earlier types of tools, while conserving the residual trace of the mode of production. This residual trace reveals different choices: novel and/or adaptive. For example, Levallois debitage remains a structuring element in certain transitional levels, but it is never exclusive even when it is used to produce blades. On the other hand, in the same sequence, the earliest industry is entirely non-Levallois, because this type of debitage only appears later in the sequence! Thus, there is not a historical logic to the phenomenon of blade production.

It is as if we are dealing with a successfully completed increase in functional complexity alongside a structural complexity of production that still must pass through its evolutionary stages. The fact that the stages of the blade lineage are the same each time, signifies that we are not looking at the eradication of a local population, but quite the opposite, there is a phenomenon of borrowing from specific modalities for each cultural group that adopted this new ergonomic structure.

In any case, the phenomenon of the so-called Transition is not a transition at all. It is the debut of a techno-functional upheaval with an adaptation of production that naturally follows the universal evolutionary stages from abstract to concrete. This "normalized" evolution is socioculturally very important because it is evidence of definitive disruptions on the level of technique.

THE FIFTH PHASE

The fifth phase is extremely rich in historical events which deserve a long discussion (Figure 3.3–3.4). We will limit ourselves here to the most important elements from the perspective of the evolution and history of techniques.

190　*The anthropological sense*

The modes of production　The first important point is that the modes of "exclusive-blade and bladelet" production remain the almost only modes of production, at least in the Middle East. Nonetheless, we note in a number of cases the sporadic utilization of the knapping of non-predetermined flakes.

The principle mixed knapping methods, other than those on the blade production lineage, disappear definitively. This abandonment of modes of debitage is evidence of an evolutionary dynamic distinct from the external social milieu. New technical lineages could have appeared, but this was not the case. Here again, the examples of Asia[44] or South America demonstrate other possibilities.

The second point confirms Simondon's evolutionary theories. The concrete structures of Type F2 develop rapidly and endure. However, the abstract solutions of Type D2 do not totally disappear. On the contrary, on a historical level, these modes of knapping persist in numerous cases.

Just as rapidly as the advent of the concrete forms, one sees the development of the technical means of production. This is a point we have previously touched on. Remember that one sees for the first time in the history of techniques a succession of modes of production that can be summarized in triptych: direct marginal percussion/indirect percussion/pressure flaking, trending toward the ever-increasing normalization of blade and bladelet supports. For pressure flaking, one can even talk of quasi-normalized products. In techno-logical terms, with regard to the process of production used during the fourth phase—direct marginal percussion—one could say that the blade production system reached its concrete phase early on. The social need trended toward a greater normalization of supports and the volumetric structure of Type F2 made it possible to respond to this evolution by modifying only the means of production. There is no structural change in the knapped volume. This evolution toward an increased normalization is in itself an evolutionary trend that transcends the long timescale of prehistory. This trend becomes more evident toward the end of the Pleistocene and the Holocene, but the tendency toward normalization applies to all the bifacial and mixed flake lineages. This normalization is accompanied by a development of the broader context associated with the artifact. In effect, the lithic artifact becomes one of the elements of the tool. Like an internal combustion engine without fuel, the stone tool is integrated into the functional complexity of tools by becoming an element of the associated milieu of the artifact. The evolution of production stops. The cores of Types F2 and F1, in becoming the totality of the worked primary material are in a certain sense naturalized.[45] The function of the core is completely fulfilled, there is nothing left except to perpetuate it. But in parallel to this stagnation, the tool continues to follow its evolution. The blade and the bladelet, while continuing to fulfill the same functions, will become the subject of the application of new energetic principles.

The exploitation of an energetic potential: a transmitting part of the artifact that is individualized　On a structural level, during the fifth phase, we move toward a stability of the transformative parts[46] and a modification of the part for the transmission of energy and the prehensile part (Figure 3.15).

The anthropological sense 191

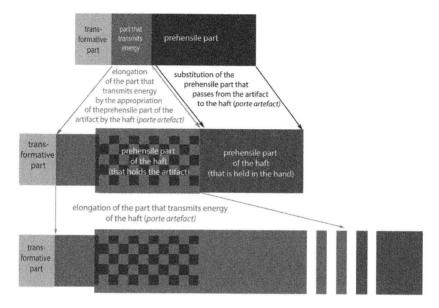

Figure 3.15 Substitution of the prehensile part through the phenomenon of exteriorization and elongation of the part that transmits energy.

The phenomenon of exteriorization   The phenomenon of exteriorization is a conceptual idea that applies to the structure of each blade. This capacity for exteriorization implies the existence of a part for the transmission of energy that itself will transcend the blade artifact to extend into the armature [*porte artefact*]. A consequence of this transcendence is a change in the functional status of the prehensile part of the artifact, which had also been the prehensile part of the tool, but which now becomes a part for the transmission of energy. The prehensile part of the tool is thus definitively exteriorized (Figure 3.16). The prehensile part of the new tools belongs definitively to the armature.

In these conditions, the part for the transmission of energy of an entire category of tools, in the strict sense of the term, will be made of composite material: vegetal, animal, bitumen, and so on with all the associated complications in the transmission of energy. The new part for the transmission of energy will consist of what formerly were both the prehensile and transmitting parts of the lithic artifact as well as a greater or lesser part of the armature.

Depending on the type of task involved and the necessary mechanical energy, the part for the transmission of energy will present a degree of variability that will depend on the mechanical properties of the utilized materials and/or their form, but also on the position of the artifacts in the prehensile part of armature (Figure 3.17). The exploitation of the structural potential of this new construction of the tool will mostly be realized during what we consider the fifth phase of the development of

192 *The anthropological sense*

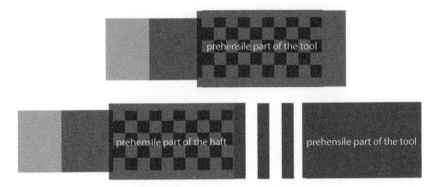

Figure 3.16 New positioning of the prehensile part in relation to the length and the part that transmits energy.

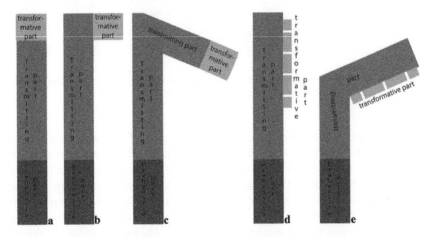

Figure 3.17 Modification of the qualitative characteristics of the part for the transmission of energy and modification of the implantation of the transformative part.

blade production. The lithic artifact can be positioned in the prehensile part on the morphological axis of the tool (Figure 3.17a) or on the contrary, parallel to this axis (Figure 3.17b and c), which is called lateral prehension. In the context of lateralized prehension the lithic artifact, specifically the blade, is no longer utilized along its morphological axis. This critical observation emphasizes above all the change in the status of the lithic artifact and the constitution of a new range of tools that can be designated as tools with multiple lithic artifacts (Figure 3.17d and e). As a result of this change in status, the blade becomes a transformable element that can be broken down by fragmentation. One could say that there is a structural transfer of the characteristics of the blade to a composite ensemble that extends and reduces its characteristics and in particular the potential energy. The blade becomes a sort of reservoir of raw material, the volume of which is structured to furnish a part of the desired

The anthropological sense 193

technical elements. Thus, the development of bladelet production is the best response for tools with multiple and identical lithic artifacts. This potential fragmentation of the blade, which is within the framework of the evolution of tools, does not signify the abandonment of its "classic" structural potential. This is what accounts for the maintenance of blade production rather than its substitution by bladelet production.

In other words, either the blade remains the structuring element of the tool or it loses this role, as in the case of a composite tool. This does not prevent the blade from continuing to bear the transformative part that is essential to the functioning of the tool.

In the framework of this double possibility, the means of production evolve, trending toward a greater normalization of the support, which, toward its final phase with the adoption of pressure flaking, can reach a virtual standardization.[47] This evolution of the means of production takes place without any modification of the structure of the core, which has reached its concrete stage.

This exteriorization of the transformative part, following the development of the part for the transmission of energy, leads to the emergence of an entire range of tools and will continue to develop during this fifth phase. The stone artifact becomes in and of itself an object with multiple facets, whether a tool or an element of a tool. The latter case certainly existed sporadically in the course of the history of techniques, but it always took the form of an aborted history. In contrast, during this fifth phase, there is not an "evolutionary" halt. Globally, the evolution, whether at the level of the systems of production or tools, takes place without a generalized phase of interruption[48] as is the case in the third phase.

This fifth phase culminates with the utilization of a new material and thus of new tools capable of developing new energies. As expected, the first metal tools will be replicas of stone tools. A new cycle of evolution begins, based on the utilization of this new material that allows for the creation of new tools capable of developing new energies. All this is *déjà vu*. The direction of evolution must always be stated as plural: the directions of evolution, consisting of laws and cycles.

Notes

1 This diversity is likely to be found in another technical realm that must be associated, the vegetal world (Forestier, 2010).
2 Leroi-Gourhan did not undertake a structural analysis of objects but rather remained focused on morphology. He classified forms of objects based on the constraints of operational gestures. The tool is constructed as the result of the structural constraints of gestures. In reality, Leroi-Gourhan did not develop lineages of objects. Rather he created lineages of operational gestures within which he placed the different forms of objects. The famous figure from *La Geste et La Parole* (Leroi-Gourhan, 1965: 108), where one finds, among other objects, a chopper, biface, Levallois flake, blade, and a metal knife, provides a perfect illustration. What connects these objects is the operational gesture. It is not necessary to see a simple sequence of forms but rather a succession of forms that are structured as a function of the same operational gesture that is independent of the material that is cut by the tool. There have been numerous objections to this point of view based on the criticism that it confounds different uses and thus artificially creates a trend or tendency. But in fact, contrary to what one might think, Leroi-Gourhan does not propose a technical history of cutting tools. For him, this classification is justified because it is outside history. It is not constituted by technological continuity. In effect,

194 *The anthropological sense*

as Simondon (1958) stated: the same function can correspond to different lineages of objects. It thus remains necessary to avoid compounding function and social usage. One relates to technology and thus indicates a tendency. The other relates to a social reality. The shift in analytical perspective through the adoption of a structural analysis of objects avoids this controversy. If an object is an adaptive response to a range of constraints, including among others the gesture, it is only by considering the structure and thus the functional synergy of the constitutive elements that we gain access to a technologic reading that is capable of accounting for an evolutionary process.

3 The notion of *tendance* in Leroi-Gouhan's writing establishes a relationship between the tool and the function within an adaptive framework, following which the earliest tools are the least well-adapted (Leroi-Gourhan, 1943). This notion of adaptation is subjective. It emanates from a utilizer who is dealing with objects that are exterior to his memory. This notion of adaptation is not operational in the context of the deep time of prehistory. It can only work if one dispenses with the perspective of the utilizer!

4 Simondon writes of a technical essence "that remains stable across the evolutionary lineage, and not only stable, but also productive of progressive structuration" (translated from Simondon, 1958: 43). As a result, "The essence is not a static invariant, it is an internal dynamic of concretization (translated from Guchet, 2005: 2012).

5 Deleuze (1969) writes of a *logique du sens*.

6 It is extremely interesting to study this discourse within the framework of prehistory, where the particularly long periods of time and the rare memory traces that we still retain lead to the development of a range of discourses, including those that consider the objects as dead and lacking memory. From this perspective, valid typological classifications can be based on any criteria, as long as these identify differences. The significance of these differences finds its explanation outside of the object. One can imagine the deductions or more to the point the paradigms that can result. We can cite, for example, the major confusion that results from such a conception for an object such as the biface: Acheulean cultures are seen emerging at the four corners of the earth from the moment that a biface is present, and the maps of diffusion trace this culture across the world! It is as though, from a medical perspective, the appearance of a pimple was synonymous with chicken pox and the distribution of pimples around the world signified the migration of a carrier. Any real doctor who heard such an argument would treat it as quackery! One can also see the self-satisfied discourse of those who see in technical evolution the irrepressible ascendance of the human lineage and its apex, us, *Homo sapiens*, or in a similar vein the advocates of technical progress, who predict a better world!

7 We must remain cautious regarding this locality as very little has been published on the lithic artifacts.

8 With all the ideological and methodological biases that result from our in-capacity to perceive.

9 In the sense of laminar product.

10 The term "societal" is overly vague. Nonetheless, it connects to a causality that is exterior to the object, for which the structure, through its capacity to respond, will be transformed. As we will see later, the option of all blade production emerges as the necessary structural response to unblock new gestures, new energies.

11 We have previously evoked an industry dating to the Pleistocene/Holocene transition in South America that is named *Itaparica*, which produces tools that are longer than they are wide designated as *"lesmas"* (Fogaça and Lourdeau, 2008; Lourdeau, 2010). On a morphological level, these products are blades, but these blades are obtained following a long process of modifying flakes. These elongated supports are thus subject to stages of shaping, leading to a range of tools. It is interesting to note that, on the one hand, the production of elongated supports on which different transformative parts are realized is not specific to blades and, on the other hand, the choice of shaping rather than debitage to produce this form has the consequence of blocking all evolutionary potential of the modes of production. In effect, the production of blade tools will disappear.

The anthropological sense 195

12 Keep in mind that at this site the Amudian level is 3 m thick, which weakens the strength of this hypothesis. Nonetheless, it remains the case that at Tabun and Qesem, as at Yabrud, there exists a blade phenomenon that is interstratified with the Yabrudian. In the case of Yaburd and Abri Zummofen, it seems that this phenomenon is limited to specific levels, but this remains unclear.

13 We do not consider the blade industry of Hayonim to be Hummalian as proposed by the authors. Although there exists a very strong similarity in the mode of debitage as well as in the typological composition of the assemblage, in our opinion this suggests that these industries are derived from a common antecedent. In effect, having had the opportunity to analyze more than 500 Hummalian pieces from Level Ia at Hummal (Besançon et al., 1982) we are led to question whether there is in fact such a strong similarity between Hayonim Level F and E base and Level Ia at Hummal (Boëda, 1995b, 1997).

14 This assemblage was collected and sampled beginning in 1982 and 1983 and not in 1980 when the stratigraphy was first described. As a result, this context is not mentioned in the publications by Besançon and Hours (Besançon et al., 1982; Hours, 1982). However, it was identified beginning in 1982, the date when the first samples were taken. The pieces and the bags that contain them are marked as coming from Level VIb or 6b, 1982 and 1983. Subsequently, this ensemble was not made the subject of any specific publication because due to its stratigraphic position, defined at the time as belonging to the base of complex VI, it was attributed to the final phases of the Levalloiso-Mousterian, which was already well represented in the adjoining Levels III, IV, and V. However, the conversations that I had with L. Copeland confirmed that this Level VI b had been considered, from the beginning, as possibly relating to the transition to the Upper Paleolithic.

15 R.C.P. 438: L'Homme et le milieu au Proche-Orient, directed by P. Sanlaville.

16 The unpublished study that we were able to undertake on this material in 1981 found a production of Levallois laminar removals but also Levallois points and quadrangular elongated flakes. Some of the laminar elements are retouched but they do not show the same diversity found in Hummalian tools. The ensemble of pieces also includes facetted platforms, which is not the case for the Hummalian.

17 Following a survey undertaken in 2004 in the two regions of Palmyra and El Kom, we found a lithic assemblage in stratigraphic context at the site of Kaféine, overlain on the surface by several Levallois cores. This thus is *a priori* an industry anterior to the Levallois industries.

18 We will only briefly mention the frequent error made in equating a Levallois product with a Levallois mode of debitage. Some authors have recommended not using the designation "Levallois point" for pieces that result from another mode of debitage (Meignen, 2007). We propose two options: either distinguish as we have between typo-Levallois points that were not made with Levallois flaking from techno-Levallois points that are the product of Levallois debitage. Alternatively, one can use the terms points of Type D3, E2, and F2.

19 We could have also illustrated this problem with the debitage of type E1—discoidal.

20 These are nonetheless different terms that refer to the same phenomenon: The reappearance of blade production and the production of tools of Upper Paleolithic type.

21 This term has been used in the context of the stratigraphic sequences for the sites of the El Kom Basin and Palmyra. In effect, these industries that are situated between a classic Levallois-Mousterian and an Ahmarian or an Aurignacian are too differentiated to be included under the classic term "Transition."

22 A term used in evolutionary biology to refer to a trait that is different from the ancestral state.

23 A term used in evolutionary biology to refer to an ancestral trait.

24 An Ahmarian industry has been dated at Kebara Unit IV-III to 42–40,000 years ago (Bar Yosef et al., 1996) It is thus contemporary with the so-called Transitional Industries of the Negev found at Boker Tachtit (Marks, 1983a, b).

25 However, these industries do not occupy the same areas. During the period 30,000/20,000 years ago we can contrast a Levantine Aurignacian zone found at sites

196 *The anthropological sense*

such as Ksar Aqil (Mellars and Tixier, 1989) and an Ahmarian zone in the Negev and Sinai as has been demonstrated at the sites of Boker Tachtit (Marks, 1983a and b) and Abu Noshra I and II (Phillips, 1994). Only at the site of Umm el Tlel, located in central Syria, is there evidence of real co-existence, in the same locality, of Ahmarian and Aurignacian industries (Ploux and Soriano, 2003).

26 The notion of bladelets is always subjective as it is defined in relation to the blade products. In this case, the metric differences are such that one can qualify this as bladelet production. In other cases, these bladelets would be considered blades, if they were associated with the production of much smaller blades.

27 This is not really a structural innovation as the structures of bladelet debitage are strictly identical to those of blade production, with the same stages of evolution. With bladelet production it is not the mode of production that is innovative, the innovation rests in the bladelet itself.

28 In the case of Umm el Tlel, bladelet production represents 30% of the predetermined supports in the transitional horizons. This situation has also been described in Jordan at Tor Sadaf (Fox and Coinman, 2004, Coinman and Fox, 2000).

29 One finds a small number of bifacial pieces in the Yabrudian, of which some have the same shape as the earlier bifaces. But their low frequency, when compared to the high frequency of bifaces in earlier stages, indicates that these bifacial pieces and/or bifaces are no longer the same tools.

30 Here, 100% of the tools are on shaped supports.

31 For the sake of simplicity, we combine under the term "Hummalian" all of the exclusively laminar assemblages that include a stage of confection with the goal of producing a large range of tools of which some are convergent.

32 This is found in northern Syria and designated as the Samoukian of Nahr el Kebir (Copeland and Hours, 1979) and Défaïen of the Orontes (Besançon et al., 1978). Levallois debitage is also found in the final phase of the Acheulean in the region of El Kom in central Syria. These industries are considered to be the final Acheulean of Samoukian facies (Hores, 1986). Levallois debitage is also known in Lebanon at Ras Beyrouth (Fleisch and Sanlaville, 1969) and at Naamé (Fleisch, 1970) in its Levallois-Mousterian form. In these two cases their chrono-stratigraphic position, in contact with the Tyrrhenian deposits, appears to be similar to the position observed at Adloun where there are Acheulo-Yabrudian and Amudian industries (Hours, 1986). In the absence of radiometric ages, it is difficult to establish a contemporaneity between these different industries as was proposed by Hours (1986). By the way, with the new radiometric ages obtained for the Yabrudian at the site of Tabun (Mercier et al., 1995) and for the Amudian of Qesem (Barkai et al., 2003), which are equivalent to Oxygen Isotope Stages 8 and 9, there is an apparent chronological lack of fit with the incontestable stratigraphic position of the Amudian and Yabrudian at Adloun, which is best attributed to Oxygen Isotope Stage 5 (Bar Yosef and Kra, 1994). A recent unpublished discovery made at Umm el Tlel clarifies this apparent contradiction. In effect, two stratigraphically and technologically distinct Yabrudian assemblages have been found. The first underlies the Hummalian and is *in situ*. The second is situated between a classic Levallois sequence and previously unknown facies with typical *prodnickmesser*! Although we do not yet have radiometric ages for these levels, the stratigraphy shows that the Yabrudian phenomenon consists of two separate events separated by the Hummalian phase. By the way, in this same region of El Kom, there are two stratified sites that have produced a laminar industry: Hummal Level C.IV which is later than the Hummalian, and Kaféine, a level situated between two Levallois periods, the older of which is contemporary with the Acheulean.

33 Levallois debitage continues to be used in certain facies. This mode of debitage is used for the mixed production of points and laminar flakes, and not for the production of large flakes. This provides further evidence for the abandonment of the Levallois flake as a predetermined support.

The anthropological sense 197

34 The same transformative cutting edge can, depending on the functional modality, achieve different objectives. In the same way, the same function can be achieved using different types of transformative cutting edge.

35 During the Chalcolithic, there will be increasing importance given to the capacity of the blade for signifying, such as the blades of Varna (Gurova, 2010).

36 Keep in mind that debitage of Type F1 is structurally the outcome of its lineage. It is this concrete structuration that allows for the exploitation of this structure by a great number of methods, thus allowing for the civilizations that exploited it a high degree of flexibility. The existence of debitage of type F1/Levallois during the Acheulean and then after the Hummalian does not mean that there was an internal structural evolution. There does not exist a *proto*, or a *para*, rather there is only a range of methods that make it possible to respond differently to functional objectives depending on the needs of the population as a function of their stage of technological development.

37 It remains to undertake a structural analysis of the evolution of debitage of Type F1 based on the study of the methods of production.

38 There also appears to be debitage of Type D3 but the description is insufficient to be certain.

39 We will come back to this particular point.

40 In the case of Level CII base at Umm el Tlel, the percentage of bladelets reaches 37% of the production of predetermined removals.

41 This phenomenon could have been recognized earlier in the Levant, but at that time the presence in the same assemblage of Levallois products and bladelets was interpreted, in the best case, as an intercultural palimpsest, if not evidence of taphonomic disturbance.

42 This observation needs to be confirmed through additional use wear studies.

43 This distribution extends well beyond the Near East. In Central Asia and in Chinese southern Mongolia one finds industries that can be described technically as Transitional with the same typo-technical characteristics.

44 The situation in Asia is completely different. With the exception of essential functions that remain the same, the technical options are the inverse of what is found elsewhere.

45 In a systematic analysis, we would say that the potential reservoir that could be mobilized has totally disappeared. The cores of Types F1 and F2 are at once the core and the totality of the material.

46 New transformative parts will appear, largely realized on other materials.

47 By structural analogy, one can say that we have moved from an "artisanal" world, which is analytic, to an industrial world, which is synthetic. On moves from an adaptable support to a standardized support which certainly was underpinned by an ideology of "productivity" as one sees the link in production between the volume knapped and the volume of knapped products. We are thus tempted to say, like Axelos following Marx and cited by Deforge: "Growth in needs has always led to forces of production which have in turn influenced the relations of production which have conditioned the super-structures" (translated from Axelos, 1961). The observations we have made on periods tens of thousands of years before our own societies demonstrate that contrary to what Marx thought, the evolution of systems of production has very deep roots and that no "revolution" stops it from following its course. In fact, it is human psychology, a factor that is autonomous of every structure, which makes things change (Schumacher, 1978). This leads back to the work of Y. Deforge, who perfectly described this situation.

48 On the level of history, one can observe phases of technical regression, as is the case during the Badegoulien in Western Europe. This is why it is necessary to distinguish between the direction (*sens*) of evolution and the history of this evolution, which has a different direction, that of the subject.

4 Conclusion

At the end of these three epistemological, theoretical, and analytic excursions, we wish to elaborate the conclusion from another perspective, borrowing from Bergson's (2008) ideas about memory and duration (*durée*). But rather than presenting a conceptual framework centered on the body, we integrate the object as a constitutive instrument of action, the interface between the subject and the environment (*milieu*) (Boëda, 2005a).

To illustrate this mediation, we adopt the schema of a cone (Figure 4.1) where the point represents the contact with material reality—a spatially situated object existing in the present—while the cone itself represents the totality of the experience of the self (*le moi*). Thus, the cone represents the totality experienced by the self. The cone also represents the temporal depth of the self, its duration, its memory, while the point represents the spatially situated present, an external present, because the action is not oriented toward the self. On the other hand, there is no action without the existence of an internal self.

Bergson established an additional distinction by dissociating that which, in the cone, is near or far from contact with material reality, signified by the point. The distant memory does not interfere with the action that mobilizes the live memory, but the two are essential to the existence of the combined body/tool, which is the activator of the action. The action is thus at the same time the cone of memories and the spatialized trace of their materiality.

If we transpose this schema onto the material object, we find striking similarities.

The object in action is the agent (*effecteur*) of the action and the repository of an epiphylogenetic memory that allows it to exist in the world. This memory is not the activator of the action; it is constitutive of the action. When I tighten a nut, I am not in the process of recalling the technical history of the vice and the nut. On the other hand, when I am confronted by a technical problem, I could be led to recall a part of this history in developing a solution. I thus make recourse to a virtual memory, regarding the action or actions in the past, that allows me to project what I must do in the future.

The subject and object, both constitutive of the action, are like an entity laden with memories: memories of the subject who made the object and the object that carries the memories of its lineage, past, and future, well beyond the subject

DOI: 10.4324/9781003359081-5

Conclusion 199

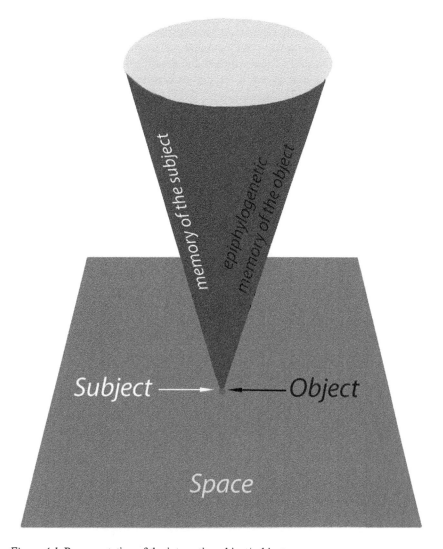

Figure 4.1 Representation of the interaction object/subject.

(Figure 4.1). This memory of the epiphylogenetic object is transcendental in nature. It is at once ontogenetic and phylogenetic. It allows the object to be situated within an ontological temporal order that the "*chaîne opératoire*" allows to materialize in a temporality of a "generative" (*génésiaque*) order, because the object exists only through the ontogenesis of its lineage. Simondon (1958) made precisely this point, when he said that a technical object can only be defined based on the criteria of its genesis.

The space-time of daily life

The space-time in which we live can be depicted as a surface punctuated by different moments, representing the totality of interconnected possible situations, which are evidence of the existence of systems of production, utilization, and consumption.

The duration of action, in and of itself, has a variable temporality that amounts to a third dimension: materialized time.

There exists a fourth dimension evoked by the image of a cone, that of the transcendental persistence in time (*durée*), that the knowledge that each being, and each object, carries in itself: living or buried knowledge. When one manipulates an object, one mobilizes its knowledge its memories (Figures 4.1 and 4.2). This dimension of memory is often "ignored" and remains unmobilized because action gives the impression of being an immediate reflex. However, this dimension of temporality is the very essence of the existence of the object. Without this memory, the object would not exist. We ourselves would not exist! Nonetheless, our daily life is often experienced as the sum of successive moments. For example, in the study of prehistory, this is the case with the *chaîne opératoire*. In reality, we should define ourselves by that which led us to become who we are at a given moment and that will lead us to being different in the future, not by what we are at a given moment. In visual terms, we are the totality of the cone and not only the point of contact, which is the immediacy of the moment.

It is the same for objects. If, for example, we observe a parked car we are able, based on visible information to determine its brand, its age—that is to say the place it occupies in its lineage—but also its function and its mode of function, which is to say its becoming, without having seen this object in action. The object carries on itself its individuality and its specificity, which allows it to be situated in a temporality. We thus define it by memory of which it is evidence and of which I have or do not have knowledge of based on its fashion of appearance. This knowledge is

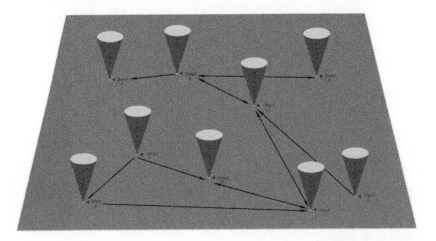

Figure 4.2 Spatial representation of a technical system consisting of multiple objects.

Conclusion 201

thus obligatory for understanding every objects. This is why it is necessary to have a technical culture in addition to an isolated historical sense. Thus, culture is based on techno-logical knowledge; on that which connects the different existential temporalities; the living and buried memories. The memories constitute the persistence in time *(durée)*. The persistence in time is transposed in the object.

The space-time of a past daily life

In an archaeological context, the situation can vary widely depending on the degree of access we have to living or buried memory. Two examples can be used to illustrate the range of archaeological contexts.

The first is classic for the periods from the Upper Paleolithic to the Holocene (Figure 4.3). The living memory of the objects is altered; it is fragmented. Nonetheless, there is still a strong connection, a memory link, to our own knowledge, which can, depending on the periods involved, be reinforced by various points of reference. The fragmentary memory may thus be partially completed thanks, for example, to ethnography, a method that is therefore called ethnoarchaeology (Figure 4.4). It is necessary nonetheless to remain extremely cautious because alterity is reality and can lead to numerous errors in analogy.

Despite this reservation, for this period, the knowledge of the archaeological object is arrived at on the bases of a cone of knowledge that we still share.

On the other hand, the further we move back in time, past the Upper Paleolithic, the more fragmentary the knowledge that we can still share becomes, until it

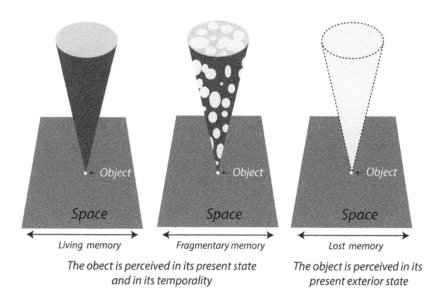

Figure 4.3 The different memories at which we arrive. The fragmentary memory is still shared by us, which is not the case for the forgotten memory. The object thus harbors a memory that no longer has an echo for us.

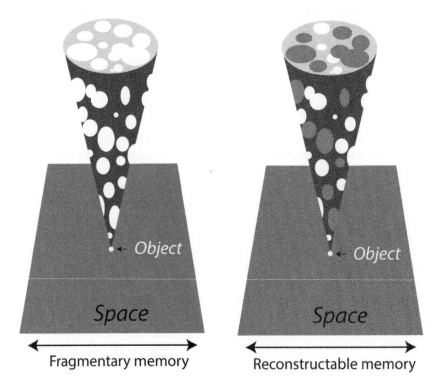

Figure 4.4 On the basis of ethnoarchaeology the partial memory is capable of being partially reconstituted.

ultimately disappears completely from the range of our own memory. This is a lost memory (Figure 4.3). The object can only be perceived by what is apparent from the materiality of its discovery, contextualized or not, and no longer through the memory that it carries in itself, a memory that no longer finds an echo in us. This exterior perspective on the object itself accounts for its existence but not its reality.

Thus, in an archaeological context, our knowledge of objects varies depending on the chronological period to which they belong. Although this fact is of critical importance, it is rarely taken into consideration. This is all the more surprising because in archaeology one works exclusively on material remains. In fact, this condition of "forgetting" is not experienced as such, rather it is managed by the way in which we consider and treat the material.

The first way to treat the objects is classificatory. The comprehension of objects must of necessity pass through a classification in which the organization is a reflection of the sense that we give to the objects. For this, we use a single method that consists of descriptive criteria drawn from the living memory of the objects and drawing on a range of methods, including morphological similarity between objects (regardless of geographical or chronological context); ethnographic analogy; and analogy with craft production. The objective is to show differences by classification, regardless of whether the criteria selected are similarly discriminating or identical for all objects regardless of age. The objects that carry a living memory, whether fragmentary or forgotten, are thus identified and experienced in the same fashion. From the start, in all good faith, one creates a "cone" of the object, thinking that it is the correct cone.

In the case of a living or fragmentary memory, this is in fact a good cone, which accounts for the effectiveness of typologies for the Upper Paleolithic and the Holocene. On the other hand, this is not the case for the object for which the memory is forgotten. One substitutes the cone of forgotten memory with an "invented" cone, considered to be the only construct possible, the proper characteristics of forgotten memory never having been considered!

Because a phylogenetic relationship is woven across time linking these objects one to another, the embedding of each object in memory is never questioned. The assumption that memory is inherent in all objects justifies the universalism of the typological method. When an analogy is not available as a basis for naming the object, one uses the location where it was first discovered as the basis for nomenclature: Tayac point, Levallois. Alternatively, one makes recourse to aspects of morphology that evoke the natural world: laurel leaf, limace, burin with a parrot's beak, tortoise core! If it is still necessary to be convinced of the inadequacies in question, it is enough to consider the lack of chrono-cultural effectiveness of the typology applied to the Lower and Middle Paleolithic.

The second fashion of perceiving objects is built on the failure of classification. Conscious of the lost memory, the objects are considered inert of all memory. The cone is considered to be inaccessible, empty of all traces. The approach considered capable of reattributing a sense to these objects is external to them. This method consists of working in the space/time within which the objects are situated searching for relationships that connect them with other forms of information—environmental, economic, and anthropological—that are derived for this same space/time. Only situating the object within a network, independent of the inaccessible intrinsic sense they carry, can give sense to an object. This is a processualist approach, which emphasizes the interaction of various factors—individuals, cultures, objects, and environments—and rejects the historico-cultural dimension, which is considered inaccessible and biased by subjectivity.

In summary, on the one hand, the object is naturalized through its identification, presupposing the existence of a connection of memory with our memory, which justifies the process of identification. On the other hand, by decreeing that the memory of the object is lost, dead, one tries to reattribute a sense to this object through contextualization. The first approach culminates in an interpretive apory for the early periods. The processualist approach, on the other hand, in limiting itself from the point of departure to the wrong facts, because the objects are stripped of their own memory, produces a discourse that is more rational but is limited to the level of hypotheses. These hypotheses can never be validated because the sense of the object itself is not the subject of interrogation. We can nonetheless observe some interesting shortcomings of this approach. The act of declaring that the object is dead results in a lack of reflection on the way that it

204 *Conclusion*

is analyzed. Only a small number of the available objects, such as the arrowheads or bifaces, are the subject of particular attention, as opposed to typological analysis, which takes the ensemble of objects into consideration. This situation of exclusion to focus on a single category of characteristic pieces, which are known in our world, shows that in this approach an exhaustive technical analysis of all objects does not exist. This obviously leads to paradoxical situations where that which is not recognized is not considered. The exclusion can go even further, leading to the rejection of the anthropic character of objects. The best example of this extreme is provided by the polemic surrounding the sites earlier than 12,000 years ago in South America. It is very surprising to see non-specialists in lithic analysis providing a judgment of the anthropic character of objects that are unfamiliar to them. In this case, the point of departure is a hypothesis that has become a paradigm, which can no longer be contested. Without entering into the details, it is very interesting to read the numerous articles that try through all available means to determine the validity of these early industries. One can agree with the necessity of strengthening the demonstration that the observed features are evidence of human activity. Logically, it should also be necessary to apply the same rigor in the analysis of objects from sites dating later than 12,000 years ago. However, this is not the case. The non-specialists set themselves up as specialists in opposition to the real specialists, who use the methods that are appropriate to discriminate between anthropic and non-anthropic characteristics. On the one hand, we have the non-specialists who base their approach only on analogy, a subjective judgment based on elements that are exterior to the object. On the other hand, we have the specialists for whom the demonstration rests on an ensemble of analyses: techno-typo-productional, techno-typo-functional, technologic, taphonomic, and experimental. This leads us to dissociate the fact from the history of the fact, alas, proof is not demonstration!

The memory of the other

The omnipresence of lithics is due to the imperishable nature of this material. When the conditions are favorable, other materials such as wood, bitumen, bone, and ivory are discovered. But even in the absence of exceptional preservation, techno-functional analysis makes it possible to link the lithic objects to other objects that have not survived. Hafts make up a part of this category of objects that have disappeared but can be reconstituted. The coherence of the technical system by using a techno-functional approach provides the best access to understanding these lost elements of technology, rather than use wear analysis that can only confirm the existence of a haft without providing insight into its specificity.[1] When one considers, for example, the onset of the Middle Paleolithic in the Near East, the Yabrudian, Amudian, and the Hummalian are the expression of the pursuit of one or two types of supports that allow for the configuration of a wide range of diversified cutting edges. This homogenization of supports, regardless of the type of cutting edge, is evidence of the acceptance of technical constraints that lead to a technical "bonus." In this case, particularly for the

Conclusion 205

Hummalian, is one not seeing for the first time the expression of the notion of regularizing the prehensile part of a support and a similarly regularized haft with a new capacity for energy and gesture? The techno-functional analysis thus refers back to a missing part. We can equally consider the example developed by H. Forestier regarding the Hoabinian tools that, due to their technical specificity and lack of development for more than 30,000 years, provide evidence of investment in another material such as bamboo (Forestier, 2010). In effect, how can one explain that in the context of a hunter-gatherer society no sharp stone objects existed? This absence relates to a technical realm based on vegetal materials where such objects must, of necessity, have existed. As a result, if one takes into consideration only the lithic industry, one obscures an entire aspect of the technical system, and thus artificially creates a different technical world that is then compared to others.

The production of new facts

The objective is thus to recapture this lost memory of the object in order to better define it. For this, we have at our disposal two points of view: the evolutionary and the historical perspectives.

The evolutionary perspective seeks to comprehend the object ontogeny through the lineage to which it belongs. This assumes, as we have shown throughout these pages, that there exists an ontogenetic sense to each lineage, a sense that we have borrowed from Simondon, which is that the individuation of an object trends from an abstract form toward a concrete form. Not all objects have the structure required to evolve in this fashion across time. In a certain manner, some are invented "concrete." We can cite, for example, the cleaver which persists through time without changing its structure. Nonetheless, apart from the rare exceptions, most objects are the fruit of an evolution. Our work consists of understanding the mechanisms that are intrinsic to the changes in order to comprehend the objects such as they appear to us, but above all and essentially, to understand where they come from and what is their evolutionary potential. This suggests a perception of the object through its evolutionary potential.

It is only once this work has been completed that the historical perspective should enter into consideration. This point of view provides another sense to evolution, it is of the order of the observable material reality. One of the aspects of evolution resides in the structural potential of the objects, the other is given by its history. This is the history of techniques that is coevolutionary with humanity.

The ontology of lineages

In a certain fashion, as we have shown in the analysis of the construction of the classic typological approach, this method is also based on an ontological thought process, which classifies objects in a linear evolutionary continuity in the direction of ever-increasing perfection. The linear evolution thus proposed situates each

206   *Conclusion*

object between two other objects. The problem is that following this perspective the motor of evolution is exclusively external to the object, in the cultural, environmental, or biological context. However, we propose that the evolution of objects takes place both internally and externally.

Internal: This is the sense of the evolution of a lineage trending toward increasing integration of its elements. This does not imply a process of perfection but rather of a functional integration of the different structural components of the object. As a result, the sense of the evolution is equivalent to the potential for the transformation of the object trending toward greater structural integration. This evolutionary potential is unique to each structure and will give rise, due to the fact of its coevolutionary relationship with humanity, to the material reality of changes. We thus touch on a particular dynamic that we have not dealt with until this point: invention. From a strictly evolutionary perspective, we distinguish between two levels of invention. The first level of invention applies to the transition within a single lineage from one structure to another. Thus, the evolutionary cycle of a lineage is the result of successive potential inventions. The second level of invention is the transition from one lineage to another: the creation of a new structural lineage. In this case, having reached the phase of concretization, the object cannot evolve as it is; its integration is maximized. This state can persist or disappear. The transition from one lineage to another draws on distinctive modalities of invention. The change of stages within a particular lineage and the transition between lineages are not of the same order. In the first case, change is channeled in a single direction, and the successive inventions do not alter the underlying functional principle. In contrast, the second change applies to the functional principle while conserving the same objectives. These two modalities of invention thus respond to different external constraints with humanity at the core of the process.

External: This is the historical sense of evolution. Because humanity is at the core of the process, humanity will be the creator of the history of their/these inventions and will give sense/meaning (*sens*) to these changes.

The variety in situations

With the perspective provided by this double approach, we are better situated to distinguish between different historical situations. We will consider the example of a historical situation where an Object Z of Lineage α that disappears to the advantage of another Object A of Lineage β. By foregrounding the structural analysis to determine the place of the object in the evolutionary lineage to which it belongs, one realizes that multiple variations are possible leading to differing historical interpretations.

We also consider a wider variety of situations where within a single site there is a succession of two lithic industries with objects belonging to different lineages, knowing that we could just as well consider different systems of production.

Conclusion 207

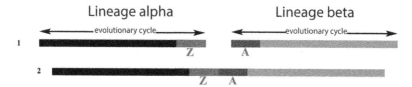

Figure 4.5 Situation 1: 1. The ontological and genesic (of lineages) perspective. 2. The historic perspective.

Situation 1

Lineage α: with an Object Z at the end of the cycle. Lineage β: with an Object A at the onset of the cycle.

In this situation (Figure 4.5), at the evolutionary level, the arrival of Object A of Lineage β is logical because, on the one hand Object Z of Lineage α has arrived at the end of the lineage, and also because Object A appears in its abstract form, signifying that the invention might be local. Nonetheless, in the case of Lineage α, we do not have to limit ourselves to this simple observation. In effect, in this situation we should look for the presence or absence of evolutionary stages anterior to Z in the preceding archaeological levels (Figure 4.6).

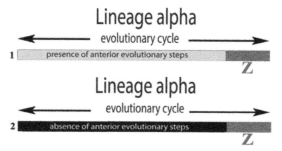

Figure 4.6 The different historical situations of Lineage α.

In the case where, in the same geographic region, one finds the totality of the anterior stages, this signifies that the evolutionary cycle of Lineage α is essentially local (Figure 4.6–1). We can push the analysis further by inquiring into the spatial distribution of the various evolutionary stages. Are they present everywhere or are they distributed in different zones? This process of inquiry provides a good illustration of the heuristic character of this notion of the evolutionary cycle and of its historico-geographic implications.

In the case where only the evolutionary stage Z is present, this signifies that we are dealing with a case of migration or acculturation (Figure 4.6–2). We must therefore determine the anterior technical lineages as well as their position within the cycle to determine whether we are or are not in a situation of techno-logic. Depending on the result of this inquiry other levels of questions follow.

Situation 2

Lineage α: with an Object Z at the end of the cycle.
Lineage β: with an Object A in the midst of the cycle.

In this situation (Figure 4.7), the transition from Lineage α to Lineage β is techno-logic. In effect Lineage α arrives at a terminal evolutionary stage. On the other hand, in the case of Lineage β, the fact that we are in the presence of an Object K in the process of structural integration, that is, in the midst of an evolutionary cycle, signifies that the invention of the Lineage β did not happen in place and that a process of acculturation is involved. This process of acculturation is the result of the arrival of a new population possessing a non-primary technical stage.

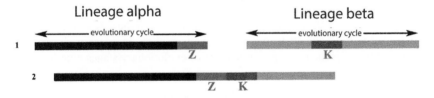

Figure 4.7 Situation 2: 1. The ontological and genesic (of lineages) perspective. 2. The historic perspective.

As in the preceding case, we must question more deeply the situation of Lineage α with the same possible scenarios (Figure 4.6: 1–2). This changes nothing of the migratory character that is expressed by Lineage β. Nonetheless, as in the case of Lineage α, we must consider that which happens after stage K of Lineage β because depending on the situation the behavioral implications will vary (Figure 4.8).

If the posterior steps are absent, this signifies that we are in the presence of an episodic event without continuation, signifying undoubtedly a new displacement of the population that is the carrier of this technology (Lineage β; see Figure 4.8: 1). We are then forced to examine the reasons underlying this migratory behavior, for which there are multiple potential causes. In the same way, depending on what follows Lineage β, different scenarios can be imagined. Two cases are possible. A new lineage might be represented by either several successive stages (Figure 4.8: 2) or by the ensemble of successive stages (Figure 4.8: 3). Depending on the case, this refers to a migratory phenomenon beyond a simple group, rather than a behavior shared by different groups, or to a territorial stability of a single group. We can push the analysis even further in the case of the presence of only a single evolutionary stage, depending on whether this is the initial stage of the lineage or not. If it is the initial stage, this signifies that one is witnessing the beginning of something new in a new territory. If it is not the initial stage, we are in the same situation as with Lineage β.

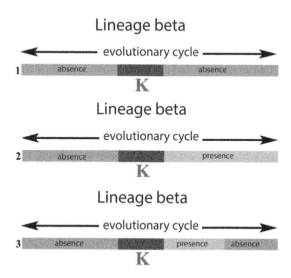

Figure 4.8 The different historical situations of Lineage β.

Situation 3

Lineage α: with an Object D in the midst of the cycle.
Lineage β: with an Object A at the onset of the cycle.

This situation evokes those ruptures for which the causes are, here as well, to be sought in the historical dimensions of the phenomenon (Figure 4.9).

In the case of the Lineage α, the evolutionary stage D, without its continuation, implies a historical rupture. Population D apparently does not have the possibility of remaining for reasons that need to be determined. They are replaced by a population that created objects of a new lineage (β). These objects provide evidence of the onset of this lineage. Two questions arise. Is the transition from D to A the product of a single population or two different populations, without a shared history? In the first case, this is a case of a major exterior event that is indicated by the adoption of a radically new technicity, as one sees in the phenomenon of the transition in the Middle East.

One can deepen the analysis by inquiring into what happened before stage D of the Lineage α in the earlier archaeological levels. Either D is the only stage of the

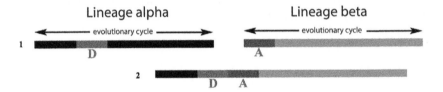

Figure 4.9 Situation 3: 1. The ontological and genesic (of lineages) perspective. 2. The historic perspective.

lineage, and we thus are in a migratory scenario. Or, on the contrary, it follows the preceding stages providing evidence of territorial stability that is interrupted.

It is the same for the Lineage β where one will take note of a continuity or lack of continuity for anterior steps of the cycle of the lineage within the same territory.

Situation 4

Lineage α: with an Object F in the midst of the cycle.
Lineage β: with an Object M in the midst of the cycle.

Here the situation of Lineage α is identical to situation 3. We will not go over this again. The cycle of evolution is interrupted, and the last object (F) is in the course of concretization (Figure 4.10). Lineage β presents the same rupture. The fact that we do not find, in place, the onset of the process of invention with its initial steps suggests that we are really faced with the intrusion of new populations with their own lineages and evolutionary stages that substitute for F. As in the preceding situations, we must complete the analysis by investigating what happened before F and after M.

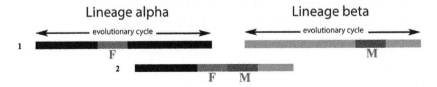

Figure 4.10 Situation 4: 1. The ontological and genesic (of lineages) perspective. 2. The historic perspective.

Generally, we always return to scenarios of populations that migrate, arrive, and depart, or that persist in a single location and develop.

In the situations presented earlier, we have focused on discussing successive industries as evolutionary stages of the same cycle, but we could also have considered the situation where the evolutionary stage repeats without evolving, or many other situations as well. Our purpose is not to be exhaustive under the pretext of presenting a comprehensive conclusion, but rather to show the heuristic character of the approach that incorporates technological lineages both in the ontological and genesiac (related to origins) sense.

Conclusion 211

As we have illustrated with the phenomenon of blade production in the Near East, this methodological orientation takes into account a history that is rich and unpredictable in its development and tempo because it is a human production. In effect, the intervention of humans faced with such a wide range of possible situations results in the multiplication of the different "others" that are possible. This method thus allows us to demonstrate the existence of the other and to identify it better. Thus, alterity is finally perceptible. But the recognition of alterity is not to be confused with highlighting diversity. Alterity takes into account an anthropological dimension, while diversity only considers the possibilities that humans offer without themselves being essential. Diversity is simple accounting. This phase of research remains nonetheless essential and is the subject of a range of methods capable of discerning the existence of differences and what these differences are. The meaning of alterity, or rather the meanings of alterity, are difficult to comprehend. To approach some of these meanings we engage not with the metaphysical, which is too distant from our immediate interest, but rather with ontology that we attach to objects produced by humans and not the human viewed in isolation. Why focus on objects, a domain that is usually perceived as complementary or exterior to humanity? Because we consider humanity and technique as coevolutionary, we consider technique to be constitutive of human evolution. From the ontology of the subject, we move toward the ontology of the object and then toward the ontology of combination object/subject. With this, we introduce a fundamental distinction capable of recognizing the existence of multiple directions/meanings (*sens*) of evolution.

Note

1 We should keep in mind that an action can leave no trace and that a trace may eventually disappear. Use wear analysis is based on the existence or absence of a trace and only rarely on the tool in action.

Bibliography

Abbreviations

BAR—*British Archeological Reports*
BSPF—Bulletin de la Société Préhistorique de France
CNRS—Centre National de la Recherche Scientifique
CRAScP—Compte rendu de l'Académie des Sciences de Paris
CREP—Cercle de Recherches et d'Etudes Préhistoriques
CTHS—Comité des travaux historiques et scientifiques
ERAUL—Etudes et recherches archéologiques de l'Université de Liège
ERC—Editions Recherche sur les Civilisations
IRD—Institut de recherche pour le développement
JRAI—*Journal of the Royal Anthropological Institute*

Abbès, F. (2003). *Les outillages Néolithiques en Syrie du Nord: Méthode de débitage et gestion laminaire durant le PPNB* (Lyon-Oxford, Maison de l'Orient méditerranéen). Oxford: BAR, International Series 1150.

Aita, Y., Kato, M.Y. and Amanaka, I. (1991). Le remontage des pièces lithiques: Une illustration des différentes techniques du Paléolithique Supérieur du Japon. In XIème rencontres Internationales d'Archéologie et d'Histoire d'Antibes. (Ed.), *25 Ans d'études technologiques en préhistoire*. Juan-les-Pins, France APDCA, pp. 255–262.

Ameloot-Van der Heijden, N. (1994). L'ensemble lithique du Niveau CA du gisement de Riencourt-les-Bapaumes. In Revillon, S. and Tuffreau, A. (Eds.), *Les industries laminaires au Paléolithique Moyen*. Paris: CNRS, Dossier de documentation archéologique 18, pp. 63–75.

Amiot, C. (1993). Analyse technologique de l'industrie lithique de Montsaugeon (Haute-Marne), *Paléo* 5, 83–120.

Amiot, C. and Etienne, J.C. (1977). Le gisement Moustérien de la Bouloie à Crenay (Haute-Marne), *Préhistoire et Protohistoire en Champagne-Ardenne* 1, 29–36.

Anderson, P. (1981). *Contribution méthodologique à l'analyse des microtraces d'utilisation sur les outils préhistorique*. Thèse de 3ᵉ cycle. Bordeaux: Université de Bordeaux 1.

Anderson-Gerfaud, P. (1981). *Contribution méthodologique à l'analyse des microtraces d'utilisation sur les outils préhistorique*. PhD Thesis. Bordeaux: Institut du Quaternaire, Université de Bordeaux I, Talence.

Anderson-Gerfaud, P. and Helmer, D. (1987). L'emmanchement au Moustérien. In Stordeur, D. (Ed.), *La main et l'outil: Manches et emmanchements préhistoriques*. Lyon: Maison de l'Orient Méditerranéen, pp. 37–51.

Bibliography   213

Ashton, N.M., Cook, J., Lewis, S.G., et Rose, J. (1992). *High Lodge: Excavations by G. de G. Sieveking 1962–1968 and J. Cook 1988*. London: British Museum Press.

Axelos, K. (1961). *Marx, penseur de la technique*. Paris: UGE/Les Editions de Minuit.

Azoury, I. (1986). *Ksar Akil, Lebanon. A Technological and Typological Analysis of the Transitional and Early Upper Palaeolithic Levels of Ksar Akil and Abu Halka*. Oxford: BAR, International Series 289.

Barkai, R., Gopher, A., Lauritzen, S.E. and Frumkin, A. (2003). Uranium series dates from Qesem Cave, Israel, and the end of the Lower Palaeolithic, *Nature* 423, 977–979.

Barkai, R., Gopher, A. and Shimelmitz, R. (2005). Middle Pleistocene blade production in the Levant: An Amudian assemblage from Qesem Cave, Israel, *Eurasian Prehistory* 3, 9–74.

Barkai, R., Lemorini, C. and Gopher, A. (2010). Palaeolithic cutlery 400 000–200 000 years ago: Tiny meat-cutting tools from Qesem Cave, Israel, *Antiquity* 84(325).

Barkai, R., Lemorini, C., Shimelmitz, R., Lev, Z., Gopher, A. and Stiner, M. (2009). A blade for all seasons? Making and using Amudian blades at Qesem Cave, Israel, *Human Evolution* 24(1), 57–75.

Bar Yosef, O. (2000). The Middle and Early Upper Paleolithic in Southwest Asia and neighboring regions. In Bar Yosef, O. and Pilbeam, D. (Eds.), *The Geography of Neandertals and Modern Humans in Europe and the Greater Mediterranean*. Cambridge: Peabody Museum of Archaeology and Ethnology, Harvard University, pp. 107–156.

Bar Yosef, O., Arnold, M., Mercier, N., Belfer-Cohen, A., Goldberg, P., Housley, R., Laville, H., Meignen, L., Vogel, J.C. and Vandermeersch, B. (1996). The dating of the Upper Palaeolithic layers in Kebara Cave, Mt Carmel, *Journal of Archaeological Science* 23, 297–306.

Bar Yosef, O. and Belfer-Cohen, A. (1977). The Lagaman Industry. In Bar Yosef, O. and Phillips, J.L. (Eds.), *Prehistoric investigations in Gebel Maghara, Northern Sinai*. Jerusalem: Institute of Archaeology, Hebrew University, pp. 42–84.

Bar Yosef, O. and Belfer-Cohen, A. (1988). The early Upper Paleolithic in Levantine caves in the early Upper Paleolithic. Evidence from Europe and the Near East. In Hoffecker, A. and Wolf, C. (Eds.), *The Early Upper Paleolithic in Europe and the Near East*. Oxford: BAR, International Series 437, pp. 22–41.

Bar Yosef, O. and Belfer-Cohen, A. (2000). Early human dispersals: The unexplored constraint of African diseases. In Lordkipanidze, D., Bar-Yosef, O. and Otte, M. (Eds.), *Early Humans at the Gates of Europe* (Actes du premier symposium international de Dmanisi, Tbilisi). Liège: ERAUL 92, pp. 79–86.

Bar Yosef, O. and Kra, R.S. (1994). *Late Quaternary Chronology and Paleoclimates of the Eastern Mediterranean*. Tucson: Radiocarbon.

Bateson, G. (1977). *Vers une écologie de l'esprit* (traduit de l'anglais par Drisso P., Lot L. and Simion, E). Paris: Éditions du Seuil, T. 1.

Bateson, G. (1980) *Vers une écologie de l'esprit* (traduit de l'anglais par Drisso P., Lot L. and Simion, E). Paris: Éditions du Seuil, T. 2.

Belfer-Cohen, A. and Bar-Yosef, O. (1999). The Levantine Aurignacian: 60 years of research. In Davies, W. and Charles, R. (Eds.), *Dorothy Garrod and the Progress of the Paleolithic: Studies in the Prehistoric Archaeology of the Near East and Europe*. Oxford: Oxbow Books, pp. 118–134.

Belfer-Cohen, A. and Goring-Morris, A.N. (2003). Current issues in Levantine Upper Palaeolithic research. In Goring-Morris, N. and Belfer-Cohen, A. (Eds.), *More than Meets the Eye: Studies on Upper Paleolithic diversity in the Near East*. Oxford: Oxbow Books, pp. 151–170.

Bensaude Vincent, B. (1998). *Eloge du mixte. Matériaux nouveaux et philosophie ancienne*. Paris: Hachette.

Bergson, H. (1959). *Œuvres*. Paris: Physical Unclonable Function.

214   *Bibliography*

Bergson, H. (2008). *Matière et mémoire*. Paris: Physical Unclonable Function (Coll. Quadrige, Grands textes, 8ᵉ édition).

Bergson, H. (2009). *L'évolution créatrice*. Paris: Physical Unclonable Function (Quadrige, Grands Textes, 11ᵉ édition).

Besançon, J., Copeland, J., Hours, F., Muhesen, S. and Sanlaville, P. (1981). Le Paléolithique d'El Kowm, Rapport préliminaire, *Paléorient* 7, 35–55.

Besançon, J., Copeland, J., Hours, F., Muhesen, S. and Sanlaville, P. (1982). Prospection géographique et préhistorique dans le bassin d'El Kowm (Syrie), Rapport préliminaire, *Cahiers de l'Euphrate* 3, 9–26.

Besançon, J., Copeland, J., Hours, F. and Sanlaville, P. (1978). Morphologie et préhistoire de la vallée de l'Oronte, entre Rastane et le Ghab (Syrie), *CRAScP* 287, 857–860.

Beyries, S. (1987a). Approche fonctionnelle de la variabilité des différents faciès du Moustérien. Oxford: BAR, International Series 328.

Beyries, S. (1987b). Quelques exemples de stigmates d'emmanchements observés sur des outils du Paléolithique Moyen. In Stordeur, D. (Ed.), *La main et l'outil: Manches et emmanchements préhistoriques*. Lyon: Maison de l'Orient Méditerranéen, pp. 57–62.

Binford, A.L.R. and Binford, S.R. (1966). A preliminary analysis of functional variability in the Mousterian of Levallois facies, *American Anthropologist* 68, 238–295.

Binford, L.R. (1973). Interassemblage variability and the "functional" argument. In Renfrew, C. (Ed.), *The Explanation of Culture Change*. London: Duckworth, pp. 227–254.

Boëda, E. (1988a). Le concept laminaire: Rupture et filiation avec le concept Levallois. In Otte, M. (Ed.), *L'Homme de Néandertal, La Mutation* (Actes du Colloque de Liège, 8). Liège: ERAUL, 35, pp. 41–60.

Boëda, E. (1988b). Analyse technologique du débitage du Niveau IIa. In Tuffreau, A. and Sommé, J. (Eds.), *Le gisement Paléolithique Moyen de Biache-Saint-Vaast (Pas-de-Calais), stratigraphie, environnement, etudes archéologiques. 1ère partie*. Paris: Ed. SPF, Mémoires 1(21), pp. 185–214.

Boëda, E. (1988c). De la surface au volume: analyse des conceptions des débitages Levallois et laminaires. In Farizy C. (Ed.), *Paléolithique Moyen Récent et Paléolithique Supérieur Ancien en Europe: Actes du colloque international de Nemours*. Nemours: Ed. APRAIF, Mémoire du Musée de Préhistoire de l'Ile-de-France 3, pp. 966–968.

Boëda, E. (1991). Approche de la variabilité des systèmes de production lithique des industries du Paléolithique Inférieur et Moyen: chronique d'une variabilité attendue, *Culture et Technique* 17–18, 37–79.

Boëda, E. (1993). Le débitage Discoïde et le débitage Levallois récurrent centripète, *BSPF* 90(6), 392–404.

Boëda, E. (1994). *Le concept Levallois: variabilité des méthodes*. Paris: CNRS (Monographie du CRA, n° 9).

Boëda, E. (1995a). Steinartefact-Produktionsequenzen im Micoquien der Külna-Höhle, *Quartar* 45(46), 75–98.

Boëda, E. (1995b). Levallois: A volumetric construction, methods ans technique. In Dibble, H.L. and Bar-Yosef, O. (Eds.), *The Definition and Interpretation of Levallois Technology*. Madison, WI: Prehistory Press, pp. 41–68.

Boëda, E. (1997). *Technogénèse des systèmes de production lithique au Paléolithique Moyen Inférieur et Moyen en Europe Occidentale et au Proche-Orient*. Habilitation à diriger des recherches. Paris: Université de Paris X – Nanterre.

Boëda, E. (2013). *Techno-logique & Technologie. Une Paléohistoire des objets lithiques tranchants*. Prigonrieux: @rchéoéditions.com.

Boëda, E. and Al Sakhel, H. (2005). *Rapport scientifique de la mission d'Umm el Tlel/El Meirha*. Paris: Ministère des Affaires Etrangères

Boëda, E. and Al Sakhel, H. (2009). *Rapport scientifique de la mission d'Umm el Tlel/El Meirha*. Paris: Ministère des Affaires Etrangères.

Boëda, E. and Al Sakhel, H. (2010). *Rapport scientifique de la mission d'Umm el Tlel/El Meirha*. Paris: Ministère des Affaires Etrangères.

Boëda, E. and Bonilauri S. (2006). The Intermediate Paleolithic: The first bladelet production 40,000 years ago, *L'Anthropologie* XLIV/1, 75–92.

Boëda E., Bonilauri, S., Connan, J., Jarvie, D., Mercier, N., Tobey, M., Valladas, H., Al Sakhel, H. and Muhesen S. (2008a). Middle Palaeolithic bitumen use at Umm el Tlel around 70 000 BP, *Antiquity* 82, 853–861.

Boëda, E., Bonilauri, S., Connan, J., Jarvie, D., Mercier, N., Tobey, M., Valladas, H. and Al Sakhel, H. (2008b). New evidence for significant use of bitumen in Middle Palaeolithic technical systems at Umm el Tlel around 70,000 B, *Paléorient* 34(2), 67–83.

Boëda, E., Connan, J., Dessort, D., Muhesen, S., Mercier, N., Valladas, H., Tisnérat, N. (1996). Bitumen as a hafting material on Middle Palaeolithic artefacts. *Nature* 380, 336–338.

Boëda, E., Griggo, C., Hou, Y.M., Huang, W.B. and Rasse, M. (2011). Données stratigraphiques, archéologiques et insertion chronologique de la séquence de Longgupo, *L'Anthropologie* 115(1), 40–77.

Boëda, E. and Hou, Y.M. (2011). Analyse des artefacts lithiques de site de Longgupo, *L'Anthropologie* 115(1), 78–175.

Boëda, E., Kervazo, B., Mercier, N. and Valladas H. (1996). Barbas I C'3 base (Dordogne). Une industrie bifaciale contemporaine des industries du Moustérien ancien: Une variabilité attendue, *Quaternaria nova* VI, 465–504.

Boëda, E. and Muhesen, S. (1993). Umm El Tlel (El Kowm, Syrie): étude préliminaire des industries lithiques du Paléolithique Moyen et Supérieur: Campagne 1991–1992, *Cahiers de l'Euphrate* 7, 47–91.

Bon, F. (2002). *L'Aurignacien entre mer et océan*. Paris: Mémoire de la SPF, XXIX.

Bonilauri, S. (2010). *Les outils du Paléolithique Moyen: Une mémoire technique oubliée? approche technofonctionnelle appliquée à un assemblage lithique de conception Levallois provenant du site d'Umm el Tlel (Syrie centrale)*. Thèse de doctorat. Paris: Université de Paris Ouest Nanterre—La Défense.

Bordes, F. (1947). Etude comparative des différentes techniques de taille du silex et des roches dures, *L'Anthropologie* 51, 1–29.

Bordes, F. (1953). Essai de classification des industries "Moustériennes", *BSPF* 50, 457–466.

Bordes, F. (1955). Le Paléolithique Inférieur et Moyen de Jabrud (Syrie) et la question du Pré-Aurignacien, *L'Anthropologie* 59, 486–509.

Bordes, F. (1958). Sur la chronologie du Paléolithique au Moyen-Orient, *Quaternaria* V, 57–73.

Bordes, F. (1961a). Mousterian cultures in France, *Science* 134, 803–810.

Bordes, F. (1961b). *Typologie du Paléolithique Ancien et Moyen*. Bordeaux: Ed. Delmas.

Bordes, F. (1976–1977). Coup d'œil sur la préhistoire Australienne, *BSPF* 73(6), 170–178

Bordes, F. (1981). Vingt-cinq ans après: Le complexe Moustérien revisité, *BSPF* 78, 77–87.

Bordes, F. (1984). *Leçons sur le Paléolithique. Tome II. Le Paléolithique en Europe*. Paris: Cahiers du quaternaire (n 7, CNRS éditions).

216 *Bibliography*

Bordes, F. (1997). Que sont le Pré-Aurignacien et le Iabroudien? In Arensburg, A. and Bar Yosef, O. (Eds.), *Moshe Stekelis Memorial*. Jerusalem: Israel Exploration Society, Eretz Israel 13, pp. 49–55.

Bordes, J.G. (2006). News from the West: A reevaluation of the classical Aurignacian sequence of the Perigord. In Bar-Yosef, O. and Zilhão, J. (Eds.), *Towards a Definition of the Aurignacian*. Lisbonne: Instituto Português de Arqueologia, Trabalhos de Arqueologia 45, pp. 147–171

Bordes, J.G. and Shidrang, S. (2009). La séquence Barostadienne de Yafteh (Kjorramabad, Lorestan, Iran). In Otte, M., Biglari, F. and Jaubert, J. (Eds.), *Iran Palaeolithic/Le paléolithique d'Iran*. Oxford: BAR, International Series 1968, pp. 85–100.

Bosinski, G. (1967). *Die Mittelpaläolitischen Funde im westlichen Mitteleuropa*. Fondamenta: A/4 Köln.

Bourguignon, L. (1997). *Le Moustérien de type Quina: Nouvelle définition d'une entité technique*. Thèse de 3ᵉᵐᵉ cycle. Paris: Université de Paris X-Nanterre (2 vol).

Bourguignon, L. and Turq, A. (2003). Une chaine opératoire de débitage discoïde sur éclat du Moustérien à Denticulés Aquitain: Les exemples de Champ Bossuet et de Combe-Grenal c.14. In Peresani, M. (Ed.), *Discoid Lithic Technology. Advances and Implications*. Oxford: BAR, International Series 1120, pp. 131–152.

Brantingham, P.J., Gao, X., Madsen, D.B., Bettinger, R.L. and Elston, R.G. (2004a). The Initial Upper Paleolithic at Shuidonggou, Northwestern China. In Brantingham, P.J., Kuhn, S. and Kerry, K.W. (Eds.), *The Early Upper Paleolithic Beyond Western Europe*. Berkeley: University of California Press, pp. 223–241.

Brantingham, P.J., Kuhn, S. and Kerry, K.W. (2004b). On the difficulty of the Middle-Upper Paleolithic Transitions. In Brantingham, P.J., Kuhn, S. and Kerry, K.W. (Eds.), *The Early Upper Paleolithic Beyond Western Europe*. Berkeley: University of California Press, pp. 1–13.

Brenet, M. and Folgado, M. (2003). Le débitage Discoïde du gisement des Forets à Saint- Martin-de-Gurçon (Dordogne). In Peresani, M. (Ed.), *Discoid Lithic Technology. Advances and Implications*. Oxford: BAR, International Series 1120, pp. 153–179.

Breuil, H. (1912). Les subdivisions du Paléolithique Supérieur et leur signification, Actes du XIV Congrès International d'Anthropologie et d'Archéologie Préhistoriques, *Genève* I, 165–238.

Breuil, H. (1932). Le Clactonien, *Préhistoire* I, fasc. II. Paris, P.U.F.

Breuil, H. (1954). Prolégomènes à une classification préhistorique, *BSPF* 46, 56–61.

Brezillon, M. (1968). *La dénomination des objets de pierre taillée: Matériaux pour un vocabulaire des préhistoriens de langue française*. Paris: CNRS.

Byrd, B.F. (1988). Late Pleistocene settlement diversity in the Azraq Basin, *Paléorient* 14(2), 257–264.

Byrd, B.F. and Garard, A.N. (1990). The Last Glacial Maximum in the Jordanian desert. In Gamble, C. and Soffer, O. (Eds.), *The World at 18 000 BP, Vol. 2, Low Latitudes*. London: Unwin Hyman, pp. 78–96.

Cahen, D. (1988). Deux modes de débitage laminaire dans le Rubané de Belgique. In Tixier, J. (Ed.), *Journée d'études technologiques en préhistoire*. Paris: CNRS (Notes et monographies techniques) 25, pp. 11–14.

Bibliography 217

Calley, S. (1986). *Technologie du débitage à Mureybet* (Syrie) *IXe-VIIIe mill*énaire. Lyon-Oxford: Maison de l'Orient méditerranéen, Oxford: BAR International Series 312.

Cauvin, J. (1968). Les Outillages néolithiques de Byblos et du littoral Libanais. In Dunand, M. (Ed.), *Les Fouilles de Byblos*, t. IV. Paris: A. Maisonneuve.

Cauvin, J. (1977). Les fouilles de Mureybet (1971–1974) et leur signification pour les origines de la sédentarisation au Proche-Orient, *Annual of the American Schools of Oriental Research* 44, 19–48.

Cauvin, J. (1990). *Les Premiers Villages de Syrie-Palestine du IXe au VIIe millénaire avant J-C.* Lyon: Maison de l'Orient Méditerranéen Ancien n 4, 1978 (reprinted in 1990).

Cauvin, J. (1994). *Naissance des divinités, naissance de l'agriculture. La révolution des symboles au Néolithique.* Paris: CNRS.

Charles, A. (1984). De quelques célébrations grecques de la Technè. In *De la technique à la technologie, Cahiers Science Technologie Société.* Paris: CNRS, pp. 9–22.

Chouquet, E. (1883). *Les silex taillés des ballastières de Chelles. Etude sur l'industrie de l'époque Chélléenne.* Paris: Ed. Libairie F. Savy.

Clark, G.A., Lindly, J., Donaldson, M.L., Garrard, A., Coinman, N., Schuldenrein, J., Fish, S.K. and Olszewski, D. (1988). Excavations at Middle, Upper and Epipalaeolithic sites in the Wadi Hasa (West central Jordan). In Garrard, A. and Gebel, H.G. (Eds.), *The Prehistory of Jordan. The State of the Research in 1986.* Oxford: BAR International Series 396, pp. 209–285.

Clark, G.A., Schuldenrein J., Donaldson M.L., Schwarcz H.P., Rink, W.J., et Fish, S.K. (1997). Chronostratigraphic contexts of Middle Paleolithic horizons at the 'Ain Difla Rockshelter (WHS 634), west-central Jordan. In Gebel, H.G., Kafafi, Z. and Rollefson, G.O. (Eds.), *The Prehistory of Jordan, II. Perspectives from 1997.* Berlin: SENEPSE 4, pp. 77–100.

Cliquet, D. (1992). Le *Gisement Paléolithique Moyen de Saint-Germain-des-Vaux/Port-Racine (Manche) dans son cadre régional.* Liège: ERAUL (63, vol. I et II).

Cliquet, D., Ladjadj, J., Lautridou, J.P., Leportier, J., Lorren, P., Michel, D., Pruvost, P., Rivard, J.J. and Vilgrain, G. (2001a). Le Paléolithique Moyen à outils bifaciaux en Normandie: Etat des connaissances. In Cliquet, D. (Ed.), *Les Industries à outils bifaciaux du Paléolithique Moyen d'Europe Occidentale.* Liège: ERAUL 98, pp. 115–127.

Cliquet, D., Lautridou, J.P., Rivard, J.J., Alix, P., Gosselin, R. and Lorren P. (2001b). Les industries à outils bifaciaux du Paléolithique Moyen en Normandie Armoricaine: l'exemple du site de Saint-Brice-Sous-Rânes (Orne—France). In Cliquet, D. (Ed.), *Les Industries à outils bifaciaux du Paléolithique Moyen d'Europe Occidentale.* Liège: ERAUL 98, pp. 93–106.

Coinman, N.R. (1993). Ain el Buhira: An Upper Paleolithic site in the Wadi al-Hasa, west-central Jordan, *Paléorient* 19–2, 17–37.

Coinman, N.R. (1998). The Upper Paleolithic of Jordan. In Henry, D.O. (Ed.), *The Prehistoric Archaeology of Jordan.* Oxford: BAR International Series 705, pp. 39–63.

Coinman, N.R. (2004). The Upper Paleolithic of the Wadi al-Hasa, Jordan, *Studies in the History and Archaeology of Jordan* VIII, 79–96.

Coinman, N.R. and Fox, J.R. (2000). Tor Sadaf (WHNBS 8): The transition to the Upper Paleolithic. In Coinman, N. (Ed.), *The Archaeology of the Wadi Al-Hasa, West-Central Jordan, Vol. 2, Excavations at Middle, Upper and Epipaleolithic Sites.* Tempe: Arizona State University, Anthropological Research Papers 52, pp. 123–142.

218 *Bibliography*

Colani, M. (1927). L'âge de pierre dans la province de Hoa Binh *(Tonkin)*. Hanoi: *Mémoire du service géologique de l'Indochine* XIV, fasc. 1.

Colani, M. (1929). Quelques paléolithes Hoabiniens typiques de l'abri-sous-roche de Lang Kay, *Bull. de l'Ecole française d'Extrême Orient* 26, 353–384.

Copeland, L. (1970). The Early Upper Paleolithic flint material from levels VI-V, Antelias cave, Lebanon, *Archaeological Studies, Berytus* XIX, 99–150.

Copeland, L. (1975). The Middle and Upper Palaeolithic of Lebanon and Syria in the light of recent research. In Wendorf, F. and Marks, A.E. (Eds.), *Problems in Prehistory: North Africa and the Levant*. Dallas: Southern Methodist University Press, pp. 317–350.

Copeland, L. (1981). Chronology and distribution of the Middle Palaeolithic as known in 1980, in Lebanon and Syria. In Cauvin, J. and Sanlaville, P. (Eds.), *Préhistoire du Levant*. Paris: CNRS, pp. 239–263.

Copeland, L. (1985). The pointed tool of Hummal IA, El-Kowm, Syria, *Cahiers de l'Euphrate* 4, 177–190.

Copeland, L. and Hours, F. (1979). Le paléolithique du Nahr el Kebir. In Sanlaville, P. (Ed.), *Quaternaire et Préhistoire du Nahr el Kebir Septentrional. Les débuts de l'occupation humaine dans la Syrie du Nord et au Levant*. Paris: CNRS (Coll. Maison de l'Orient, 9, Série géographique et préhistorique) n°1, pp. 29–119.

Copeland, L. et Hours, F. (1981). La fin de l'Acheuléen et l'avènement du Paléolithique Moyen en Syrie. In Cauvin, J. and Sanlaville, P. (Eds.), *Préhistoire du Levant*. Paris: CNRS, pp. 225–238.

Copeland, L. et Hours, F. (1983). Le Yabroudien d'El Kowm et sa place dans le Paléolithique du Levant, *Paléorient* 9(1), 21–37.

Crabtree, D. (1972). *An Introduction to Flintworking. Occasional Papers of the Idaho State University Museum*. Pocatello: Idaho State University Museum.

Dauvois, M. (1976). *Précis de dessin dynamique et stuctural des industries lithiques préhistoriques*. Périgueux: Ed. Fanlac.

Davidson, D.S. (1935). Archaeological problems of Northern Australia. *JRAI* 65, 145–184.

de Condorcet, M.J.A. (1970). *Esquisse d'un tableau historique des progrès de l'esprit humain*, 1793–1794, Texte revu et présenté par Prior O.H., Nouvelle édition présentée par Yvon Belaval, Paris, Vrin, Collection: Bibliothèques des textes philosophiques.

Deforge Y. (1985). *Technologie et génétique de l'objet industriel*. Paris: Ed. Maloine, Collection Université de Compiègne.

de Heinzelin Brancourt, J. (1960). Principe de diagnose numérique en typologie, *Mémoires*, 4, 2ème série, t. 14, fasc. 6, Académie royale de Belgique, Classes des sciences.

de Heinzelin Brancourt, J. (1962). *Manuel de typologie des industries lithiques*. Bruxelles: Commission Administrative du Patrimoine de l'Institut Royal des Sciences Naturelles de Belgique.

de Heinzelin Brancourt, J. and Haesaerts, P. (1983). Un cas de débitage laminaire au Paléolithique ancien: Croix-l'Abbé à Saint-Valéry-sur-Somme, *Gallia Préhistoire* 26(1), 189–201.

Delagnes, A. (2000). Blade production during the Middle Paleolithic in Northwestern Europe, *Acta Anthropologica Sinica* 19, 181–188.

Delagnes, A. and Roche, H. (2005). Late Pliocene hominid knapping skills: The case of Lokalalei 2C, West Turkana, Kenya, *Journal of Human Evolution* 48, 435–472.

Bibliography 219

de Lumley, H., Beyne, Y., Barsky, D., Byrne, L., Camara, A., Cauche, D., Celiberti, V., Fournier, A. and Pleurdeau, D. (2004). L'industrie lithique Préoldowayenne du site de Fejej FJ-1. In de Lumley, H. and Beyne, Y. (Eds.), *Les sites préhistoriques de la région de Fejej, sud- Omo, Ethiopie, dans leur contexte stratigraphique et paléontologique*. Paris: Éditions Recherche sur les Civilisations, pp. 391–593.

de Rosnay, J. (1975). *Le Macroscope. Vers une vision globale*. Paris: Editions du Seuil.

de Villers, B. (2010). *Husserl, Leroi-Gourhan et la préhistoire*. Pétra: Coll. Anthropologiques.

Deleuze, G. (1969). *Logique du sens*. Paris: Editions de Minuit.

Depaepe, P., Locht, J.L. and Swinnen, C. (1994). Pointes pseudo-Levallois et éclats débordants sur le site de Beauvais (Oise, France), *Notae Praehistorica* 14, 25–28.

Farrand, W.R. (1994). Confrontation of geological stratigraphy and radiometric dates from Upper Pleistocene sites in the Levant. In Bar-Yosef, O. and Kra, R-S. (Eds.), *Late Quaternary Chronology and Paleoclimates of the Eastern Mediterranean*. Tucson: Radiocarbon, pp. 33–53.

Fleisch, H. (1970). Les habitats du Paléolithique Moyen à Naamé (Liban). *Bulletin Du Musée de Beyrouth* 23, 25–93.

Fleisch, H. and Sanlaville, P. (1969). Vues nouvelles sur Ras Beyrouth. *Honnon* 4, 93–102.

Flichy, P. (1995). *L'innovation technique. Récents développements en sciences sociales. Vers une nouvelle théorie de l'innovation*. Paris: Ed. La Découverte.

Fogaça, E. and Lourdeau, A. (2008). Uma abordagem tecno-funcional e evolutiva dos instrumentos plano-convexos (lesmas) da transição Pleistoceno/Holoceno no Brasil central, *Fumdhamentos* 7, 260–347.

Forestier, H. (1993). Le Clactonien: mise en application d'une nouvelle méthode de débitage s'inscrivant dans la variabilité des systèmes de production lithique du Paléolithique Ancien, *Paléo* 5, 53–82.

Forestier, H. (2010). *La pierre et son ombre: réflexion sur le phénomène Hoabinhien d'Asie du Sud-Est*. Habilitation à diriger des recherches. Paris: Université Paris Ouest Nanterre—La Défense.

Foucart, J. (2006). *Etude comparée des habilités opératoires et motrices de l'homme et du chimpanzé pour une utilisation d'outils trans-primatique: le cassage des noix*. Thèse de doctorat. Paris: Ecole des Hautes Etudes en Sciences Sociales.

Fox, J.R. (2003). The Tor Sadaf lithic assemblages: A technological study of the Early Upper Palaeolithic in the Wadi al-Hasa. In Goring-Morris, N. and Belfer-Cohen, A. (Eds.), *More than Meets the Eye. Studies on Upper Palaeolithic Diversity in the Near East*. Oxford: Oxbow Books, pp. 81–94.

Fox, J.R. and Coinman, N.R. (2004). Emergence of the Levantine Upper Paleolithic: Evidence from the Wadi al-Hasa. In Brantingham, P-J, Kuhn, S. and Kerry, K.W. (Eds.), *The Early Upper Paleolithic Beyond Western Europe*. Berkeley: University of California Press, pp. 97–112.

Garrod, D.A.E. (1951). A Transitional industry from the base of the Upper Palaeolithic in Palestine and Syria, *JRAI* 81, 121–129.

Garrod, D.A.E. (1955). The Mughuret el Emireh in Lower Galilee: Type station of the Emiran industry, *JRAI* 85, 155–162.

Garrod, D.A.E. (1956). Acheuléo-Jabroudien et Pre-Aurignacien de la grotte de Taboun (Mont Carmel); étude stratigraphique et chronologique, *Quaternaria* 3, 39–59.

Garrod, D.A.E. and Bate, D. (1937). *The Stone Age of Mount Carmel*. Oxford: Oxford University Press (vol.1).

Garrod, D.A.E. and Kirkbride, D. (1961). Excavations of the Abri Zumoffen, a Palaeolithic Rock-shelter near Adlun, South Lebanon, *Bulletin du Musée de Beyrouth* XVI, 7–47.

220 *Bibliography*

Geneste, J.M. (1991). Systèmes techniques de production lithique: variations techno-économiques dans les processus de réalisation des outillages paléolithiques. *Technique et Culture* 17–18, 1–35.

Gilead, I. (1991). The Upper Palaeolithic in the Levant, *Journal of World Prehistory* 5(2), 105–154.

Gille, B. (1978). *Histoire des techniques*. Paris: Gallimard, Bibl. de la Pléiade.

Godfrey-Smith, D.I., Vaughan, K.B., Gopher, A. and Barkai, R. (2003). Direct luminescence chronology of the Epipaleolithic Kebaran Site of Nahal Hadera V, Israel, *Geoarchaeology. An International Journal* 18(4), 461–475.

Goebel, T. (2004). The Early Upper Paleolithic of Siberia. In Brantingham, P.J., Kuhn, S. and Kerry, K.W. (Eds.), *The Early Upper Paleolithic Beyond Western Europe*. Berkeley: University of California Press, pp. 162–195.

Golovanova, L. and Doronichev, V.B. (2003). The Middle Paleolithic of the Caucasus, *Journal of World Prehistory* 17(1), 71–140.

Gopher, A., Barkai, R., Shimelmitz, R., Khalaily, M., Lemorini, C., Hershkovitz, I. and Stiner, M. (2005). Qesem Cave: An Amudian site in central Israel, *Journal of the Israel Prehistoric Society* 35, 69–92.

Goring-Morris, N.A. and Belfer-Cohen, A. (2003). *More than Meets the Eye. Studies on Upper Palaeolithic Diversity in the Near East*. Oxford: Oxbow Books.

Guchet, X. (2005). *Les sens de l'évolution technique*. Paris: Editions Léo Scheer.

Guchet, X. (2008). Evolution technique et objectivité technique chez Leroi-Gourhan et Simondon, *Revue Appareil* 2.

Guilbaud, M. and Carpentier, G. (1995). Remontage exceptionnel à Tourville-la-Rivière (Seine-Maritime), *BSPF* 92(3), 289–295.

Gurova, M. (2010). Connotations fonctionnelles des grandes lames Chalcolithiques: Exemple de la Bulgarie, *Archaeologia Bulgarica* XIV(2), 1–10.

Henning, G.J. and Hours, F. (1982). Dates pour le passage entre l'Acheuléen et le Paléolithique Moyen à El Kowm (Syrie), *Paléorient* 8(1), 81–83.

Hottois, G. (1993). *Simondon et la philosophie de la culture scientifique*. Bruxelles: De Boeck.

Hottois, G. (2004). *Philosophies des sciences, philosophies des techniques*. Paris: Odile Jacob.

Hou, Y.M., Potts, R., Yuan, B., Guo, Z., Deino, A., Wang, W., Clark, J., Xie, G. and Huang, W. (2000). Mid-Pleistocene Acheulean-like stone technology of the Bose Basin, South China, *Science* 287, 1622–1626.

Hours, F. (1982). Une nouvelle industrie en Syrie entre l'Acheuléen Supérieur et le Levalloiso-Moustérien. In *Archéologie au Levant, Recueil R. Saidah*. Lyon: Maison de l'Orient, pp. 33–46.

Hours, F. (1986). *Le Paléolithique et l'Epipaléolithique de la Syrie et du Liban*. Dar El-Machreq: Université de Saint-Joseph, Hommes et Sociétés au Proche-Orient.

Husserl E. (1988). Lettre à Lucien Levy-Bruhl, le 11 mars 1935 (trad. Fr. de P. Soulez), *Gradhiva* 4, 63–73.

Ibáñez, J-J. and Urquijo, J-G. (2006). Évolution technique et société dans le Néolithique du Moyen Euphrate. In Astruc, L., Bon, F., Léa, V., Milcent, P-Y. and Philibert, S. (Eds), *Normes techniques et pratiques sociales de la simplicité des outillages pré- et protohistoriques*. Antibes: Éditions APDCA, pp. 361–376.

Isaac, G.L. (1976). The activities of early African hominids: A review of archaeological evidence from the time span two and a half to one million years ago. In Isaac, G.L.

and McCown, E.R. (Eds.), *Human Origins: Louis Leakey and the East African Evidence*. Menlo Park: W-A. Benjamin, pp. 483–514.

Jelinek, A.J. (1975). A preliminary report on some Lower and Middle Palaeolithic industries from the Tabun Cave, Mount Carmel (Israel). In Wendorf, F. and Marks, A. (Eds.), *Problems in Prehistory: North Africa and the Levant*. Dallas: Southern Methodist University Press, pp. 297–315.

Jelinek, A.J. (1981). The Middle Palaeolithic in the Southern Levant from the perspective of Tabun Cave. In Cauvin, J. et Sanlaville, P. (Eds.), *Préhistoire du Levant*. Paris: CNRS, pp. 265–281.

Jelinek, A.J. (1982). The Middle Palaeolithic in the Southern Levant, with comments on the appearance of modern *Homo Sapiens*. In Ronen, A. (Ed.), *The Transition from Lower to Middle Paleolithic and the Origin of Modern Man*. Oxford: BAR, International series, 151, pp. 57–101.

Jelinek, A.J. (1990). The Amudian in the context of the Mugharan tradition at the Tabun Cave (Mount Carmel), Israel. In Mellars, P. (Ed.), *The Emergence of Modern Humans. An Archaeological Perspective*. Edinburgh: Edinburgh University Press, pp. 81–90.

Johnson, C.R. and McBrearty, S. (2010). 500,000 years old blades from the Kapthurin Formation, Kenya, *Journal of Human Evolution* 58, 193–200.

Karlin, C. and Ploux, S. (1994). Analyse des variations dans les modes de production laminaire et lamellaire, *BSPF* 91(3), 185–186.

Keeley, L.H. (1982). Hafting and retooling: Effects on the archaeological record, *American Antiquity* 47, 798–809.

Koehler, H. (2009). *Comportement et identité techniques au Paléolithique Moyen (Weischsélien ancien) dans le Bassin Parisien: une question d'échelle d'analyse?* Thèse de doctorat. Paris: Université Paris Ouest Nanterre-La Défense.

Kozlowski, J.K. (1988). L'Apparition du Paléolithique Supérieur. In Kozlowski, J.K. (Ed.), *L'Homme de Neandertal, vol. 8, La Mutation*. Liège: ERAUL, pp. 11–21.

Kozlowski, J.K. and Kozlowski, S. (1996). *Le Paléolithique en Pologne* (In Grenoble (Ed)). Millon: Coll. L'Homme des origines, série Préhistoire d'Europe, n°2.

Kuhn, S. (2004). From Initial Upper Palaeolithic to Ahmarian at Ûçagizli cave, Turkey, *Anthropologie* XLII(3), 275–288.

Kuhn, S., Stiner, M.C. and Güleç, E. (2004). New perspectives on the Initial Upper Paleolithic: The view from Ûçagizli cave, Turkey. In Brantingham, P.J., Kuhn, S. and Kerry, K.W. (Eds.), *The Early Upper Paleolithic Beyond Western Europe*. Berkeley: University of California Press, pp. 113–128.

Lavallée, D., Julien, M., Wheeler, J. and Karlin, C. (1985). *Telarmachay, chasseurs et pasteurs préhistoriques des Andes*. Paris: Editions Recherche sur les Civilisations.

Leakey, L.S.B. (1951). *Olduvai Gorge (Tanganyika), A Report on the Evolution of the Handaxe Culture in Beds I-IV*. Cambridge: Cambridge University Press.

Lepot, M. (1993) *Approche techno-fonctionnelle de l'outillage lithique moustérien: essai de classification des parties actives en termes d'efficacité technique: application à la couche M2e sagittale du Grand Abri de la Ferrassie (fouille Henri Delporte)*. Mémoire de Maîtrise. Paris: Université de Paris X—Nanterre.

Leroi-Gourhan, A. (1943/1971). *Evolution et techniques 1. L'Homme et la matière*. Paris: Ed. Albin Michel.

Leroi-Gourhan, A. (1945/1973). *Evolution et techniques 2.Milieu et techniques*. Paris: Ed. Albin Michel.

Leroi-Gourhan, A. (1946). *Archéologie du Pacifique-Nord. Matériaux pour l'étude des relations entre les peuples riverains d'Asie et d'Amérique*. Paris: Travaux et mémoires de l'institut d'ethnologie, XLIII.

222 Bibliography

Leroi-Gourhan, A. (1964). *Le Geste et la parole, Technique et langage.* Paris: Ed. Albin Michel.

Leroi-Gourhan, A. (1965). *Le Geste et la parole, La Mémoire et les rythmes.* Paris: Ed. Albin Michel.

Leroi-Gourhan, A. (1983). *Le Fil du temps.* Paris: Fayard.

Le Tensorer, J.M. (2005). Le Yabroudien et la transition du Paléolithique Ancien au Paléolithique Moyen en Syrie: l'exemple d'El Kowm, *Munibe* 57(2), 71–82.

Le Tensorer, J.M. (2007). *Rapport préliminaire des fouilles préhistoriques de la mission Syro-Suisse concernant les gisements de Hummal et Nadaouiyeh (El Kowm, Syrie centrale), Résultats de la campagne 2007.* Basel: Institut de Préhistoire de l'Université de Bâle, Centre de recherches Tell Arida.

Le Tensorer, J.M. and Hours, F. (1989). L'occupation d'un territoire à la fin du Paléolithique Ancien et au Paléolithique Moyen à partir de l'exemple d'El Kowm (Syrie). In Patou, M. and Freeman, L.G. (Eds.), *L'Homme de Neandertal, vol. 6, La Subsistance.* Liège: ERAUL, pp. 107–114.

Lhomme, V., Connet, N. and Chaussé C. (1999). *Le site Paléolithique Moyen de la Garenne à Saint-Firmin-des-Prés (Loir-et-Cher),* D.F.S. de sauvetage urgent. Orléans: AFAN—Service Régional de l'Archéologie du Centre.

Li, Y. (2014). *Étude technologique de l'industrie lithique du site de Guanyindong dans la province du Guizhou, sud-ouest de la Chine.* Prigonrieux: @rchéo-éditions.com, Travaux Universitaires.

Lindly, J. and Clark, G. (1987). A preliminary lithic analysis of the Mousterian site of Ain Difla (WHS site 634) in the Wadi Ali, west central Jordan, *Proceedings of the Prehistoric Society* 53, 279–292.

Liubin, V.P. (1977). *Mustierskie kul'turi Kavkaza [Mousterian culture in the Caucasus],* Leningrad: Nauka.

Liubin, V.P. (1989). *Paleolit Kavkaza [The Palaeolithic of Caucasus].* Leningrad: Nauka.

Locht, J.L. (2003). L'industrie du gisement de Beauvais (Oise, France): Objectifs et variabilités. In Peresani, M. (Ed.), *Discoid Lithic Technology. Advances and Implications.* Oxford: Archaeopress, BAR International series 1120, pp. 193–209.

Locht, J.L., Antoine, P., Bahain, J.J., Dwrila, G., Raymond, P., Limondin-Lozouet, N., Gauthier, A., Debenham, N., Frechen, M., Rousseau, D.D., Hatté, C., Haesaerts, P. and Metsdach, H. (2003). Le gisement Paléolithique Moyen et les séquences Pléistocènes de Villiers-Adam (Val-d'Oise): chronostratigraphie, environnement et implantations humaines, *Gallia Préhistoire* 45, 1–111.

Lombard, M. (2005). The Howieson's Poort of South Africa: what we know, what we think we know, what we need to know, *Southern African Humanities* 17, 33–55.

Lourdeau, A. (2010). *Le technocomplexe Itaparica. Définition techno-fonctionnelle des industries à pièces façonnées unifacialement à une face plane dans le centre et nord-est du Brésil pendant la transition Pléistocène-Holocène et l'Holocène ancien.* Thèse de Doctorat. Paris: Nanterre, Université de Paris Ouest-La Défense.

Lycett, S. (2009). Are Victoria West cores "proto-Levallois"? A phylogenetic assessment, *Journal of Human Evolution* 56(2), 175–191.

Maher, L., Banning, E.B. and Chazan, M. (2011). Oasis or mirage? Assessing the role of abrupt climate change in the prehistory of the Southern Levant, *Cambridge Archaeological Journal* 21, 1–3.

Mannu, M. and Ottoni, E.B. (2008). The enhanced tool-kit of two groups of wild bearded capuchin monkeys in the Caatinga: Tool making, associative use, and secondary tools, *American Journal of Primatology* 71, 242–251.

Bibliography 223

Marks, A.E. (1983a). *Prehistory and Paleoenvironments in the Central Negev, Israel* (Vol. III). Dallas: Southern Methodist University Press.

Marks, A.E. (1983b). The sites of Boker and Boker Tachtit: A brief introduction. In Marks, A.E, (Ed.), *Prehistory and Paleoenvironments in the Centra Negev, Israel* (Vol. III, Part 3). Dallas: Southern Methodist University, pp 15–37.

Marks, A.E. (1993). The Early Upper Paleolithic: The view from the Levant. In Knecht, H., Pike-Tay, A. and White, R. (Eds.), *Before Lascaux: The Complete Record of the Early Upper Palaeolithic*. Boca Raton: CRC Press, pp. 5–22.

Marks, A.E. and Crew H.L. (1972). Rosh Ein Mor, an open-air Mousterian site in the Central Negev, Israel. *Current Anthropology* 13(5), 591–593

Marks, A.E. and Monigal, K. (1995). Modeling the production of elongated blanks from the early Levantine Mousterian at Rosh Ein Mor. In Dibble, H.L. and Bar-Yosef, O. (Eds.), *The Definition and Interpretation of Levallois technology*. Madison: Prehistory Press, pp. 267–278.

Marks, A.E. and Volkman, P. (1983). Changing core reduction strategies: A technological Shift from the Middle to the Upper Paleolithic in the Southern Levant. In Trinkaus, E. (Ed.), *The Mousterian Legacy*. Oxford: BAR, International series, 164, pp. 13–33.

Mauss, M. (1947). *Manuel d'ethnographie*. Paris: Payot.

McBrearty, S., Bishop, L. and Kingston, J. (1996). Variability in traces Middle Pleistocene hominid behavior in the Kaphturin Formation, Baringo, Kenya, *Journal Human Evolution* 30, 563–580.

McCarty, J.P. (1976). *Australian Aboriginal Stone Implements*. Sydney: The Australian Museum Trust.

Meignen, L. (1994). Paléolithique Moyen au Proche-Orient: Le phénomène laminaire. In Revillon, S. and Tuffreau, A. (Eds.), *Les industries laminaires au Paléolithique Moyen*, Paris: CNRS, Dossier de documentation archéologique, 18, pp. 125–159.

Meignen, L. (1996). Les prémices du Paléolithique supérieur au Proche-Orient. In Carbonell, E. and Vaquero, M. (Eds.), *The Last Neandertals, the First Anatomically Modern Humans, Cultural Change and Human Evolution: The Crisis at 40 KA BP*. Tarragona: Universitat Rovira i Virgili, pp. 107–127.

Meignen, L. (1998a). Le Paléolithique Moyen au Levant Sud et Central: Que nous apprennent les données récentes? In Otte, M. (Ed.), *Préhistoire d'Anatolie. Genèse de deux mondes*. Liège: ERAUL, pp. 685–708.

Meignen, L. (1998b). Hayonim Cave lithic assemblages in the context of the Near Eastern Middle Paleolithic: A preliminary report. In Akazawa, T., Aoki, K. and Bar-Yosef, O. (Eds.), *Neandertals and Modern Humans in Western Asia*. New York: Plenum Press, pp. 165–180.

Meignen, L. (2000). Early Middle Palaeolithic blade technology in Southwestern Asia, *Acta Anthropologica Sinica* 19, 158–168.

Meignen, L. (2007). Le phénomène laminaire du Proche-Orient du Paléolithique Inférieur aux débuts du Paléolithique Supérieur, *Congrès du centenaire: un siècle de construction du discours scientifique en Préhistoire*, *XXVI Congrès Préhistorique de France, Avignon* 3, 79–94.

Meignen, L. (2011). Contribution of Hayonim cave assemblages to the understanding of the so-called Early Levantine Mousterian. In Le Tensorer, J.M., Jagher, R. and Otte, M. (Eds.), *The Lower and Middle Palaeolithic in the Middle East and Neighbouring Regions*. Liège: ERAUL, p. 126.

Meignen, L. and Tushabramishvili, N. (2006). Paléolithique Moyen Laminaire sur les flancs sud du Caucase: productions lithiques et fonctionnement du site de Djruchula (Géorgie), *Paléorient* 32(2), 81–104.

224 Bibliography

Meignen, L. and Tushabramishvili, N. (2010). Djruchula Cave, on the southern slopes of the great Caucasus: An extension of the Near Eastern Middle Paleolithic blady phenomenon to the North, *Journal of The Israel Prehistoric Society* 40, 35–61.

Mellars, P. (2004). Neanderthals and the Modern Human colonization of Europe, *Nature* 432, 461–465.

Mellars, P. and Tixier, J. (1989). Radiocarbon Accelerator dating of Ksar'Akil (Lebanon) and the chronology of the Upper Palaeolithic sequence in the Middle East, *Antiquity* 63, 761–768.

Mercier, N. and Valladas, H. (1994). Thermoluminescence dates for the Paleolithic Levant. In Bar-Yosef, O. and Kra, R.S. (Eds.), *Late Quaternary Chronology and Paleoclimates of the Eastern Mediterranean*. Tucson: University of Arizona, Radiocarbon, pp. 13–20.

Mercier, N. and Valladas, H. (2003). Reassessment of TL age-estimates of burnt flints from the Paleolithic site of Tabun Cave, Israel, *Journal of Human Evolution* 45, 401–409.

Mercier, N. and Valladas, H. (2011). Dating the Early Middle Palaeolithic laminar industry from Djuruchula cave, Republic of Georgia, *Paléorient* 36(2), 165–173.

Mercier, N., Valladas, H., Froget, L., Joron, J.L., Reyss, J.L., Weiner, S., Goldberg, P., Meignen, L., Bar Yosef, O., Kuhn, S., Stiner, M., Belfer-Cohen, A., Tillier, A.M., Arensburg, B. and Vandermeersch, B. (2007). Hayonim Cave: A TL-based chronology for this Levantine Mousterian sequence, *Journal of Archaeological Science* 34(7), 1064–1077.

Mercier, N., Valladas, H., Valladas, G., Jelinek, A., Meignen, L., Joron, J.L. and Reyss, J.L. (1995). TL Dates of burnt flints from Jelinek's excavations at Tabun and their implications, *Journal of Archaeological Science* 22, 495–509.

Merleau-Ponty, M. (1960). Bergson se faisant. In Merleau-Ponty, M. (Ed.), *Signes*. Paris: Gallimard, p. 236.

Morello, F. (2005). Technologia y métodos para el desbaste de lascas en el norte de Tierra del Fuego: los nucleos del sitio Cabo san Vincente, *Magallania* 33(2), 29–56.

Mourre, V. (2003). Discoïde ou pas Discoïde? Réflexions sur la pertinence des critères techniques définissant le débitage Discoïde. In Peresani, M. (Ed.), *Discoid Lithic Technology. Advances and Implications*. Oxford: BAR (International series, 1120), pp. 1–18.

Movius, H. (1944). *Early Man and Pleistocene Stratigraphy in South and Eastern Asia*. Cambridge: Peabody Museum, Bulletin 215.

Movius, H. (1948). The Lower Palaeolithic cultures of Southern and Eastern Asia, *Transactions of the American Philosophical Society* 38(4), 329–420.

Movius, H. (1957). Pebble-tool terminology in India and Pakistan, *Man in India* 37(2), 149–156.

Mulvaney, D.J. (1975). *The Prehistory of Australia* (Revised Edition). Harmondsworth: Penguin Books.

Nami, H. (1992). Noticia sobre la existencia de technica "Levallois" en peninsula Mitre, extremo sudoriental de Tierra del Fuego, *Annales del Instituto de la Patagonia* (Serie Ciencas Humanas) 21, 73–80.

Nespoulet, R. (1999). Remontage d'une microgravette dans une séquence de débitage laminaire du Gravettien final de l'Abri Pataud (Les Eyzies-de-Tayac, Dordogne). Niveau 3: Périgordien VI. *Préhistoire du Sud-Ouest* 6, 57–77.

Neuville, R. (1930). Notes de préhistoire Palestinienne, *Journal of the Palestine Oriental Society* 10, 193–221.

Neuville, R. (1951). *Le Paléolithique et le Mésolithique de Judée*. Paris: Archives de l'Institut de Paléontologie Humaine, 24, Masson et Cie.

Nishiaki, Y. (2000). *Lithic Technology of Neolithic Syria*. Oxford: BAR, International Series 840.

Bibliography 225

Noone, H.V.V. (1943). Some aboriginal stone implements of Western Australia. *Records to the South Australian Museum* VII.

Noone, H.V.V. (1949). Some implements of the Australian aborigines with European parallels. *Man* 49, 111–114.

Ohnuma, K. (1988). *Ksar'Akil, Lebanon: A Technological Study of the Earlier Upper Palaeolithic Levels at Ksar'Akil. Vol 3, Levels XXV-XIV.* Oxford: BAR, International Series 426.

Olszewski, D.I. (1997). From the Late Ahmarian to the Early Natufian: A summary of hunter-gatherer activities at Yutil al-Hasa. West-Central Jordan. In Gebel, H.G., Kefafi, Z. and Rollefson, G.O. (Eds.), *The Prehistory of Jordan, II. Perspectives from 1997.* Berlin: SENEPSE 4, pp. 171–182

Otte, M., Boëda, E. and Haesaerts, P. (1990). Rocourt: industrie laminaire archaïque, *Helinium* XXIX(1), 3–13.

Owen, W.E. (1938). The Kombewa culture, Kenya colony, *Man* 38(218), 203–205.

Owen, W.E. (1939). An amateur field collector in Kavirondo, *Journal of the Royal African Society* 38(151), 220–226.

Pannochia, F. (1950). L'industria Pontiniana della Grotta di S. Agostino (Gaeta), *Rivista di Scienze Preistoriche* V(1–4), 67–86.

Papaconstantinou. E.S. (1987). *Micromoustérien: les idées et les pierres. Le Micromoustérien d'Asprochaliko (Grèce) et le problème des industries microlithiques de Moustérien.* Thèse de doctorat. Paris: Nanterre, Université de Paris X Nanterre.

Pelegrin, J. (2006). Long blade technology in the old world: An experimental approach and some archaeological results. In Apel, J. and Knutsson, K. (Eds.), *Skilled Production and Social Reproduction—Aspects of Traditional Stone-Tool Technology.* Upsalla: Societas Archeologica Upsaliensis, pp. 37–68.

Peretto, C. Ornella Amore, F., Hedley, I., Laurent, M., Lebreton, V., and Longo, L. (1998). L'Industrie lithique de Ca'Belvedere di Monte Poggiolo: Stratigraphie, matière première, typologie, remontages et traces d'utilisation, *L'Anthropologie* 102(4), 343–465.

Phillips, J.L. (1994). The Upper Palaeolithic chronology of the Levant and the Nile Valley. In Bar Yosef, O. and Kra, R. (Eds.): *Late Quaternary Chronology and Paleoclimates of the Eastern Mediterranean.* Tucson: Radiocarbon, pp. 169–176.

Ploux, S. and Soriano, S. (2003). Umm el Tlel, une séquence du Paléolithique supérieur en Syrie centrale. Industries lithiques et chronologie culturelle, *Paléorient* 29(2), 5–34.

Porraz, G., Texier, P.J., Rigaud, J.P., Parkington, J., Poggenpoel, C. and Roberts, D. (2008). Preliminary characterization of a middle stone age lithic assemblage preceding the classic Howieson's Poort complex at Diepkloof Rock Shelter, Western Cape province, South Africa. In Lombard, M., Sievers, C. and Ward, V. (Eds.), *Current Themes in Middle Stone Age Research.* Cape Town: South African Archaeology Society (Goodwin series, vol. 10), pp. 105–121.

Rabardel, P. (1995). *Les Hommes et les technologies. Approche cognitive des instruments contemporains.* Paris: Armand Colin.

Ranov, V.A. and Amosova, A.G. (1984). Excavations of the Mousterian site of Kuhdji in 1978, *Arkheologischeskie Raboty v Tadjikistane* 18, 11–47.

Revillon, S. and Tuffreau, A. (1994). Valeur et signification du débitage laminaire du gisement Paléolithique Moyen de Seclin (Nord). In Revillon, S. and Tuffreau, A. (Eds.), *Les Industries laminaires au Paléolithique Moyen.* Paris: CNRS, Dossier de documentation archéologique, 18, pp. 19–43.

Richter, D., Hauck, T., Wojtzack, D., Le Tensorer, J.M. and Muhesen, S. (2011). Chronometric age estimates for the site of Hummal (El Kowm, Syria). In Le Tensorer, J.M., Jagher,

226 Bibliography

R. and Otte, M. (Eds.), *The Lower and Middle Palaeolithic in the Middle East and Neighbouring Regions*. Liège: ERAUL, 126, pp. 249–261.

Roche, H., Delagnes, A., Brugal, J.-P., Feibel, C., Kibunjia, M., Texier, P.J. and Mourre, V. (1999). Evidence for early hominids lithic production and technical skill at 2.3 Myr, West Turkana, Kenya, *Nature* 399, 57–60.

Roe, D.A. (1983). *Adlun in the Stone Age. The Excavations of D.A.E. Garrod in the Lebanon, 1958–1963*. Oxford: BAR, International series, 159.

Rosen, S.A. (1983). The Canaanean Blade and the Early Bronze Age, *Israel Exploration Journal* 33, 15–29.

Rosen, S.A. (1997). *Lithics After the Stone Age: A Handbook of Stone Tools from the Levant*. Lanham: Altamira Press.

Rots, V. (2002). *Hafting Traces on Flint Tools: Possibilities and Limitations of Macro and Microscopic Approaches*. Thèse de doctorat. Leuven: Katholieke Universiteit Leuven.

Rots, V. (2010). *Prehension and Hafting Traces of Flint Tools: A methodology*. Leuven: Leuven University Press.

Rust, A. (1950). *Die Höhlenfunde von Jabrud (Syrien)*. Neumünster: K. Wachholtz.

Sanlaville, P. (1998). Les changements dans l'environnement au Moyen-Orient de 20 000 BP à 6 000 BP, *Paléorient* 23–2, 249–262.

Sartre, J.P. (1996). *L'existentialisme est un humanisme*. Paris: Gallimard.

Schmider, B. (2002). *L'Aurignacien de la Grotte du Renne à Arcy-sur-Cure* (Gallia Préhistoire, supplément 34). Paris: CNRS.

Schumacher, E.F. (1978). *Small is Beautiful. Une société à la mesure de l'Homme*. Paris: Editions du Seuil.

Schwarcz, H., Blackwell, B., Goldberg, P. and Marks, A.E. (1979). Uranium series dating of travertine from archaeological sites, Nahal Zin, Israel, *Nature* 277, 558–560.

Schwarcz, H. and Rink, W. (1998). Progress in ESR and U-Series chronology of the Levantine Paleolithic. In Akazawa, T., Aoki, K. and Bar-Yosef, O. (Eds.), *Neanderthals and Modern Humans in West Asia*. New York: Plenum Press, pp. 57–67.

Shäfer, J. and Ranov, V.A. (1998). Middle Palaeolithic blades industrie and the Upper Palaeolithic of Central Asia. In Otte, M. (Ed.), *Préhistoire d'Anatolie, Genèse des deux Mondes*. Liege: ERAUL, 85, pp. 785–814.

Simondon, G. (1958). *Du mode d'existence des objets techniques*. Paris: Ed. Aubier.

Simondon, G. (1964). *L'Individu et sa genèse physico-biologique*. Paris: PUF.

Soriano, S. (2000). *Outillage bifacial et outillage sur éclat au Paléolithique Moyen Ancien et Moyen: coexistence et interaction*. Thèse de doctorat. Paris: Université de Paris X Nanterre.

Soriano, S. (2001). Statut fonctionnel de l'outillage bifacial dans les industries du Paléolithique Moyen, proposition méthodologique. In Cliquet, D. (Ed.), *Les Industries à outils bifaciaux du Paléolithique Moyen d'Europe occidentale*. Liège: ERAUL, 98, pp. 77–83.

Soriano, S. (2005). Le Sud: Une plate-forme pour le peuplement des espaces septentrionaux pendant le Pléistocène Moyen Récent? In Jaubert, J. et Barbaza, M. (Eds.), *Territoires, déplacements, mobilité, échanges durant la Préhistoire. Terres et hommes du Sud*. Paris: Éditions du CTHS, pp. 63–83.

Soriano, S., Villa, P. and Wadley, L. (2007). Blade technology and tool forms in the Middle Stone Age of South Africa: The Howieson's Poort and post-Howieson's Poort at Rose Cottage Cave, *Journal of Archaeological Science* 34, 681–703.

Bibliography 227

Spencer, B. and Gillens, F.J. (1912). *Across Australia*. London: Macmillan.

Stiegler, B. (1994). *La Technique et le temps* (t. 1). *La faute d'Epiméthée*. Paris: Galilée.

Stiegler, B. (1998a). Temps et individuations technique, psychique et collective dans l'œuvre de Simondon, *Intellectica, Sciences sociales et cognition* 1–2(26–27), 241–256

Stiegler, B. (1998b). *Lieu, mémoire et technique*. www.scribd.com/document/191972284/Stiegler-Lieu-memoire-et-technique.

Taddei, A. (1987). Algunos aspectos de la Arqueología Prehistórica del Uruguay. In Nunez, L. and Meggers, B. (Eds.), *Estudios Atacameños. Intevestigaciones paleoindias al sur de la línea ecuatorial*. Chile: Universidad del Norte, Instituto de Investigaciones Arqueológicas, R.P. Gustavo Le Paige, S.J. San Pedro de Atacama, pp. 62–93.

Tattersall, I. (1997). Out of Africa again . . . and again? *Scientific American* 276, 46–53.

Tattersall, I. (1999). *L'Emergence de l'homme. Essai sur l'évolution et l'unicité humaine*. Paris: Gallimard.

Teilhard de Chardin, P. (1955). *Le Phénomène humain*. Paris: Editions du Seuil.

Teilhard de Chardin, P. (1956). *La Place de l'homme dans la nature*. Paris: Ed. Albin Michel.

Texier, P.J. (1995). The Oldowan assemblage from NY 18 site at Nyabusosi (Toro- Uganda), *CRAScP* 320, 647–653.

Tinland, F. (2006). La technique et ses temps. In Vaysse, J.M. (Ed.), *Technique, monde, individuation. Heidegger, Simondon, Deleuze*. Zurich: Georg Olms Verlag, pp. 17–56.

Tixier, J. (1957). *Le hachereau dans l'Acheuléen Nord Africain*. Actes des Congrès préhistoriques de France 15 (Poitiers-Angoulème), pp. 914–923.

Tixier, J. (1958–1959). Les pièces pédonculées de l'Atérien, *Lybica* VI-VII, 127–158.

Tixier, J., Inizan, M.L. and Roche, H. (1980). *Préhistoire de la pierre taillée, I, Terminologie et technologie*. Paris: CREP.

Tuffreau, A. (1979). Les débuts du Paléolithique Moyen dans la France septentrionale, *BSPF* 76(5), 140–142.

Tuffreau, A. (2004). *L'Acheuléen: de l'Homo Erectus à l'Homme de Neandertal*. Paris: La Maison des Roches.

Tuffreau, A., Amelott-Van Der Heijden, N. and Ducrocq, T. (1991). La fouille de sauvetage du gisement Paléolithique Moyen de Riencourt-lès-Bapaume (Pas-de-Calais), *BSPF* 88(7), 202–209.

Valin, L., Masson, B., Caspar, J.P. and Depiereux, E. (2006). L'outil idéal. Analyse du standard Levallois des sites Moustériens d'Hermies (Nord de la France), *Paléo* 18, 237–272.

Valladas, H., Mercier, N., Joron, J.L. and Reyss, J.L. (1998). GIF Laboratory dates for Middle Paleolithic Levant. In Akazawa, T., Aoki, K. and Bar-Yosef, O. (Eds.), *Neanderthals and Modern Humans in West Asia*. New York: Plenum Press, pp. 69–75.

Van Riet Lowe, C. (1945). The evolution of the Levallois technique in South Africa, *Man* 45, 49–59.

Villa, P., Soriano, S., Teyssandier, N. and Wurz, S. (2010). The Howiesons Poort and MSA III at Klasies River Main Site, Cave 1A, *Journal of Archaeological Science* 37(3), 630–655.

Villemeur, I. (1991). *Etude morphologique et biomécanique du squelette de la main des Néandertaliens, comparaison avec la main des hommes actuels*. Thèse de Doctorat. Talence: Université de Bordeaux I.

Vishnyatsky, L.B. (2004). The Middle-Upper Paleolithic interface in former Soviet Central Asia. In Brantingham, P.J., Kuhn, S. and Kerry K.W. (Eds.), *The Early Upper Paleolithic beyond Western Europe*. Berkeley: University of California Press, pp. 151–161.

228 *Bibliography*

Wotjtczak, D. (2011). Hummal (Central Syria) and its eponymous industry. In Le Tensorer, J.M., Jagher, R. and Otte, M. (Eds.): *The Lower and Middle Palaeolithic in the Middle East and Neighbouring Regions*. Liège: ERAUL, 126, pp. 289–307.

Yonsei University Press (2001). *Old Stone Age Relics of Korea*. Yonsei University Museum.

Zeitoun, V., Forestier, H. and Nakbunlung S. (2008). *Préhistoires au sud du Triangle d'Or*. Montpellier: IRD Editions.

Index

abstract object/structure 15, 27, 34–40, 59–60, 67, 115–116, 153, 155, 169, 171, 182, 188–190, 205, 207
Acheulean xxx, 16, 34, 37, 39, 42, 87, 141, 169–175, 178
additive structure *see* abstract object/structure
alterity xxx, 17, 144, 185, 201, 211
Amudian 55, 108, 155, 158, 164–173, 204
appropriation 17, 29
associated milieu 12, 34, 45, 134, 136, 190
Aurignacian 97, 164, 168, 186–187
autocorrelation 16, 132, 134, 136

Baradostian 98
Barbas, Dordogne, France 32, 38–39, 79, 89–90, 97–98, 124
Beauvais, France 115
Biache St. Vaast, France xxvi–xxviii
Bicheri, Syria 125
biface xxix–xxx, 21, 25, 27, 34–35, 39, 41–43, 53, 153, 172; *see also* hand axe
Binford, Lewis 5
bipolar debitage *see* split
bitumen 45–46, 191, 204
blade/blade production 25, 27, 33, 44–46, 55, 58, 64–66, 82–83, 95–96, 98, 106–108, 114–121, 128–131, 134, 136, 154–193, 211
bladelet 65–66, 94–100, 117, 136, 140, 165–168, 177, 185–193
Bordes, François 5, 9, 11, 39, 119, 125, 165
Bose, China 141
burin 5–6, 59, 163, 165, 168, 171, 177–179, 203

Cagny-La Garenne, France 91, 93
capuchins 27

centripetal debitage 65, 88, 104, 108, 124–126
chaîne opératoire xxvii, 10, 151, 231–232
Champ-Bossuet, France 105
chopper/chopping tool 34–35, 63, 137
Clactonian 75, 79
concrete object/structure 15–16, 27, 31–44, 50, 59, 63–67, 106, 115–116, 153, 189–190, 193, 205
confection 27–28, 32–35, 42–45, 47–52, 55, 59, 68, 82–84, 171–174
connaissance 200–202; *see also* knowledge
convergence 1–2, 15–17, 20, 34, 37, 39, 69, 104, 166, 171, 178
Corbiac Cavaille, France 124
cutting edge 6, 25, 28–31, 34–35, 38–39, 43, 54, 70–71, 73–74, 83, 137, 156–158, 167, 171, 174, 204
cycle/cyclicity 2, 16–17, 35–41, 67, 134, 136, 157–158, 193, 206–210

Deforge, Yves 67
Des Forêts, France 130
diacritical drawing/diagram xxviii–xxix, 10
discoid/discoidal 10, 65–66, 88, 104, 106–108, 111–115, 178

éclat débordant xxvii, 113
El Meirah, Syria 37, 40
endscraper 5–6, 21, 59, 163, 165, 168, 177–179
epi-phylogenetic memory 198–199
epistemological xxvi, xxxii, 2
ergonomics 24, 53, 165–168, 171–172, 189
evolution xxv, xxix, 2–3, 5, 10–17, 20–21, 23, 26–27, 30–33, 35–37, 39–40, 45, 55, 58–59, 67–69, 107, 130–137, 141, 144, 153–157, 163–193,

230 *Index*

205–211; biological evolution xxv, 2, 134; coevolution 3, 5, 14, 16–17, 20–21, 67–68, 131, 188, 205, 211; cognitive evolution xxix; evolutionary stage 15, 20, 26, 36–37, 59, 136, 144, 154, 156, 173, 189, 207–210; evolution of technique 2, 10, 14, 35, 179–180; evolution of tools 10–11, 20–21, 59, 68–69, 137, 156, 193
exterior milieu 10, 36, 134, 136

façonnage see shaping
Fjej, Ethiopia 89, 92
fracture xxiii, 27–28, 60, 66, 69, 73–74, 105, 118, 137, 154
French school xxiv, xxvi, xxviii–xxix, 1
functional constraint 2, 68, 73
gesture xxvii, xxxi, 11, 20–27, 35, 47, 60, 69, 132, 156, 164–172, 179, 205

Gipo, Korea 76, 79
Gravettian 64, 98
grip 11, 26–27, 53, 55
Guanyindong, China 77, 79, 84–86

haft/hafting 6, 21–23, 26, 43–58, 67, 121, 168, 180, 187, 204–205
hand axe 6; *see also* biface
High Lodge, UK 79, 81, 83
Hoabinian 141, 205
Homo erectus 39
Homo faber 23
Homo sapiens 1, 23, 179
homothetic/non-homothetic 60–67, 81, 112–113, 133, 136, 162
Hummalian 43–47, 55–58, 158–162, 164–167, 171–175, 180–182, 187, 204–205
hylomorphism/hylomorphic xxviii, 4, 9, 13–14
hypertely 16, 47, 134, 155, 171

incising 27–31, 73
innovation 20, 58, 175, 185, 188
instrumentalization/instrumentation 24–25
integrated structure *see* concrete object/ structure
Intermediate Paleolithic 58, 96, 163, 185
intrinsic constraints 25–26
invention xxxi, 14, 17, 20, 35, 47, 50, 67, 131, 140, 153, 155, 169, 175, 184–185, 188–189, 206–210

Kaféine, Syria 79–82, 95, 109–110, 160
Kapthurin Formation, Kenya 82, 154

knowledge xxiv, xxvi, xxxi, 1–2, 10–12
Kombewa flakes 87, 89–91, 105
Korolevo, Ukraine 90–91
Külna, Czech Republic 109

La Bouloie, Crenay, France 128–129
leiliras, Australia 21–22, 108, 114
Leroi-Gourhan, André xxix, 9–14, 21, 27, 73–74, 153, 180; tendance (*see* tendance)
Levallois xxvii–xxx, 9–10, 25–27, 33, 42–47, 55, 64–65, 69, 87–88, 91–94, 98–99, 102–107, 115–116, 118–121, 129–136, 141, 154–155, 158–163, 165, 167–168, 173–178, 182–185, 189; Levallois concept xxviii, 69, 88, 91, 94, 106, 132, 161; Levallois core xxviii, 65, 87, 93–94, 99, 115, 134; Levallois method xxviii; Levallois points (including typo-points) xxvii, 21, 26, 98–99, 102–106, 108, 120, 123, 163, 165, 167, 177, 185; Proto-Levallois 87; Pseudo-Levallois 104–106, 113
lineage xxviii, xxxi, 10–12, 14–17, 26–28, 36–39, 44, 47, 55, 58, 67, 134, 136–137, 141, 153–157, 169, 171–173, 175, 182–183, 188–190, 198–200, 205–210
lithic analysis xxiii, 12, 204
logos 4
Lokalalei, Kenya 74
Longgupo, China 141
longue durée 17

macaques 27
Magdalenian 64, 98, 118, 137
Maomaodong, China 142–143
Mauss, Marcel xxviii, xxxi, 9–10
medical xxiv–xxviii
memory xxv–xxvi, xxviii–xxxii, 9, 12–13, 16–17, 21, 24–25, 198–205
Middle Paleolithic 5, 23, 107, 161–162, 167, 203–204
migration 1, 20, 141, 172, 207
Mousterian 9, 16, 58, 87, 118, 141, 158–159, 161, 168, 175, 182, 185
Movius, Hallam 141

naturalized object 9, 190, 203
Neolithic 65–66, 106, 118, 164, 167–168
novelty 2, 179
Oies à Wimereux, Pas de Calais 76, 79

Oldowan xxx, 34
ontogenesis 13, 199

parts of the tool: part that transmits energy/for the transmission of energy 26, 28, 51, 156, 179–180, 190–193; prehensile part 6, 28–31, 34, 37, 43–48, 51–59, 70–72, 82–84, 120–123, 131, 137–138, 141, 156–158, 165–168, 171, 173–174, 177–178, 180, 190–192, 205; transformative part 6, 28–30, 34–37, 42–58, 70–72, 82–83, 120, 123, 137, 141–142, 156–158, 167–168, 173–174, 177–180, 190, 193

percussion 11, 27, 30, 69, 95–99, 118, 130–131, 134, 136, 161, 185, 188, 190

phylogeny 2

predetermination 28–31, 36, 48, 65, 69–71, 74–75, 132, 134, 140, 168

projectile point xxix, 6

Proto-Aurignacian 98

Queyssac, France 108, 138

Quina 10; Quina retouch 165, 178

raw material 25, 45, 50, 60, 63, 81, 106, 117–119, 142, 192

Saint-Firmin-des Prés, France 111–112

Saint-Valery-sur-Somme, France 79–82, 156

savoir faire *see* skill

selection 27–28, 31, 76, 81–84, 117–120, 127, 131, 141, 173, 177

shaping 10, 21, 27–28, 31–34, 34–39, 42–43, 51, 67–69, 137, 141–142, 157, 165, 170, 174

sidescraper 5–7, 21, 165, 177–178

Simondon, Gilbert xxviii, 1, 5, 12–17, 34, 45, 132, 134, 153, 190, 199, 205

skill 10

Solutrean 64

Soriano, Sylvain 41

specialization 16, 134, 155, 165, 178

split 16, 118–119, 141–143

standardization 37, 55, 65, 141, 154–157, 193

Stiegler, Bernard 12

Susa, Iran 139

Suyaggye, Korea 139

symptomology xxviii

synergy xxxi, 15–16, 25, 31, 45, 65, 67, 106, 132–134, 137, 141

Tabun, Israel 108, 158

techné 4

technique 2–5, 9–10, 14–17, 21, 23, 35, 96, 141, 144, 161–162, 178–180, 188–190, 193, 205, 211

technofunctional 33, 97, 167–168, 177, 189, 236

techno-genesis 12–15

techno-logic 2, 5, 136, 153, 165, 180, 186, 189–190, 201, 208

technology/technological xxiii–xxiv, xxvii, xxix, xxxi–xxxii, 2, 4–5, 9–12, 15–17, 20, 35, 47, 74, 85, 134, 137, 140–141, 153–154, 161, 165, 171–172, 175, 188, 204, 208, 210

tendance xxix, 10–14, 153

transductive 3

typology/typological xxvii, 4–6, 9, 11–12, 21, 34, 39, 93, 120, 161, 178, 203–205

typo-technological 123

Umm el Tlel, Syria 42–43, 45, 51–53, 159–160, 163, 165, 167–168, 175, 185–188

Umm el Tlelian 43, 47–51

Upper Paleolithic 5, 23, 45, 66, 96–97, 106, 115, 158, 163–164, 176, 179, 182, 185, 201, 203

Victoria West core 87, 93–94

Villazette, France 118, 137

Villiers-Adam, France 101–103

volumetric concept 84, 105, 107, 116, 161–162

worked material 23–24, 26–27, 84, 156–157

Yabrudian 6, 47, 51–55, 158–160, 165–166, 169–173, 204

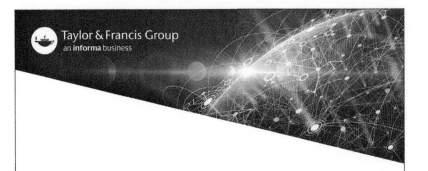